EARTHCARE

EARTHCARE

WOMEN AND THE ENVIRONMENT

CAROLYN MERCHANT

ROUTLEDGE   NEW YORK

1995

Published in 1996 by

Routledge
29 West 35th Street
New York, NY 10001

Published in Great Britain by

Routledge
11 New Fetter Lane
London EC4P 4EE

Library of Congress Cataloging-in-Publication Data
Merchant, Carolyn.
    Earhtcare: women and the environment / by Carolyn
Merchant.
        p.   cm.
    Includes bibliographical references.
    ISBN 0-415-90887-6 (alk. paper). —ISBN 0-415-90888-
5 (alk. paper)
        1. Ecofeminism. 2. Women environmentalists. 3.
Environmentalism. 4. Human ecology. I. Title.
HQ1233. M46 1995
333. 7'082—dc20

Cover: Teresa Fasolino's 1990 "Garden of Eden" re-envisions
Albrecht Dürer's Adam and Eve as mutual caretakers of the
earth. The snake is absent and both humans hold an apple.

TO THE WOMEN WHO WILL
CARE FOR AND DEFEND
THE EARTH IN THE THIRD
MILLENNIUM FROM THOSE
WHO HAVE DONE SO IN THE
RECENT AND DEEP PAST

CONTENTS

PART THREE / PRACTICE

LIST OF ILLUSTRATIONS

AND TABLES

TABLES

ACKNOWLEDGMENTS

Over the past two and a half decades, I have been deeply engaged with issues concerning the relationship between women and nature that comprise the chapters of *Earthcare*. The book probes the complexities of theory, history, and practice that connect symbols, representations, and constructions of nature as female with women's labor in the earth and their subsequent efforts to save it from destruction. There is no simple relationship between the ways in which nature has been gendered both positively and negatively as female over the past two and a half millennia and the roles of women in society. Nature has been revered as animate mother, feared and degraded as unpredictable witch, and plowed as virgin land. Yet forces such as the socialization of women as caretakers and nurturers, the degradation of women's livelihoods and bodies, and the double burden borne by women as workers and homemakers in capitalist, socialist, and colonized countries has often propelled them to act to preserve both nonhuman nature and themselves.

How, when, where, and in what contexts cultural symbols and social forces that connect women to nature seem to reinforce each other, in both positive and negative ways, is explored in the following pages. The outcome of these investigations into the cultural and historical associations between women and nature has led me to conclude the book with a proposal for an ethic of earthcare that neither genders nature as female nor privileges women as caretakers, yet nonetheless emerges from women's experiences and connections to the earth and from cultural constructions of nature as unpredictable and chaotic. In that conclusion, I offer an ethic of partnership between people and nature that could lead to a sustainable world in the next century.

In thinking through these ideas and proposals for sustainability, I have been assisted over the years by many women and men who have taken the time and trouble to talk with me, read drafts of my written work, and engage in debate over issues. Without the help of these professional colleagues, students, friends, editors, and anonymous referees this book would be much impoverished. Colleagues in the United States who have influenced my thinking, helped me to conceptualize my thoughts, and suggested references and quotations include Morris Berman, Zelda Bronstein, Baird Callicott, Claudia Carr, Anthony Chenells, William Cronon, Helen Denham, Irene Diamond, Giovanna Di Chiro, Jeffery Ellis, Barbara Epstien, Yaakov Garb, Florence Gardner, Katherine Hayles, Debora Hammond, Donna Haraway, David Igler, Evelyn Fox Keller, Ynestra King, Annette Kolodny, David Kubrin, James McCarthy, Alan Miller, Kenneth Olwig, Gloria Orenstein, Victor Rotenberg, Londa Schiebinger, Arnold Schultz, Candace Slater, Karen Warren, Hayden White, and Donald Worster.

As a Fulbright scholar in Sweden in 1984, and on a subsequent visit in 1986, I benefited from the knowledge and collaboration of Abby Peterson who co-authored Chapter 8, "Peace with the Earth." Colleagues and friends throughout Sweden who assisted us and have continued to provide valuable continuity and information on Sweden's environmental movement include: Ronny Ambjörnsson, Boel Berner, Stina Deurell, Lena Eskilsson, Tore Frängsmyr, Flore Gate, Margareta Gisselberg, Brigitta Hambreus, Elisabet Hermodsson, Sven Hultman, Sif Johansson, Kjell Jonsson, Sara Lidman, Ingegerd Lündstrom, Christina Mörtberg, Gunilla Olsson, Marit Paulson, Sverker Sörlin, Ingrid Stjernquist, Sven Wahlberg, and Birgitta Wrenfelt.

In 1991, I was fortunate to be selected by Patsy Hallen and Murdoch University in Perth, Australia to be the first external ecofeminist scholar for the decade under a grant to teach and lecture on ecofeminisim at Murdoch. While there, I traveled throughout the country and enjoyed the hospitality and assistance of many women and men who, along with my students at Murdoch, supplied valuable information and materials for Chapter 9, "The Ecological Self." In addition to Patsy Hallen, whose ideas and enthusiasm greatly influenced my own work, I am particularly indebted to: Genn Albrecht, Diane Bell, Janis Birkeland, Pat Brewer, Lex Brown, Carla Catterall, Mary Dykes, Robyn Eckersley, Frank Fisher, Brian Laver, Leslie Instone, Freya Mathews, Alan Roberts, Val Plumwood, Ariel Salleh, Christine Sharp, Kate Short, Sandra Taylor, Ian Tyrell, Virginia Westbury, Jo Vallentine, and John Young.

In 1992, at the invitation of the Brazilian Women's Coalition, I attended and presented a paper in the session on "The Code of Ethics and Accountability" at the Earth Summit's "Global Forum" in Rio de Janeiro, which became the basis for the concluding chapter, "Partnership Ethics." I am particularly indebted for ideas and support from Bella Abzug, Thais Corral, Corine Kumar D'Souza, Rosiska Darcy de Oliveira, Vandana Shiva, and the Women's Congress for a Healthy Planet, held in Miami, Florida, November, 1991.

The work represented in this book was supported by fellowships, grants and travel to domestic and international conferences by the University of California at Berkeley, the United States Agricultural Experiment Station, the Fulbright Commission, the National Endowment for the Humanities, the California Council for the Humanities, the National Science Foundation, the American Council of Learned Societies, the Nathan Cummings Foundation, and the Center for Advanced Study in the Behavioral Sciences. I appreciate their contributions, as well as the assistance given by librarians, research assistants, and secretarial staff at the University of California, Umeå University in Sweden, and Murdoch University in Australia. I extend deep appreciation to Celeste Newbrough who prepared the index of this and previous books and to Cecelia Cancellaro and Claudia Gorelick at Routledge for editorial assistance and advice.

I wish to thank the following publishers and journals for permission to reprint previously published materials here: Routledge for portions of Chapter 1; W.W. Norton and Antipode for Chapter 2; *Isis* the History of Science Society, and the University of Chicago Press for portions of

Chapter 3; HarperCollins for Chapter 4; the University of North Carolina Press for Chapter 5; *Environmental History Review* for Chapter 6, and *Women's Studies International Forum*, Elsevier Science Limited, and Abby Peterson for Chapter 8.

Finally, I would like to thank my husband and colleague Charlie Sellers and my sons David Iltis and John Iltis for stimulating conversations, healthy debates, and moral support.

Carolyn Merchant
Berkeley, California
October 1994

INTRODUCTION

Earthcare responds to a growing perception in the late twentieth century that the planet has seen better days. Taking care of the earth, however, is a human concern, not just a women's issue. Why then a book that links women with the environment and an ethic of earthcare? Does not such a connection essentialize women as planetary caretakers and green cleaners? Does it not keep women in their place as caretakers of the earth's household—the *oikos,* or Greek word meaning the human home? Is it the case, as Sherry Ortner asked in 1974, that female is to male as nature is to culture?[1] As this book shows, there is a multitude of complex dimensions to these issues and no straightforward, easy answers.

Earthcare explores the many aspects of the association of women with nature in Western culture and their roles in the contemporary environmental movement. It looks at the age-old connections between women and nature, symbols of nature as female, and women's practices and daily interactions with the earth. The complexity of these symbols and practices over time precludes any simple essentialism that women's nature is to nurture. Indeed both history and practice reveal the positive, negative, and problematical ways in which both women and nature have been constructed over time by science and culture—projects in which both women and men have participated to varying degrees. Each chapter in this book engages a theoretical, historical, or practical aspect of these connections between women and the environment.

In Part I, I raise a number of theoretical issues concerning women, the earth, and female symbols of nature. Gaia from the Greek tradition, Eve from the Christian religion, and Isis from Egyptian history are exemplars of nature as female with differing implications for the treatment of women and the earth. Gaia, the Greek deity who brought forth the earth from chaos (or the void), symbolizes for both the feminist and environmental movements a potentially powerful force for change. Ecofeminism in its various forms—liberal, cultural, social, and socialist—envisions ways to save the planet and achieve social justice, while environmentalism enlists Gaia as a symbol for a scientific theory that sees the planet as a living organism. Both approaches have problematical aspects, however, implying that women and nature are both super-green-cleaners who will take care of environmental problems.

Eve, likewise, is a female symbol with a variety of potential implications for the environment. As virgin, Eve represents pristine, untouched nature; as fallen Eve, she symbolizes a barren desert wanting improvement; as mother, she implies a planted garden, an improved land, a ripened, fruitful world. Yet each symbol contains within it a narrative trajectory that propels colonial and capitalist development of New World and Third World lands. The fall from Eden into a wasteland sets up Western culture's project of recovering the Garden, using science, technology, and capitalism to recreate it on earth. The whole earth is developed and improved via the removal of its forested wildlands, the irrigation of its deserts, and the cultivation of its soils, not for usufruct by the many, but for profit by the few.

Finally, Isis, Egyptian bringer of new life as the Nile floods and crops are planted each spring, becomes for Western science a symbol of knowing nature by extracting the secrets hidden beneath her robe. Science's method of knowing through the disembodied mind's eye of calculation and the empirical eye of observation combines logical positivism with ocularcentrism. If Isis is also nonwhite, as the debate over the black African origins of science and culture suggests, then the racial and sexual dimensions of the investigation of "nature's body" are metaphorically and historically linked. The history of science reveals that studies of racial and sexual differences can lead to policies and practices that privilege white over black and male over female. In such cases, a scientific method deriving from positivism, ocularcentrism, and Eurocentrism can lead to the domination of nature, women, and minorities.

Yet alternatives to domination suggested by the iconographies of Gaia, Eve, and Isis are possible without a simple reversal of cultural dualisms. Social changes in the relations between ecology, production, and reproduction, as well as new narratives about nature, partial perspectives in science, dialectical systems approaches, chaos theory, and partnership ethics are among the possibilities explored in the following chapters. Nevertheless, positive aspects of icons such as Gaia, Eve, and Isis may be sources of inspiration for an age weary of seeing nature as a vast machine that can be fixed by engineers and technicians. An ethic of earthcare that views both nature and people as real, live, active entities can be embraced by women and men, scientists and environmentalists alike, in personal as well as politically-responsible terms.

In Part II, I look at the history of associations between women and nature, the ways women have interacted with the earth, and the ways they have conserved its resources. In "The Death of Nature" (an excerpt from my 1980 book), I argue that the organic world view of the Renaissance, in which the cosmos was alive and the earth was considered a nurturing mother, contained ethical constraints against the exploitation of the earth. During the rise of mercantile capitalism and the Scientific Revolution of the seventeenth century, the world was reconceptualized as a machine made of dead atoms, God was an engineer, and society a sum of self-interested individuals. An environmental ethic of restraint gave away to a sanction for the domination of nature.

During the same period, across the Atlantic in New England, a native American culture that was also animistic and organic was being transformed by the introduction of European mercantile capitalism and colonialism. Over a period of 250 years, the role women played in the southern New England landscape moved from one of corn mothers to moral mothers. Native American women, whose food products constituted about 85 percent of the tribal diet, interacted directly with the earth through planting, tending, and harvesting corn, beans, and squash, offering the first fruits of their labor to a corn mother deity. Colonial women, whose culture took over Indian lands, likewise had an immediate interaction with the earth through their outdoor labor in providing family subsistence. With the transformation to an industrial—capitalist economy in the nineteenth century, women's farm work lessened, while wage and home labor increased. Simultaneously, women became symbols of the moral counterpart of workplace amorality. Women and their country farms represented refuges from polluted cities and factory stress. In the same period, many middle-class women found time to engage in the study and teaching of nature and to participate in rural outings and wilderness adventures. Out of such activities grew women's contributions to the conservation and preservation movements of the late nineteenth century.

At the turn of the century in the United States, women worked to save the nation's parks, forests, and wilderness areas. While men have received most of the credit for conservation, it was women's visionary, intellectual, and organizational skills that pushed through many of the nation's reserved lands. Over a million women across the country engaged in cooperative efforts to preserve trees, birds, and wildlands and to clean up harbors and rivers. Although these middle-class women volunteers justified their actions within a framework that conserved the ideals of the middle-class home and family, they also developed lobbying and organizational techniques that dovetailed with and drew on the emancipatory efforts of the woman suffrage and women's rights movements.

Taken as a whole, the three chapters in Part II argue that as organic societies in England and New England, which had female imagery as core components, gave way to mercantile and then industrial capitalism, a mechanistic science and world view arose that legitimated continued market expansion and the truncation of women's outdoor work. Although women's direct interaction with nature to produce family subsistence declined, capitalism produced a middle class of women who studied, appreciated, and conserved the natural world, shielding large areas from further exploitative development.

Part III examines the environmental movement of the 1960s through the 1990s in three industrial-capitalist, First World countries—the United States, Sweden, and Australia, countries in which I have had an opportunity to live for periods of time and share the thoughts and activities of women engaged in the struggle to preserve nature. In each case I look at the connections between women's philosophical and activist approaches to saving the environment. Women become activists in part because their bodies, or the bodies of those with whom they have a caring relationship, are threatened by toxic or radioactive substances or when land or another species about which they care deeply is threatened with extinction.

As activists, women in all three countries have protested the development of nuclear power and nuclear weapons, sought to curtail the use of pesticides and the dumping of hazardous wastes, promoted alternative forms of farming, forestry, and the use of environmentally benign technologies, educated children in how to care for nature, analyzed the connections between First and Third World resource flows, and engaged in implementing green political change. As thinkers and philosophers, they have questioned the assumptions of the dominant mechanistic, positivist paradigm through which much environmentally problematic research has been done, developed the foundations for ecological feminism, and formulated alternative approaches to earthcare. In the process of assuming leadership roles, they have also liberated themselves as dynamic and powerful forces for change.

In the conclusion, I develop an ethic of earthcare based on the concept of a partnership between people and nature. Rather than seeing nature as more powerful than and dominant over human beings (whether as goddess or witch), as was usually the case in premodern societies, or seeing humans as dominant over nature through science and technology, as has been the view of most modern societies, a dynamic balance may be attained through a partnership ethic. Nature, as was once represented by Gaia, Eve, and Isis, is real, active, and alive. Human beings, especially women and minorites, as amply illustrated by their actions on behalf of the earth, are also real, active, autonomous beings. A partnership relationship means that a human community is in a dynamic relationship with a nonhuman community. Each has power over the other. Nature, as a powerful, uncontrollable force, has the potential to destroy human lives and to continue to evolve and develop with or without human beings. Humans, who have the power to destroy nonhuman nature and potentially themselves through science and technology, must exercise care and restraint by allowing nature's beings the freedom to continue to exist, while still acting to fulfill basic human material and spiritual needs. An earthcare ethic, which is premised on this dynamic relationship, is generated by humans, but is enacted by listening to, hearing, and responding to the voice of nature. A partnership ethic thus emerges as a guide to practice.

Throughout this book, I use the concepts of ecology, production, reproduction, and consciousness within a framework of dialectical interacting systems (see Table 1). I assume that the world is real, material, and in constant dynamic change. Science makes it possible to know (through mathematical description and experimentation) a limited domain. But chaos and complexity theories indicate a limit to that knowledge, hence a limit to predictability and management. Moreover, feminist epistemologies of science challenge positivist ways of knowing nature based solely on the mind's eye and the empirical eye.

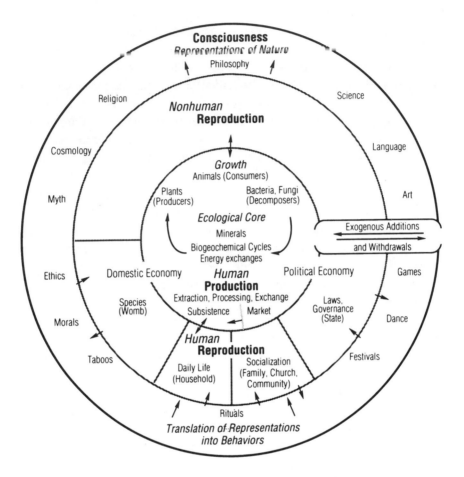

Consciousness
Representations of Nature
Philosophy

Religion

Science

Cosmology

Language

Nonhuman
Reproduction

Myth

Art

Growth
Animals (Consumers)

Plants
(Producers)

Bacteria, Fungi
(Decomposers)

Ecological Core
Minerals
Biogeochemical Cycles
Energy exchanges

Exogenous Additions
and Withdrawals

Ethics

Domestic Economy

Human
Production
Extraction, Processing, Exchange

Political Economy

Games

Species
(Womb)

Subsistence

Market

Laws,
Governance
(State)

Morals

Dance

Human
Reproduction

Taboos

Daily Life
(Household)

Socialization
(Family, Church,
Community)

Festivals

Rituals
*Translation of Representations
into Behaviors*

TABLE 1 / CONCEPTUAL FRAMEWORK
FOR INTERPRETING ECOLOGICAL
REVOLUTIONS.

Ecology, production, reproduction, and consciousness interact over time to bring about ecological transformations. The innermost sphere represents the ecological core within the local habitat, the site of interactions between ecology and human production. Plants (producers), animals (consumers), bacteria and fungi (decomposes), and minerals exchange energy among themselves and with human producers in accordance with the laws of thermodynamics and the biogeochemical cycles. Introductions and withdrawals of organisms and resources from outside the local habitat can alter its ecology. Human production (the extraction, processing, and exchange of resources and commodi-

ties) is oriented toward immediate use as food, clothing, shelter, and energy for subsistence or toward profit in mercantile trade and industrial capitalism. With increasing industrialization, the subsistence-oriented sector declines and the market-oriented sector expands (as indicated by the clockwise arrow).

The middle sphere represents human and nonhuman reproduction. The intergenerational reproduction of species and intragenerational survival rates influence ecological interactions directly in the case of nonhuman individuals or as mediated by production in the case of humans. In subsistence (or use-value) societies, production is oriented toward the reproduction of daily life in the household through the production of food, clothing, shelter, and energy (as indicated by the two-way arrow). For

c.f. v-Co.'s Interconnectedness

Consciousness as a way of knowing nature, however, is broader than the mind alone. It encompasses knowing through the body, all the senses working together—feelings, volitions, and thought. It may refer to individual or group consciousness, hence to dominant worldviews, as well as to alternative ways of representing nature. Representations of material reality are socially constructed from a real, material world by real bodies, mediated through local modes of production and reproduction (such as indigenous systems, colonialism, and capitalism). The results are partial representations reflected in images, metaphors, myths, art, dance, religion, and science. Such representations in turn convey values and ethics to individuals and communities.

Female images such as Gaia, Eve, and Isis develop in local contexts, but are often appropriated by other cultures and politics, including, among others, Western science, environmentalism, and feminism. Appropriated representations can be apolitical, ahistorical, acontextual, and essentialist. Yet most images are reinterpreted, recontextualized, and given new meaning by later societies and social movements. They can be used to show how essentialist notions, such as the conflation of nature and women, are historically constructed over time and function to keep women in their place as "natural" caretakers or green homemakers. Yet reclaiming and recontextualizing past images does not mean people are necessarily chained to the past or advocating a romantic return to it, but instead are claiming the power to change it. Images can be inspirational, as when Eve as virgin inspired the settlement of "virgin" lands for nineteenth-century colonists or when she became, for late twentieth-century feminists, the image of the first female scientist. Similarly, Gaia inspires a sense of the earth as a living organism for twentieth-century environmentalists or, as "mother earth," evokes a new earth ethic. Isis may symbolize nature as a bringer of new life or represent a precolonized, power-

---

humans, the reproduction of society also includes socialization (in the family, church, and community) and the establishment of laws and governance that maintain order in the tribe, town, state, or nation.

Human consciousness, symbolized by the outermost sphere, includes representations of nature reflected (as indicated by the arrows) in myth, cosmology, religion, philosophy, science, language, and art, helping to maintain a given society over time and to influence change. Through ethics, morals, taboos, rituals, festivals, dance, and games, they are translated into actions and behaviors that both affect and are affected by the environment, production,

and reproduction (as indicated by the arrows).

The "semipermeable" membranes between the spheres symbolize possible interactions among them. Ecological revolutions are brought about through interactions between production and ecology and between production and reproduction. These changes in turn stimulate and can be stimulated by new representations of nature and forms of human consciousness.

Source: Carolyn Merchant, "The Theoretical Structure of Ecological Revolutions," *Environmental Review* 11, no. 4 (winter 1987): 268, reprinted by permission.

ful woman of color. People are free to criticize the use of such images and to offer alternatives.

My own view is that, however inspirational, the cultural baggage associated with images of nature as female means that gendering nature is at present too problematical to be adopted by emancipatory social movements in Western societies. A view of nature as a process, one that is more powerful and longer lasting than human societies and human beings, is a sufficient basis for an ethic of earthcare. Women and men can participate in ecological movements to save the earth not only because it fulfills vital human needs, but because it is home to a multitude of other living and nonliving things, many of which are beautiful and inspiring in their own right.

PART ONE

THEORY

I

GAIA

ECOFEMINISM AND
THE EARTH

"Gaia (also called Ge) is the ancient earth-mother who brought forth the world and the human race from 'the gaping void, Chaos.'...Long before she herself was regarded as the mother of the powerful deities, she herself was the powerful deity." So Charlene Spretnak began her 1978 *Lost Goddesses of Early Greece*.[1] Spretnak, whose research was initiated in 1975 after a summer seminar on "Women and Mythology," wished to reclaim the pre-Hellenic goddess myths that existed prior to the transformation of Greece by barbarian invaders (the Ionians, Achaeans, and Dorians) and their patriarchal codification in the seventh century B.C. by Hesiod and Homer.[2] Her endeavor to reclaim Gaia as an earth-mother was part of an effort among feminists of the 1970s to create a new earth-based form of spirituality rooted in ancient traditions that revered both the earth and female deities. She drew on the work of women writing in the early twentieth century, such as Jane Ellen Harrison (1903), Helen Diner (1929), and Esther Harding (1955), as well as male pioneers such as Johann Jacob Bachofen (1854) and Robert Briffault (1927).[3] She composed a myth about Gaia that began:

> From the eternal Void, Gaia danced forth and rolled Herself into a spinning ball. She molded mountains along Her spine, valleys in the hollows of Her flesh. A rhythm of hills and stretching plains followed Her contours. From Her warm moisture She bore a flow of gentle rain that fed Her surface and brought life.[4]

Spretnak later incorporated the Gaia creation story into ecofeminism. Nature and women could be liberated through the recognition of Gaia as both the earth and the female aspect of the godhead coupled with the removal of patriarchal constructions of "women as Other and men as godlike and inherently superior."[5]

Spretnak's identification of Gaia as a powerful feminist and ecological symbol was followed in 1979 by James Lovelock's scientific popularization in his book, *Gaia: A New Look at Life on Earth*. Lovelock, whose work began with papers on "Gaia as Seen Through the Atmosphere" in 1972 and on the "Gaia Hypothesis" and homeostasis in 1973 (with Lynn Margulis) drew scientific attention to the concept of the earth as a living organism. The "Gaia hypothesis" proposed that "the entire range of living matter on Earth, from whales to viruses, and from oaks to algae, could be regarded as constituting a single living entity, capable of manipulating the earth's atmosphere to suit its overall needs and endowed with faculties and powers far beyond those of its constituent parts." Like Spretnak, Lovelock saw Gaia as part of a religious reverence for the earth: "The concept of Mother Earth, or, as the Greeks called her long ago, Gaia, has been widely held throughout history and has been the basis of a belief which still coexists with the great religions."[6]

Together, the two approaches of feminist spirituality and scientific theory recast Gaia as a compelling metaphor for a new understanding of and reverence for life on earth. The concept of "Mother Earth," revived by feminists and central to the cultures of indigenous peoples, was now reinforced by science. The idea took hold in the public imagination when it became the theme for Paul Winter's "Missa Gaia: The Earth Mass" in 1981, and concerts were held in the cathedral of St. John the Divine in New York City and in the Grand Canyon. A National Audubon Society Expeditions symposium, "Is the Earth a Living Organism?", that included scientists, historians, poets, and American Indians, was held in 1985, and the concept received scientific scrutiny through an American Geophysical Union Conference in 1988. Concerts, poetry, statues of Gaia, Gaia bookstores, whole earth images and catalogues, as well as numerous books and scientific conferences followed during the 1980s and '90s. A forceful metaphor for a new postmodern age seemed to be in the making.[7]

Yet, however unifying, Gaia is also a problematical image for both environmentalists and feminists. Its message carries cultural baggage that undercuts its inspirational power. If Gaia is a self-regulating homeostatic system, then "she" can correct problems caused by humans or even find humans expendable.

Or, as Lovelock queried, "[Which] regions of the earth are vital to Gaia's well being? Which ones could she do without?" These implications undercut environmental caretaking vital to maintaining life as we know it, as well as social justice issues relating to the diversity of peoples and regions. Gaia also raises problems for feminists. As Spretnak herself noted at the Audubon conference on Gaia, "Men in this society have this deeply imbedded idea that Mom always comes along and cleans up after them." Or, as Australian ecofeminist Val Plumwood points out, Gaia is actually a "super servant" who will keep the planet clean for humans: "It does not matter if we do not wash our dishes and throw our dirty linen on the floor because Gaia, a super housekeeping goddess operating with whiter than white homeostatic detergent, will clean it all up after us."[8] These observations about Gaia, both positive and problematical, exemplify one aspect of a much larger debate about the relationships between the domination of nature and women and the liberation of both through ecological feminism.

Ecofeminism emerged in the 1970s with an increasing consciousness of the connections between women and nature. The term, "ecofeminisme," was coined in 1974 by French writer Françoise d'Eaubonne in 1974 who called upon women to lead an ecological revolution to save the planet.[9] Such an ecological revolution would entail new gender relations between women and men and between humans and nature.

Developed by Ynestra King at the Institute for Social Ecology in Vermont about 1976, the concept became a movement in 1980 with a major conference on "Women and Life on Earth" held in Amherst, Massachusetts and the ensuing Women's Pentagon Action to protest anti-life nuclear war and weapons development.[10] During the 1980s cultural feminists in the United States injected new life into ecofeminism by arguing that both women and nature could be liberated together.

Liberal, cultural, social, and socialist feminism have all been concerned with improving the human/nature relationship and each has contributed to an ecofeminist perspective in different ways (Table 2).[11] Liberal feminism is consistent with the objectives of reform environmentalism to alter human relations with nature from within existing structures of governance through the passage of new laws and regulations. Cultural ecofeminism analyzes environmental problems from within its critique of patriarchy and offers alternatives that could liberate both women and nature.

Social and socialist ecofeminism, on the other hand, ground their analyses in capitalist patriarchy. They ask how patriarchal relations of reproduction reveal the domination of women by men, and how capitalist relations of pro-

TABLE 2 / FEMINISM AND THE ENVIRONMENT

	Nature	Human Nature	Feminist Critique of Environmentalism	Image of a Feminist Environmentalism
Liberal Feminism	Atoms Mind/Body dualism Domination of Nature	Rational Agents Individualism Maximization of self-interest	"Man and his environment" leaves out women	Women in natural resources and environmental sciences
Marxist Feminism	Transformation of Nature by science and technology for human use. Domination of nature as a means to human freedom Nature is material basis of life: food, clothing, shelter, energy	Creation of human nature through mode of production, praxis Historically specific—not fixed Species nature of humans	Critique of capitalist control of resources and accumulation of goods and profits	Socialist society will use resources for good of all men and women Resources will be controlled by workers Environmental pollution could be minimal since no surpluses would be produced Environmental research by men and women
Cultural Feminism	Nature is spiritual and personal Conventional science and technology problematic because of their emphasis on domination	Biology is basic Humans are sexual reproducing bodies Sexed by biology/gendered by society	Unaware of interconnectedness of male domination of nature and women Male environmentalism retains hierarchy Insufficient attention to environmental threats to woman's reproduction (chemicals, nuclear war)	Woman/Nature both valorized and celebrated Reproductive freedom Against pornographic depictions of both women and nature Cultural ecofeminism
Socialist Feminism	Nature is material basis of life: food, clothing, shelter, energy Nature is socially and historically constructed Transformations of nature by production and reproduction	Human nature created through biology and praxis (sex, race, class, age) Historically specific and socially constructed	Leaves out nature as active and responsive Leaves out women's role in reproduction and reproduction as a category Systems approach is mechanistic and not dialectical	Both nature and human production are active Centrality of biological and social reproduction Dialectic between production and reproduction Multileveled structural analysis Dialectical (not mechanical) systems Socialist ecofeminism

duction reveal the domination of nature by men. They seek the total restructuring of the market economy's use of both women and nature as resources.
Although cultural ecofeminism has delved more deeply into the woman–nature
connection, social and socialist ecofeminism have the potential for a more thor-
ough critique of domination and for a liberating social justice.

Ecofeminist actions address the contradiction between production and
reproduction. Women attempt to reverse the assaults of production on both
biological and social reproduction by making problems visible and proposing
solutions (see Table 1). When radioactivity from nuclear power-plant acci-
dents, toxic chemicals, and hazardous wastes threaten the biological reproduction of the human species, women experience this contradiction as assaults on
their own bodies and on those of their children and act to halt them.
Household products, industrial pollutants, plastics, and packaging wastes
invade the homes of First World women threatening the reproduction of daily
life, while direct access to food, fuel, and clean water for many Third World
women is imperiled by cash cropping on traditional homelands and by pesticides used in agribusiness. First World women combat these assaults by altering consumption habits, recycling wastes, and protesting production and disposal methods, while Third World women act to protect traditional ways of
life and reverse ecological damage from multinational corporations and the
extractive industries. Women challenge the ways in which mainstream society
reproduces itself through socialization and politics by envisioning and enact-
ing alternative gender roles, employment options, and political practices.

Many ecofeminists advocate some form of an environmental ethic that
deals with the twin oppressions of the domination of women and nature
through an ethic of care and nurture that arises out of women's culturally
constructed experiences. As philosopher Karen Warren conceptualizes it:

> An ecofeminist ethic is both a critique of male domination of both
> women and nature and an attempt to frame an ethic free of male-
> gender bias about women and nature. It not only recognizes the multi-
> ple voices of women, located differently by race, class, age, [and]
> ethnic considerations, it centralizes those voices. Ecofeminism builds
> on the multiple perspectives of those whose perspectives are typically
> omitted or undervalued in dominant discourses, for example Chipko
> women, in developing a global perspective on the role of male domina-
> tion in the exploitation of women and nature. An ecofeminist perspec-
> tive is thereby...structurally pluralistic, inclusivist, and contextualist,
> emphasizing through concrete example the crucial role context plays
> in understanding sexist and naturist practice.[12]

An ecofeminist ethic, she argues, would constrain traditional ethics based on rights, rules, and utilities, with considerations based on care, love, and trust. Yet an ethic of care, as elaborated by some feminists, falls prey to an essentialist critique that women's nature is to nurture.[13]

My own approach is a partnership ethic that treats humans (including male partners and female partners) as equals in personal, household, and political relations and humans as equal partners with (rather than controlled-by or dominant-over) nonhuman nature (see Conclusion). Just as human partners, regardless of sex, race, or class must give each other space, time, and care, allowing each other to grow and develop individually within supportive nondominating relationships, so humans must give nonhuman nature space, time, and care, allowing it to reproduce, evolve, and respond to human actions. In practice, this would mean not cutting forests and damming rivers that make people and wildlife in flood plains more vulnerable to "natural disasters"; curtailing development in areas subject to volcanos, earthquakes, hurricanes, and tornados to allow room for unpredictable, chaotic, natural surprises; and exercising ethical restraint in introducing new technologies such as pesticides, genetically-engineered organisms, and biological weapons into ecosystems. Constructing nature as a partner allows for the possibility of a personal or intimate (but not necessarily spiritual) relationship with nature and for feelings of compassion for nonhumans as well as for people who are sexually, racially, or culturally different. It avoids gendering nature as a nurturing mother or a goddess and avoids the ecocentric dilemma that humans are only one of many equal parts of an ecological web and therefore morally equal to a bacterium or a mosquito.

LIBERAL ECOFEMINISM

Liberal feminism characterized the history of feminism from its beginnings in the seventeenth century until the 1960s. It is rooted in liberalism, the political theory that accepts the scientific analysis that nature is composed of atoms moved by external forces, a theory of human nature that views humans as individual rational agents who maximize their own self-interest, and capitalism as the optimal economic structure for human progress. It accepts the egocentric ethic that the optimal society results when each individual maximizes her own productive potential. Thus what is good for each individual is good for society as a whole. Historically, liberal feminists have argued that women do not differ from men as rational agents and that exclusion from educational and economic opportunities has prevented them from realizing their own potential for creativity in all spheres of human life.[14]

Twentieth century liberal feminism was inspired by Simone de Beauvoir's *The Second Sex* (1949) and by Betty Friedan's *The Feminine Mystique* (1963). De Beauvoir argued that women and men were biologically different, but that women could transcend their biology, freeing themselves from their destiny as biological reproducers to assume masculine values. Friedan challenged the "I'm just a housewife" mystique resulting from post-World War II production forces that made way for soldiers to reassume jobs in the public sphere, pushing the "reserve army" of women laborers back into the private sphere of the home. The liberal phase of the women's movement that exploded in the 1960s demanded equity for women in the workplace and in education as the means of bringing about a fulfilling life. Simultaneously, Rachel Carson made the question of life on earth a public issue. Her 1962 *Silent Spring* focused attention on the death-producing effects of chemical insecticides accumulating in the soil and tissues of living organisms—deadly elixirs that bombarded human and non-human beings from the moment of conception until the moment of death.[15]

For liberal ecofeminists (as for liberalism generally), environmental problems result from the overly rapid development of natural resources and the failure to regulate pesticides and other environmental pollutants. The way the social order reproduces itself through governance and laws can be meliorated if social reproduction is made environmentally sound. Better science, conservation, and laws are therefore the proper approaches to resolving resource problems. Given equal educational opportunities to become scientists, natural resource managers, regulators, lawyers, and legislators, women, like men, can contribute to the improvement of the environment, the conservation of natural resources, and the higher quality of human life. Women, therefore, can transcend the social stigma of their biology and join men in the cultural project of environmental conservation.

Within the parameters of mainstream government and environmental organizations, such as the Sierra Club, are a multitude of significant opportunities for women to act to improve their own lives and resolve environmental problems. Additionally, women have established their own environmental groups. Organizations founded by women tend to have high percentages of women on their boards of directors. In California, for example, the Greenbelt Alliance was founded by a woman in 1958, the Save the Bay Association by three women in 1961, and the California Women in Timber in 1975 by a group of women. Yet most of the women in these organizations do not consider themselves feminists and do not consider their cause feminist.

Feminism as a radical label, they believe, could stigmatize their long term goals. On the other hand, groups such as Friends of the River, Citizens for a Better Environment, and the local chapter of the Environmental Defense Fund employ many women who consider themselves feminists and men who consider themselves sensitive to feminist concerns, such as equality, childcare, overturning of hierarchies within the organization, and creating networks with other environmental organizations, all within the framework of liberalism.[16]

CULTURAL ECOFEMINISM

Cultural feminism developed in the late 1960s and 1970s with the second wave of feminism (the first being the women's suffrage movement of the early twentieth century). Cultural ecofeminism is a response to the perception that women and nature have been mutually associated and devalued in western culture. Sherry Ortner's 1974 article, "Is Female to Male as Nature is to Culture?" posed the problem that motivates many ecofeminists. Ortner argued that, cross-culturally and historically, women, as opposed to men, have been seen as closer to nature because of their physiology, social roles, and psychology. Physiologically, women bring forth life from their bodies, undergoing the pleasures, pain, and stigmas attached to menstruation, pregnancy, childbirth, and nursing, while men's physiology leaves them freer to travel, hunt, conduct warfare, and engage in public affairs. Socially, childrearing and domestic caretaking have kept married women close to the hearth and out of the workplace. Psychologically, women have been assigned greater emotional capacities with greater ties to the particular, personal, and present than men who are viewed as more rational and objective with a greater capacity for abstract thinking.[17]

To cultural ecofeminists the way out of this dilemma is to elevate and liberate women and nature through direct political action. Many cultural feminists celebrate an era in prehistory when nature was symbolized by pregnant female figures, trees, butterflies, and snakes and in which women were held in high esteem as bringers forth of life. An emerging patriarchal culture, however, dethroned the mother goddesses and replaced them with male gods to whom the female deities became subservient. The scientific revolution of the seventeenth century further degraded nature by replacing Renaissance organicism and a nurturing earth with the metaphor of a machine to be controlled and repaired from the outside. The ontology and epistemology of mechanism are viewed by cultural feminists as deeply masculinist and exploitative of a nature historically depicted in the female gender. The earth is dominated by male-developed and male-controlled technology, science, and industry.[18]

Often stemming from an anti-science, anti-technology standpoint, cultural ecofeminism celebrates the relationship between women and nature through the revival of ancient rituals centered on goddess worship, the moon, animals, and the female reproductive system. A vision in which nature is held in esteem as mother and goddess is a source of inspiration and empowerment for many ecofeminists. Spirituality is seen as a source of both personal and social change. Goddess worship and rituals centered around the lunar and female menstrual cycles, lectures, concerts, art exhibitions, street and theater productions, and direct political action (web-spinning in anti-nuclear protests) are all examples of the re-visioning of nature and women as powerful forces. Cultural ecofeminist philosophy embraces intuition, an ethic of caring, and web-like human-nature relationships.[19]

For cultural feminists, human nature is grounded in human biology. Humans are biologically sexed and socially gendered. Sex/gender relations give men and women different power bases. Hence the personal is political. The perceived connection between women and biological reproduction turned upside down becomes the source of women's empowerment and ecological activism. Women's biology and Nature are celebrated as sources of female power. This form of ecofeminism has largely focused on the sphere of consciousness in relation to nature—spirituality, goddess worship, witchcraft—and the celebration of women's bodies, often accompanied by social actions such as anti-nuclear or anti-pornography protests.[20]

Much populist ecological activism by women, while perhaps not explicitly ecofeminist, implicitly draws on and is motivated by the connection between women's reproductive biology (nature) and male-designed technology (culture). Many women activists argue that male-designed and produced technologies neglect the effects of nuclear radiation, pesticides, hazardous wastes, and household chemicals on women's reproductive organs and on the ecosystem. They protest against radioactivity from nuclear wastes, power plants, and bombs as a potential cause of birth defects, cancers, and the elimination of life on earth. They expose hazardous waste sites near schools and homes as permeating soil and drinking water and contributing to miscarriages, birth defects, and leukemia. They object to pesticides and herbicides being sprayed on crops and forests as potentially affecting children and child-bearing women living near them. Women frequently spearhead local actions against spraying, water pollution, and power plant sitings and organize citizens to demand toxic clean-ups. (Figure 1.1)[21]

In 1978, Lois Gibbs of the Love Canal Homeowner's Association in Niagara Falls, New York, played a critical role in raising women's consciousness

FIG. 1.1 / CLEAN WATER DEMONSTRATION

Carol Barrett of Newport, Tennessee protests the polluting of the Pigeon River by Champion
International Corporation's paper mill at a rally along the river next to the plant. The state of North
Carolina recommended continuing a permit variance allowing discoloration of the Pigeon River by
Champion until the mill completed a modernization project. The pigeon runs from North Carolina to
Tennessee. Photograph by Jetta Fraser, Impact Visuals.

about the effects of hazardous waste disposal by Hooker Chemicals and
Plastics Corporation in her neighborhood of 1,200 homes. Love Canal is a
story of how lower-middle-class women who had never been environmental
activists became politicized by the life-and-death issues directly affecting their
children and their homes and succeeded in obtaining redress from the state of
New York. In 1983 Gibbs founded the Citizen's Clearing House for
Hazardous Waste and began publishing a newsletter, *Everyone's Backyard*.[22]

The majority of activists in the grassroots movement against toxics are
women (see Chapter 7). Many became involved when they experienced miscarriages or their children suffered birth defects or contracted leukemia or
other forms of cancer. Through networking with neighborhood women, they
began to link their problems to nearby hazardous waste sites. From initial Not
in My Backyard (NIMBY) concerns, the movement has changed to Not in

Anybody's Backyard (NIABY) to Not On Planet Earth (NOPE). Thus Cathy Hinds, whose well water in East Gray, Maine was contaminated by chemicals from a nearby industrial clean-up corporation, became "fighting mad" when she lost a child and her daughter began to suffer from dizzy spells. She eventually founded the Maine Citizens' Coalition on Toxics and became active in the National Toxics Campaign. Her motive was to protect her children. Women, she says, "are mothers of the earth," who want to take care of it.[23]

Native American women organized WARN, Women of All Red Nations to protest high radiation levels from uranium mining tailings on their reservations and the high rates of aborted and deformed babies as well as issues such as the loss of reservation lands and the erosion of the family. They recognized their responsibilities as stewards of the land and expressed respect for "our Mother Earth who is a source of our physical nourishment and our spiritual strength." (see Chapter 7).[24]

Cultural ecofeminism, however, has its feminist critics. Susan Prentice argues that ecofeminism, while asserting the fragility and interdependence of all life, "assumes that women and men…have an essential human nature that transcends culture and socialization." It implies that what men do to the planet is bad; what women do is good. This special relationship of women to nature and politics makes it difficult to admit that men can also develop an ethic of caring for nature. Second, ecofeminism fails to provide an analysis of capitalism that explains why it dominates nature. "Capitalism is never seriously tackled by ecofeminists as a process with its own particular history, logic, and struggle. Because ecofeminism lacks this analysis, it cannot develop an effective strategy for change." Moreover, it does not deal with the problems of poverty and racism experienced by millions of women around the world.[25] In contrast to cultural ecofeminism, the social and socialist strands of ecofeminism are based on a socioeconomic analysis that treats nature and human nature as socially constructed, rooted in an analysis of race, class, and gender.

SOCIAL ECOFEMINISM

Building on the social ecology of Murray Bookchin, social ecofeminism envisions the restructuring of society in humane, decentralized communities. "Social ecofeminism," states Janet Biehl, "accepts the basic tenet of social ecology, that the idea of dominating nature stems from the domination of human by human. Only ending all systems of domination makes possible an ecological society, in which no states or capitalist economies attempt to subjugate nature, in which all aspects of human nature—including sexuality and the passions as well as rationality—are freed." Social ecofeminism distinguishes itself from goddess-worshipping cultural ecofeministo who acknowledge a special historical relationship between women and nature and wish to liberate both together. Instead it begins with the materialist, social feminist analysis of early radical feminism that sought to restructure the oppressions imposed on women by marriage, the nuclear family, romantic love, the capitalist state, and patriarchial religion.

Social ecofeminism advocates the liberation of women through overturning economic and social hierarchies that turn all aspects of life into a market society that today even invades the womb. It envisions a society of decentralized communities that transcend the public-private dichotomy necessary to capitalist production and the bureaucratic state. In them women emerge as free participants in public life and local municipal workplaces.

Social ecofeminism acknowledges differences in male and female reproductive capacities, inasmuch as it is women and not men who menstruate, gestate, give birth, and lactate, but rejects the idea that these entail gender hierarchies and domination. Both women and men are capable of an ecological ethic based on caring. In an accountable face-to-face society, childrearing would be communal; rape and violence against women would disappear. Rejecting all forms of determinism, it advocates women's reproductive, intellectual, sensual, and moral freedom. Biology, society, and the individual interact in all human beings, giving them the capacity to choose and construct the kinds of societies in which they wish to live.[26]

But in her 1991 book *Rethinking Ecofeminist Politics* Janet Biehl withdrew her support from ecofeminism, and likewise abandoned social ecofeminism, on the grounds that the concept had become so fraught with irrational, mythical, and self-contradictory meanings that it undercut women's hopes for a liberatory, ecologically-sane society. While early radical feminism sought equality in all aspects of public and private life, based on a total restructuring of society, the cultural feminism that lies at the root of much of ecofeminism seemed to her to reject rationality by embracing goddess worship, to biologize and essentialize the caretaking and nurturing traits assigned by patriarchy to women, and to reject scientific and cultural advances just because they were advocated by men.[27] Social ecofeminism, however, is an area that will receive alternative definition in the future as theorists such as Ynestra King, Ariel Salleh, Val Plumwood, and Chiah Heller sharpen the critique of patriarchal society, hierarchy, and domination.

SOCIALIST ECOFEMINISM

Socialist ecofeminism is not yet a movement, but rather a feminist transformation of socialist ecology that makes the category of reproduction, rather than production, central to the concept of a just, sustainable world. Like Marxist feminism, it assumes that non-human nature is the material basis of all of life and that food, clothing, shelter, and energy are essential to the maintenance of human life. Nature and human nature are socially and historically contructed over time and transformed through human praxis. Nature is an active subject, not a passive object to be dominated, and humans must develop sustainable relations with it. It goes beyond cultural ecofeminism in offering a critique of capitalist patriarchy that focuses on the dialectical relationships between production and reproduction, and between production and ecology.

A socialist ecofeminist perspective offers a standpoint from which to analyze social and ecological transformations, and to suggest social actions that will lead to the sustainability of life and a just society. It asks:

1. What is at stake for women and for nature when production in traditional societies is disrupted by colonial and capitalist development?
2. What is at stake for women and for nature when traditional methods and norms of biological reproduction are disrupted by interventionist technologies (such as chemical methods of birth control, sterilization, amniocentesis, rented wombs, and baby markets) and by chemical and nuclear pollutants in soils, waters, and air (pesticides, herbicides, toxic chemicals, and nuclear radiation)?
3. What would an ecofeminist social transformation look like?
4. What forms might socialist societies take that would be healthy for all women and men and for nature?

In his 1884 *Origin of the Family, Private Property, and the State*, Friedrich Engels wrote that "the determining factor in history is, in the last resort, the production and reproduction of immediate life....On the one hand, the production of the means of subsistence...on the other the production of human beings themselves." In producing and reproducing life, humans interact with nonhuman nature, sustaining or disrupting local and global ecologies. When we ignore the consequences of our interactions with nature, Engels warned, our conquests "take...revenge on us." "In nature nothing takes place in isolation." Elaborating on Engels' fundamental insights, women's roles in production, reproduction, and ecology can become the starting point for a socialist ecofeminist analysis.[28]

SOCIALIST ECOFEMINISM AND PRODUCTION

As producers and reproducers of life, women in tribal and traditional cultures over the centuries have had highly significant interactions with the environment. As gatherers of food, fuel, and medicinal herbs; fabricators of clothing; planters, weeders, and harvesters of horticultural crops; tenders of poultry; preparers and preservers of food; and bearers and caretakers of young children, women's intimate knowledge of nature has helped to sustain life in every global human habitat.

In colonial and capitalist societies, however, women's direct interactions with nature have been circumscribed. Their traditional roles as producers of food and clothing, as gardeners and poultry tenders, as healers and midwives, were largely appropriated by men. As agriculture became specialized and mechanized, men took over farm production, while migrant and slave women and men supplied the stoop labor needed for field work. Middle-class women's roles shifted from production to the reproduction of daily life in the home, focusing on increased domesticity and the bearing and socialization of young children. Under capitalism, as sociologist Abby Peterson points out, men bear the responsibility for and dominate the production of exchange commodities, while women bear the responsibility for reproducing the workforce and social relations. "Women's responsibility for reproduction includes both the biological reproduction of the species (intergenerational reproduction) and the intragenerational reproduction of the work force through unpaid labor in the home. Here too is included the reproduction of social relations—socialization." Under industrial capitalism, reproduction is subordinate to production.[29]

Because capitalism is premised on economic growth and competition in which nature and waste are both externalities in profit maximization, its logic precludes sustainability. The logic of socialism on the other hand is based on the fulfillment of people's needs, not people's greed. Because growth is not necessary to the economy, socialism has the potential for sustainable relations with nature. Although state socialism has been based on growth-oriented industrialization and has resulted in the pollution of external nature, new forms of socialist ecology could bring human production and reproduction into balance with nature's production and reproduction. Nature's economy and human economy could enter into a partnership.

The transition to a sustainable global environment and an equitable human economy that fulfills people's needs would be based on two dialectical relationships—that between production and ecology and that between production and reproduction. In existing theories of capitalist development, reproduction and ecology are both subordinate to production. The transition to socialist ecology would reverse the priorities of capitalism, making production subordinate to reproduction and ecology.

SOCIALIST ECOFEMINISM AND REPRODUCTION

Socialist ecofeminism focuses on the reproduction of life itself. In nature, life is transmitted through the biological reproduction of species in the local ecosystem. Lack of proper food, water, soil chemicals, atmospheric gases, adverse weather, disease, and competition by other species can disrupt the survival of offspring to reproductive age. For humans, reproduction is both biological and social. Enough children must survive to reproductive age to reproduce the community over time, but too many put pressure on the particular mode of production, affecting the local ecology. Also, by interacting with external nature, adults must produce enough food, clothing, shelter, and fuel on a daily basis to maintain their own subsistence and sustain the quality of their ecological homes. Both the intergenerational biological reproduction of humans and other species and the intragenerational reproduction of daily life are essential to continuing life over time. Sustainability is the maintenance of an ecological—productive—reproductive balance between humans and nature—the perpetuation of the quality of all life.[30]

Biological reproduction affects local ecology, not directly, but as mediated by production. Many communities of tribal and traditional peoples developed rituals and practices that maintained their populations in a balance with local resources. Others allowed their populations to grow in response to the need for labor or migrated into new lands and colonized them. When the mode of production changes from an agrarian to an industrial base, and then to a sustainable production base, the number of children that families need declines. How development occurs in the future will help families decide how many children to have. A potential demographic transition to smaller population sizes is tied to ecologically sustainable development.

Ecofeminist political scientist Irene Diamond raises concern over the implications of "population control" for Third World women: "The most recent 'advances' in family planning techniques from injectable contraceptives and vaccines against pregnancy to a range of hormonal implants, often banned in western nations as unsafe, reduce women of the south to mindless objects and continue the imperialist model which exploits native cultures 'for their own good.'"[31] Furthermore, with the availability of prenatal sex identification techniques, feminists fear the worldwide "death of the female sex" as families that place a premium on male labor opt to abort as many as nine out of every ten female fetuses. Third, feminists argue that women's bodies are being turned into production machines to test contraceptives, for *in vitro* fertilization experiments, to produce babies for organ transplants, and to produce black market babies for sale in the northern hemisphere.

Reproductive freedom means freedom of choice—freedom to have or not to have children in a society that both needs them and provides for their needs. The same social and economic conditions that provide security for women also promote the demographic transition to lower populations. The Gabriela Women's Coalition of the Philippines calls for equal access to employment and equal pay for women, daycare for children, healthcare, and social security. It wants protection for women's reproductive capacities, access to safe contraception, and the elimination of banned drugs and contraceptives. It advocates equal, nondiscriminatory access to education, including instruction concerning consumer rights and hazardous chemicals. Such a program would help to bring about a sustainable society in which population is in balance with the fulfillment of daily needs and the use of local resources, a society that offers women and men of all races, ages, and abilities equal opportunities to have meaningful lives.

A socialist ecofeminist movement in the developed world can work in solidarity with women's movements to save the environment in the underdeveloped world. It can support scientifically-based ecological actions that also promote social justice. Like cultural ecofeminism, socialist ecofeminism protests chemical assaults on women's reproductive health, but puts them in the broader context of the relations between reproduction and production. It can thus support point of production actions such as the Chipko and Greenbelt movements in the Third World (see below), protests by Native American women over cancer-causing radioactive uranium mining on reservations, and protests by working-class women over toxic dumps in urban neighborhoods.[32]

WOMEN IN THE THIRD WORLD

Many of the problems facing women in the Third World today are the historical result of colonial relations between the First and Third Worlds. From the seventeenth century onward, European colonization of lands in Africa, India, the Americas, and the Pacific initiated a colonial ecological revolution in which an ecological complex of European animals, plants, pathogens, and people disrupted native peoples' modes of subsistence, as Europeans extracted resources for trade on the international market and settled in the new lands. From the late eighteenth century onward, a capitalist ecological revolution in the northern hemisphere accelerated the extraction of cash crops and resources in the southern hemisphere, pushing Third World peoples onto marginal lands and filling the pockets of Third World élites. In the twentieth century, northern industrial technologies and policies have been exported to the south in the form of development projects. Green Revolution agriculture (seeds, fertilizers, pesticides, dams, irrigation equipment, and tractors), plantation forestry (fast-growing, non-indigenous species, herbicides, chip harvesters, and mills), capitalist ranching (land conversion, imported grasses, fertilizers, and factory farms) and reproductive technologies (potentially harmful contraceptive drugs, sterilization, and bottle feeding) have further disrupted native ecologies and peoples.

Women of the South have born the brunt of environmental crises resulting from colonial marginalization and ecologically unsustainable development projects. As subsistence farmers, urban workers, or middle-class professionals, their ability to provide basic subsistence and healthy living-conditions is threatened. Women in the Third World, however, have not remained powerless in the face of these threats. They have organized movements, institutes, and businesses to transform maldevelopment into sustainable development. They are often at the forefront of change to protect their own lives, those of their children, and the life of the planet. While some might consider themselves feminists, and others embrace ecofeminism, most are mainly concerned with maintaining conditions for survival.

In India, nineteenth–century British colonialism in combination with twentieth–century development programs have created environmental problems that affect women's subsistence, especially in forested areas. Subsistence production, oriented toward the reproduction of daily life, is undercut by expanding market production, oriented toward profit-maximization (see Table 1). To physicist and ecofeminist Vandana Shiva the subsistence and market economies are incommensurable:

> There are in India, today, two paradigms of forestry—one life-enhancing, the other life-destroying. The life-enhancing paradigm emerges from the forest and the feminine principle; the life-destroying one from the factory and the market....Since the maximising of profits is consequent upon the destruction of conditions of renewability, the two paradigms are cognitively and ecologically incommensurable. The first paradigm has emerged from Indian's ancient forest culture, in all its diversity, and has been renewed in contemporary times by the women of Garhwal through Chipko.[33]

India's Chipko, or tree-hugging, movement attempts to maintain sustain-ability. It has its historical roots in ancient Indian cultures that worshipped tree goddesses, sacred trees as images of the cosmos, and sacred forests and groves. The earliest woman-led tree-embracing movements are three-hun-dred years old. In the 1970s women revived these chipko actions in order to save their forests for fuelwood and their valleys from erosion in the face of cash cropping for the market. The basis of the movement lay in a traditional ecological use of forests for food (as fruits, roots, tubers, seeds, leaves, petals and sepals), fuel, fodder, fertilizer, water, and medicine. Cash cropping, by contrast, severed forest products from water, agriculture, and animal hus-bandry. Out of a women's organizational base and with support by local males, protests to save the trees took place over a wide area from 1972 through 1978, including actions to embrace trees, marches, picketing, singing, and direct confrontations with lumberers and police.[34]

The Chipko movement's feminine forestry-paradigm is based on assumptions similar to those of the emerging science of agroforestry, now being taught in Western universities. Agroforestry is one of several new sci-ences based on maintaining ecologically viable relations between humans and nature. As opposed to modern agriculture and forestry, which separate tree crops from food crops, agroforestry views trees as an integral part of agri-cultural ecology. Complementary relationships exist between the protective and productive aspects of trees and the use of space, soil, water, and light in conjunction with crops and animals. Agroforestry is especially significant for small farm families, such as many in the Third World, and makes efficient use of both human labor and natural resources.[35]

In Africa, numerous environmental problems have resulted from colo-nial disruption of traditional patterns of pastoral herding, as governments imposed boundaries that cut off access to migratory routes and traditional resources. The ensuing agricultural development created large areas of deser-tified land, which negativly impacted women's economy. The farmers, most-ly women, suffered from poor yields on eroded soils. They had to trek long distances to obtain wood for cooking and heating. Their cooking and drink-ing waters were polluted. Developers with professional training, who did not understand the meaning of "development without destruction," cut down trees interfering with highways and electrical and telephone lines, even if they were the only trees on a subsistence farmer's land.

Kenyan women's access to fuelwood and water for subsistence was the primary motivation underlying the women's Greenbelt Movement. According

FIG. 1.2 / WANGARI MAATHAI. WANGARI MAATHAI OF THE GREEN BELT
ALLIANCE, KENYA, CONFERS WITH THE DALAI LAMA, TIBETAN SPIRITUAL
LEADER, AT THE EARTH SUMMIT PARLIAMENTARY FORUM, JUNE 1992.
PHOTOGRAPH BY GIANNA CARVALHO, IMAGENS DA TERRA, IMPACT VISUALS.

to founder Wangari Maathai, the movement's objective is to promote "environmental rehabilitation, conservation, and...sustainable development." It attempts to reverse humanly-produced desertification by planting trees for conservation of soil and water. (Figure 1.2)[36]

The National Council of Women of Kenya began planting trees in 1977 on World Environment Day. Working with the Ministry of the Environment and Natural Resources, they continued to plant trees throughout the country and established community woodlands on public lands. They planted seedlings and sold them to generate income. The movement promoted traditional agroforestry techniques previously abandoned in favor of "modern" farming methods that relied on green revolution fertilizers, pesticides, new seed varieties, and irrigation systems that were costly and non-sustainable. During the past ten years, the movement has planted over seven million trees, created hundreds of jobs, reintroduced indigenous tree species, educated people in the need for environmental care, and promoted the independence and a more positive image of women.[37]

"The whole world is heading toward an environmental crisis," says Zimbabwe's Sithembiso Nyoni. "Women have been systematically excluded from the benefits of planned development....The adverse effects of Africa's current so-called economic crisis and external debt...fall disproportionately on women and make their problems ever more acute." Twenty years ago good water, wood, grass, and game still existed, even on semi-arid communal lands, and women did not have to walk long distances to obtain subsistence resources. But the introduction of Green Revolution seeds and fertilizers required different soils and more water than found on the common lands. The poor—primarily women—have born the brunt of development proceeding independently of environmental consequences.[38]

According to Zimbabwe's Kathini Maloba, active in both the Greenbelt Movement and the Pan-African Women's Trade Union, many farm women suffer loss from poor crops on marginal soils, lack of firewood, polluted water, poor sanitation, and housing shortages. Women have suffered miscarriages from the use of chemical fertilizers and pesticides. In 1983, 99 percent of all farms had no protection from pesticides. Only 1 percent of employers heeded pesticide warnings and used detection kits to test pesticide levels in foods and water.

Development programs that emphasize people's needs within local environmental constraints would include: water conservation through erosion control, protection of natural springs, and the use of earthen dams and water tanks; in agriculture, the reintroduction of traditional seeds and planting of indigenous trees; in herding, the use of local grasses, seeds, and leaves for feed and driving cattle into one place for fattening before market; in homes, the use of household grey water to irrigate trees and more efficient ovens that burn less fuelwood.[39]

Latin American women likewise point to numerous environmental impacts on their lives. Both Nicaragua and Chile are countries in which socialist governments have been opposed by the United States through the use of economic boycotts and the funding of opposition leaders who supported conservative capitalist interests. Maria Luisa Robleto of the Environmental Movement of Nicaragua asserts that women are fighting to reverse past environmental damage. In Nicaragua, before the Sandinista revolution of 1979, many women worked on private haciendas that used large amounts of pesticides, especially DDT. Since the revolution the postion of women changed as part of the effort to build a society based on sustainable development. In part because of male engagement in ongoing defense of the country and in part because of the efforts of the Nicaraguan women's movement, women moved into agricultural work that was formerly masculine. Women were trained in tractor driving, coffee plantation management, and animal husbandry.

According to Robleto, women agricultural workers in Nicaragua have twenty times the level of DDT in their breast milk as non-agricultural workers. They want equal pay and an end to toxic poisoning from insecticides. If breast feeding is promoted as an alternative to expensive formula feeding, there must be a program to control toxins in breast milk. In a country where 51 percent of the energy comes from firewood, 39 percent of which is used for cooking, there must be a forestry and conservation program oriented to women's needs. A grassroots movement is the spark for ecological conservation.

Chile's Isabelle Letelier of the Third World Women's Project (widow of the Chilean ambassador to the United States who was assassinated by Pinochet agents following the overthrow of the socialist Allende government in 1973), speaks of the power of *compesina* women who created life and controlled medicine and religion. The global society, she says, is out of control. The round planet must be saved. Women must take charge, since men are not going to solve the problems. They must construct a society for both women and men. The rights of the land, the rights of nature, and women's rights are all part of human rights. Santiago is now one of the most polluted cities in the world. There are children who receive no protein and who resort to eating plastic. There is a television in every home, but no eggs or meat. There are colored sugars, but no bread. In 1983, says Letelier, women broke the silence and began speaking out for the environment. Without the help of telephones, they filled a stadium with 11,000 women. They established networks as tools; they learned to question everything, to be suspicious of everything. They learned to see. "Women give life," says Letelier. "We have the capacity to give life and light. We can take our brooms and sweep the earth. Like witches, we can clean up the atmosphere with our brooms. We can seal up the hole in the ozone layer. The environment is life and women must struggle for life with our feet on the ground and our eyes toward the heavens. We must do the impossible."

Gizelda Castro, of Friends of the Earth, Brazil, echoes the ecofeminist cry that women should reverse the damage done to the earth. "Men," she says, "have separated themselves from the ecosystem." Five hundred years of global pillage in the name of development and civilization have brought us to a situation of international violence against the land and its people. The genetic heritage of the south is constantly going to the north. Women have had no voice, but ecofeminism is a new and radical language. Women must provide the moral energy and determination for both the First and Third Worlds. They are the future and hope in the struggle over life.

In Malaysia, which received independence in 1957 as the British empire underwent decolonization, many environmental problems have resulted from a series of five-year development plans that ignored both the environment and conservation, especially the impact of development on women. "The rapid expansion of the cash crop economy, which is hailed as a 'development' success story, has plunged thousands of women into a poisonous trap," argues Chee Yoke Ling, lecturer in law at the University of Malaysia and secretary general of the country's chapter of Friends of the Earth. As land control shifted to large multinational rice, rubber, and palm oil plantations, women's usufructory rights to cultivate the land were lost to a male-dominated cash-exporting economy. They became dependent and marginalized, moving into low paying industrial and agricultural jobs. Women workers constitute 80 percent of those who spray chemical pesticides and herbicides such as paraquat on rubber and palm plantations. They pour the liquid, carry the open containers, and spray the chemicals without protective clothing, even when pregnant or nursing. The workers are usually unaware of the effects of the chemicals and often cannot read the warning labels on the packaging. Protests resulted in loss of jobs or transfer to even less desirable forms of labor. In 1985, Friends of the Earth Malaysia began to pressure the Ministry of Health to ban paraquat. They called on plantation owners and government agencies to stop using the chemical for the sake of human right to life as well as the life of waters and soils.[40]

Women in the Third World are thus playing an essential role in conservation. They are making the impacts of colonialism and industrial capitalism on the environment and on their own lives visible. They are working to maintain their own life-support systems through forest and water conservation, to rebuild soil fertility, and to preserve ecological diversity. In so doing, they are assuming leadership roles in their own communities. Although they have not yet received adequate recognition from their governments and conservation organizations for their contributions, they are slowly achieving the goals of ecofeminism—the liberation of women and nature.

WOMEN IN THE SECOND WORLD

Second World development has been informed by Marxist theory that the goal of production is the fulfillment of human needs. Yet state socialism as the method for achieving equitable distribution of goods and services has created enormous problems of pollution and depletion resulting from a series of five-year plans for rapid industrial growth. As Second World countries incorporate market economic goals, environmental problems will become increasingly complex. Can the evolving, changing Second World produce and distribute enough food and goods for its own people and also reverse environmental deterioration? The movements toward democratization in the 1990s reveal an openness to new ideas and cooperation in resolving economic and environmental problems, but many problems in implementing solutions remain.

While Second World women have shared educational and economic opportunities along with men, like First World women they have also borne the double burden of housework added to their employment outside the home. Like First World women, they have experienced the effects of industrial and toxic pollutants on their own bodies and seen the impacts on their children and husbands. Although women in the Second World have not achieved the environmental vision of Marxist feminists (see Table 2), they have used scientific and technological research and education to find ways of mitigating these problems and have participated in incipient green movements.

Second World women have assumed leadership roles in environmental affairs. In Poland, Dr. Maria Guminska, a professor of biochemistry at Krakow Medical University, helped to found the 4000 member Polish Ecology Club and served as one of its vice-presidents. She prepared a critical report on the air pollution of Poland's largest aluminum smelter and was active in the effort to reduce toxic pollutants from a Krakow pharmaceutical plant. And in Russia, Dr. Eugenia V. Afanasieva, an assistant professor at the Moscow Polytechnical Institute, was Deputy Director of the Environmental Education Center for Environmental Investigation. The Center developed a filtration system to help clean up industrial water pollution. Dr. Afanasieva works with young people to promote better environmental education. "All mankind now stands at the beginning of a new era," she states. "People must make the choice to live or to perish. Nobody can predict the future. We must save our civilization. We must change our ways of thinking. We must think ecologically." Women, she argues, play a major role in expanding environmental awareness: "It seems to me that women are more active in environmental programs than men. We give birth to our children, we teach them to take their first steps. We are excited about their future."[41]

In 1989 the First International Conference on Women, Peace, and the Environment was held in the Soviet Union. The women who attended called for greater participation by women as environmentalists and scientists to help decide the fate of the planet. They said:

> Each of us should do everything possible to promote actions for survival on local, national, and international levels.... We must work to end food irradiation, to ban all known chemicals destroying the ozone

layer, to reduce transport emissions, to recycle all reusable waste, to plant arboreta and botanical gardens, to create seed banks, etc. These are among the most urgent beginnings for a strategy of survival.[42]

Olga Uzhnurtsevaa of the Committee of Soviet Women pleads for environmental improvement in the face of her country's accelerating industrial production. A national ecological program subsidized by the government is needed to reverse ecological damage. Children are born with birth defects; air and water quality have deteriorated. In the former Soviet Union, she says, women's councils support environmental thinking. Many Soviet journalists and activists concerned over environmental problems in the Lake Baikal watershed and the Baltic Sea are women. Women are especially concerned with the need to protect nature from the arms race. This problem involves all of humanity, especially the effects on the Third World. Quoted Uzhnurtsevaa,

> Nature said to women:
> Be amused if you can,
> Be wise if possible,
> But by all means, be prudent.[43]

CONCLUSION

Although the goals of liberal, cultural, social, and socialist feminists may differ as to whether capitalism, women's culture, or socialism should be the ultimate objective of political action, shorter-term objectives overlap. Weaving together the many strands of the ecofeminist movement is the concept of reproduction construed in its broadest sense to include the continued biological and social reproduction of human life and the continuance of life on earth. In this sense there is perhaps more unity than diversity in women's common goal of restoring the natural environment and quality of life for people and other living and non-living inhabitants of our planet Gaia.

2

E V E

NATURE AND

NARRATIVE

A Penobscot Indian story from northern New England explains the origin of maize. A great famine had deprived people of food and water. A beautiful Indian maiden appeared and married one of the young men of the tribe, but soon succumbed to another lover, a snake. On discovery she promised to alleviate her husband's sorrow if he would plant a blade of green grass clinging to her ankle. First he must kill her with his ax, then drag her body through the forest clearing until all her flesh had been stripped, and finally bury her bones in the center of the clearing. She then appeared to him in a dream and taught him how to tend, harvest, and cook corn and smoke tobacco.[1]

This agricultural origin story taught Indians how to plant their corn in forest clearings and also that the earth would continue to regenerate the human body through the corn plant. It features a woman (the corn maiden) and a male lover as central actors. It begins with the state of nature as drought and famine. Nature is a desert, a poor place for human existence. The plot features a woman as saviour. Through a willing sacrifice in which her body is returned to the earth, she introduces agriculture to her husband and to the women who subsequently plant the corn, beans, and squash that provide the bulk of the food sustaining the life of the tribe. The result is an agroecological system based on the planting of interdependent polycultures in forest gardens. The story type is ascensionist and progressive. Women transform nature from a desert into a garden. From a tragic situation of despair and death, a comic, happy, and optimistic situation of continued life results. In this story, the valence of women as corn mothers is good; they bring bountiful gifts. The valence of nature ends as a good. The earth is an agent of regeneration. Death is transformed into life through a reunification of the corn mother's body with the earth. Even death results in a higher good.[2]

Into this bountiful world of corn mothers enter the Puritan fathers bringing their own agricultural origin story of Adam and Eve. The biblical myth begins where the Indian story ends—with an ecological system of polycultures in the Garden of Eden. A woman, Eve, shows "the man", Adam, how to pick fruit from the Tree of the Knowledge of Good and Evil and harvest the fruits of the garden. Instead of attaining a resultant good, the couple is cast out of the garden into a desert. Instead of moving from desert to garden, as in the Indian story, the biblical story moves from garden to desert. The Fall from paradise is caused by a woman. Men must labor in the earth by the sweat of their brow to produce food. Here a woman is also the central actress and like the Indian story it contains elements of violence toward women. But the plot is declensionist and tragic, not progressive and comic as in the Indian story. The end result is a poorer state of nature than in the beginning. The valence of woman is bad. The end valence of nature is bad. Here men become the agents of transformation. They become saviors, who through their own agricultural labor have the capacity to re-create the lost garden on earth.[3]

According to Benjamin Franklin, Indians quickly perceived the difference between the two accounts. Franklin satirically writes that when the Indians were apprised of the "historical facts on which our [own] religion is founded; such as the fall of our first parents by eating an apple, ...an Indian orator stood up,...." to thank the Europeans for their story. "What you have told us ...is all very good. It is, indeed, bad to eat apples. It is much better to make them all into cider. We are much obliged by your kindness in coming so far to tell us these things which you have heard from your mothers; in return I will tell you some of those which we have heard from ours."[4]

Historical events reversed the plots of the Indian and the European origin stories. The Indians' comic happy ending changed to a story of decline and conquest, while Euramericans were largely successful in creating a New World garden. Indeed, the story of Western civilization since the seventeenth century and its advent on the American continent can be conceptualized as a grand narrative of Fall and recovery. The concept of recovery, as it emerged in the seventeenth century, not only meant a recovery from the Fall, but also entailed restoration of health, reclamation of land, and recovery of property.[5]

The recovery plot is the long, slow process of returning humans to the Garden of Eden through labor in the earth. Three subplots organize its argument: Christian religion, modern science, and capitalism. The Genesis story of the Fall provides the beginning; science and capitalism the middle; recovery of the garden the end. The initial lapsarian moment (the lapse from innocence) is the decline from garden to desert as the first couple is cast from the light of an ordered paradise into a dark, disorderly wasteland.

The Bible, however, offered two versions of the origin story that led to the Fall. In the Genesis 1 version, God created the land, sea, grass, herbs, and fruit; the stars, sun, and moon; and the birds, whales, cattle, and beasts—after which he made "man in his own image . . .; male and female created he them." Adam and Eve were instructed, "be fruitful and multiply, and replenish the earth, and subdue it" and were given "dominion over the fish of the sea, and over the fowl of the air, and over every living thing that moveth upon the earth." In the Genesis 2 version, thought to have derived from a different and earlier tradition, God first created the plants and herbs, next "man" from dust, and then the garden of Eden with its trees for food (including the Tree of Life and the Tree of the Knowledge of Good and Evil in the center) and four rivers flowing out of it. He then put "the man" in the garden "to dress and keep it," formed the beasts and fowls from dust, and brought them to Adam to name. Only then did he create Eve from Adam's rib. Genesis 3 narrates the Fall from the garden, beginning with Eve's temptation by the serpent, the consumption of the fruit from the Tree of the Knowledge of Good and Evil (which in the Renaissance becomes an apple), the expulsion of Adam and Eve from the garden "to till the ground from which he was taken," and finally God's placement of the cherubims and flaming sword at the entrance of the garden to guard the Tree of Life.[6]

During the Renaissance, artists illustrated the Garden of Eden story through woodcuts and paintings, one of the most famous of which is Lucas Cranach's 1526 painting of Eve offering the apple to Adam, after having been enticed by the snake coiled around the Tree of the Knowledge of Good and Evil (Figure 2.1). Writers from Dante to Milton depicted the Fall and subsequent quest for paradise, while explorers searched for the garden first in the Old and then in the New Worlds. Although settlers endowed new lands and peoples with Eden-like qualities, a major effort to re-create the Garden of Eden on earth ultimately ensued. Seventeenth-century botanical gardens and zoos marked early efforts to reassemble the parts of the garden dispersed throughout the world after the Fall and the Flood.[7]

FIG. 2.1 / EVE OFFERS ADAM AN APPLE FROM THE TREE OF THE KNOWLEDGE OF GOOD AND EVIL IN THE GARDEN OF EDEN. ADAM AND EVE, LUCAS CRANACH, 1526. COURTAULD INSTITUTE GALLERIES, LONDON, REPRODUCED BY PERMISSION

But beginning in the seventeenth century and proceeding to the present, New World colonists have undertaken a massive effort to reinvent the whole earth in the image of the Garden of Eden. Aided by the Christian doctrine of redemption and the inventions of science, technology, and capitalism ("arte and industrie"), the long-term goal of the recovery project has been to turn the earth itself into a vast cultivated garden. The strong interventionist version in Genesis 1 legitimates recovery through domination, while the softer Genesis 2 version advocates dressing and keeping the garden through human management (stewardship). Human labor would redeem the souls of men and women, while cultivation and domestication would redeem the earthly wilderness. The End Drama envisions a reunification of the earth with God (the Parousia), in which the redeemed earthly garden merges into a higher heavenly paradise. The Second Coming of Christ was to occur either at the outset of the thousand year period of his reign on earth (the millennium) or at the Last Judgment when the faithful were reunited with God at the resurrection.[8]

Greek philosophy offered the intellectual framework for the modern version of the recovery project. Parmenidean oneness represents the unchanging natural law that has lapsed into the appearances of the Platonic world. This fallen phenomenal world is incomplete, corrupt, and inconstant. Only by recollecting of the pure unchanging forms can the fallen partake of the original unity. Recovered and Christianized in the Renaissance, Platonism provided paradigmatic ideals (such as that of the Garden of Eden) through which to interpret the earthly signs and signatures leading to the recovery.[9]

Modern Europeans added two components to the Christian recovery project—mechanistic science and *laissez faire* capitalism—to create a grand master narrative of Enlightenment. Mechanistic science supplies the instrumental knowledge for reinventing the garden on earth. The Baconian–Cartesian–Newtonian project is premised on the power of technology to subdue and dominate nature, on the certainty of mathematical law, and on the unification of natural laws into a single framework of explanation. Just as the alchemists tried to speed up nature's labor through human intervention in the transformation of base metals into gold, so science and technology hastened the recovery project by inventing the tools and knowledge that could be used to dominate nature. Francis Bacon saw science and technology as the way to control nature and hence recover the right to the garden given to the first parents. "Man by the Fall, fell at the same time from his state of innocency and from his dominion over creation. Both of these losses can in this life be in some part repaired; the former by religion and faith; the latter by arts and science,"

Humans, he asserted, could "recover that right over nature which belongs to it by divine bequest," and should endeavour "to establish and extend the power and dominion of the human race itself over the [entire] universe."[10]

The origin story of capitalism is a movement from desert back to garden through the transformation of undeveloped nature into a state of civility and order.[11] Natural resources—"the ore in the mine, the stone unquarried [and] the timber unfelled"—are converted by human labor into commodites to be exchanged on the market. The Good State makes capitalist production possible by imposing order on the fallen worlds of nature and human nature. Thomas Hobbes' nation state was the end result of a social contract created for the purpose of controlling people in the violent and unruly state of nature. John Locke's political theory rested on the improvement of undeveloped nature by mixing human labor with the soil and subduing the earth through human dominion. Simultaneously, Protestantism helped to speed the recovery by sanctioning increased human labor just as science and technology accelerated nature's labor.[12]

Crucial to the structure of the recovery narrative is the role of gender encoded into the story. In the Christian religious story, the original oneness is male and the Fall is caused by a female, Eve, with Adam, the innocent bystander, being forced to pay the consequences as his sons are pushed into developing both pastoralism and farming.[13] While fallen Adam becomes the inventor of the tools and technologies that will restore the garden, fallen Eve becomes the Nature that must be tamed into submission. In the Western tradition, fallen Nature is opposed by male science and technology. The Good State that keeps unruly nature in check is invented, engineered, and operated by men. The Good Economy that organizes the labor needed to restore the garden is likewise a male-directed project.

Nature, in the Edenic recovery story, appears in three forms. As original Eve, nature is virgin, pure, and light—land that is pristine or barren, but having the potential for development. As fallen Eve, nature is disorderly and chaotic; a wilderness, wasteland, or desert requiring improvement; dark and witchlike, the victim and mouthpiece of Satan as serpent. As mother Eve, nature is an improved garden; a nurturing earth bearing fruit; a ripened ovary; maturity. Original Adam is the image of God as creator, initial agent, activity. Fallen Adam appears as the agent of earthly transformation, the hero who redeems the fallen land. Father Adam is the image of God as patriarch, law, and rule—the model for the kingdom and state. These meanings of nature as female and agency as male are encoded as symbols and myths into

American lands as having the potential for development, but needing the male hero, Adam. Such symbols are not essences because they do not represent characteristics necessary or essential to being female or male. Rather, they are historically constructed and derive from the origin stories of European settlers and European cultural and economic practices transported to and developed in the American New World. That they may appear to be essences is a result of their historical construction in Western history, not their immutable characteristics.

The Enlightenment idea of progress is rooted in the recovery of the garden lost in the Fall—the bringing of light to the dark world of inchoate nature. The lapsarian origin story is thus reversed by the grand narrative of Enlightenment that lies at the very heart of modernism. The controlling image of Enlightenment is the transformation from desert wilderness to cultivated garden. This complex of Christian, Greco-Roman, and Enlightenment components touched and reinforced each other at critical nodal points. As a powerful narrative, the idea of recovery functioned as ideology and legitimation for settlement of the New World, while capitalism, science, and technology provided the means of transforming the material world.

GRECO-ROMAN ROOTS OF THE
RECOVERY NARRATIVE

In creating a recovery narrative that reversed the lapsarian moment of the Fall, Europeans reinforced the Christian image of the precipitous fall from the Garden of Eden with pagan images of a gradual decline from the Golden Age. Hesiod (8th century B.C.) told of the time of immortal men who lived on Olympus where all was "of gold" and "the grain-giving soil bore its fruits of its own accord in unstinted plenty, while they at their leisure harvested their fields in contentment amid abundance."[14] Ovid in the *Metamorphoses* (A.D. 7), pictured the Golden Age as a time when a bountiful (unplowed) mother earth brought forth grains, fruits, honey, and nectar and people were peaceful, "unaggressive, and unanxious." Only in the decline of the subsequent silver, bronze, and iron ages did strife, violence, swindling, and war set in.[15]

Whereas Hesiod and Ovid offered elements that reinforced the Fall, Virgil and Lucretius introduced components of a recovery story that moved from "savagery" to "civilization." Nature was a principle of development, deriving from the Latin word *nascere*, "to be born." Each stage of development was inherent in the preceding stage, an actualization of a prior potential. The word "nation" derived from the same word, hence the state was born from the state of nature.[16] Virgil (70-19 B.C.) depicted a narrative of development from nature to nation that moved through four stages mimicking the human life cycle: (1) death and chaos, a world filled with presocial "wild" peoples (winter); (2) birth and the pastoral, in which people grazed sheep on pastured lands, (spring); (3) youth or farming by plowing and planting gardens (summer); (4) maturity, or the city (Rome) in the Garden (fall). For Virgil these four stages were followed by a return to death and chaos, whereas in the Christian myth the recovery was followed by redemption and a return to the original garden. Yet within each of Virgil's stages lies the potential to lapse back prematurely into the earlier chaotic or "savage" state. The second or pastoral stage is like the Christian Garden of Eden—its loss is mourned and its innocence yearned for—but in the Roman story, it passes "naturally" to the third, or agricultural, stage.

Virgil's *Georgics* narrates the agricultural period in which humans actively labor in the earth to cultivate it and themselves. Both society's potential and the earth's potential are actualized and perfected. When farmers till the ground and tend their crops, nature's bounty brings forth fruits: "Father Air with fruitful rains" descended on the "bosom of his smiling bride" to feed her "teeming womb."[17] The *Aeneid* reveals the fourth stage—the emergence of Rome as a city of culture and civilization within the pastoral and agricultural landscapes—*urbs in horto*—the city in the garden. The four developmental phases of nature and nation exist both temporally as stages and spatially as zones. The city is an actualization of movement from a chaotic "wild" periphery to a pastoral outer zone, a cultivated inner zone, and a "civilized" central place. Because nature is viewed as a cyclical development, the decline and fall of Rome is preordained in the final return to winter and chaos. Yet out of chaos comes a second Golden Age as "the great line of the ages is born anew." The "virgin" (Justice) returns and a "newborn boy" appears "at whose coming the iron race shall first cease and a golden race will spring up in the whole world." At this point the Roman and Christian versions of a second return converge offering Europeans and Americans the possibility of the recovery of an Edenic Golden Age.[18]

Lucretius provides the elements for Thomas Hobbes' origin story of capitalism and the Good State as an emergence from the "state of nature." Lucretius' *De Rerum Naturum* (*Of the Nature of Things*) closely prefigures Hobbes' *Leviathan*. For both Lucretius and Hobbes the early state of human nature is disorderly, lawless, and chaotic. According to Lucretius, before the discovery of plow agriculture, wild beasts consumed humans and starvation was rampant.[19] But early civilization, nurtured by the taming of fire and the cooking of food, foundered on the discovery of gold, as human greed spawned violent wars. Just as Hobbes saw individual men in the state of nature as unruly and warlike, so Lucretius lamented that "things down to the vilest lees of brawling mobs succumbed, whilst each man sought unto himself dominion and supremacy." Just as Hobbes argued that people voluntarily gave up their ability to kill each other in the state of nature and entered into a civil contract enforced by the state, so Lucretius held that people out of their own free will submitted to laws and codes. The creation of civil law thus imposes order on disorderly humans, offering the possiblity of recovery from the state of nature.[20]

Yet Lucretius' poem, as it came down to the Renaissance, ended not in recovery, but in death, as plague and pestilence overcame Athens. The poem breaks off on a note of extreme pessimism and utter terror; piles of dead bodies burn on funeral pyres and all hope is forsaken. Like Lucretius, Hobbes (who was also deemed an atheist) offered a profoundly pessimistic view of nature, human nature, and divinity. Humans who are basically competitive and warlike contest with each other on the commons and in the marketplace in the creation of a capitalist economy.[21]

Like civilization, Nature for Lucretius ends in death and a return to the chaos of winter. As did humans, the earth "whose name was mother" went through stages of life and death. She brought forth birds, beasts, and humans. The fields were like wombs, and the earth's pores gave forth milk like a mother's breasts. Yet when the earth had aged, she was like a worn-out old woman.[22]

In the seventeenth century, the Greek cyclical stories of nature and human society that ended in death and destruction were converted to the Christian redemption story during the battle between ancients and moderns. The declensionist narrative depicting a slide downward from Golden Age to Iron Age, from original wisdom to ignorance, from human giants to midgets, was transformed by the hope of recovery. Both nature and human nature were capable of redemption. Science and technology offered the means of transforming nature, labor in the earth the means of saving human souls. The earth could be plowed, cultivated, and improved as human beings mixed their labor with the soil. (For Locke, as oppposed to Hobbes, the state of nature is good and labor has a positive valence.) Thus both the cultivated earth and cultivated humans would be prepared for the final moment of redemption, or Parousia, when earth would merge with heaven, re-creating the original oneness. With the discovery of the New World, a New Earth could be reconstructed with the image of the original garden as paradigmatic ideal.

THE AMERICAN HEROIC RECOVERY NARRATIVE

In America, the recovery narrative propelled settlement and "improvement" of the American continent by Europeans. Euramerican men acted to reverse the decline initiated by Eve by turning it into an ascent back to the garden. Using science, technology, and biblical imagery, they changed first the eastern wilderness and then the western deserts into cultivated gardens. Sanctioned by the Genesis origin story, they subdued the "wilderness," replenished the earth, and appropriated Indian homelands as free lands for settlement. Mercantile capitalism cast America as the site of natural resources, Africa as the source of enslaved human resources, and Europe as the locale of resource management. Timber, barrel staves, animal hides, herbal medicines, tobacco, sugar, and cotton were extracted from nature in the great project of "improving" the land. Men, as fallen Adam, became the heroic agents who transformed and redeemed fallen Nature.[23]

In New England, European settlers converted a "hideous and desolate wilderness" into "a second England for fertileness" in the space of a few decades. The Pilgrim migration, as recorded in the text of William Bradford, conforms to the six elements of the mythic heroic narrative identified by Russian folklorist Vladimer Propp: 1) The hero's initial absence. 2) His transference from one place to another. 3) The combat between hero and villain. 4) The hero's receipt of a gift. 5) The victory. 6) The final repair of the hero's initial absence.[24] In this case the hero, Bradford, leads his people through trials and tests in the struggle to recreate the garden in the New World.

In the first phase of the New England recovery story, the land is absent of the hero. Indian corn fields are abandoned and the Indians victims of disease. As John Cotton put it: "When the Lord chooses to transplant his people, he first makes a country ...void in that place where they reside."[25] In the second, or transferrence phase, the hero, William Bradford, is transported from Old England to New England by ship. A spatial translocation takes place between two kingdoms, that of the antichrist (the fleshpots of Old England) and the New Canaan, or promised land of New England. In the third, or combative phase, the hero is tested through struggle with the villain—the devil acting through nature. The mythic struggle between hero and villain is played out as a struggle between Bradford and the wilderness—the tempestuous ocean and the desolate forest, a land filled with "wild beasts and wild men." Bradford's faith in God and his leadership of his people are continually called on, as storms wreak havoc with the small ship, the Mayflower, and the little band of settlers struggles to survive the grim winter on the shores of an unforgiving land. In the fourth phase the hero receives a gift from a helper, in this case "a special instrument sent [from] God" through the Indian Squanto, who not only speaks the Pilgrims' own language, but shows them how to "set their corn, where to take fish, and to procure other commodities." The fifth phase is the victory of the hero, as the corn is harvested, cabins and stockade are built, and the struggling band survives its first year. Nature, as wilderness, has been defeated. In the sixth and climactic phase the hero's initial absence has been repaired, the misfortunes are liquidated, and the Pilgrims are reborn. They celebrate their triumph over wilderness by their first harvest, achieved through the miracle of the re-created garden. By filling and replenishing the land, the recovery of the garden in the New World has been launched and the American recovery myth created.[26]

Pilgrim victory was followed by Puritan victory when the Massachusetts Bay Colony added thousands of additional settlers to the new land, repeating the heroic journey across the Atlantic to advance the Edenic recovery. As the *Arabella* left England for the New World in 1629, Puritan refugees listened to John Winthrop quoting Genesis 1:28, "Be fruitful and multiply, and replenish the earth and subdue it." Boston pastor Charles Morton adhered to both the Genesis origin story and the Baconian ideal when he wrote in 1728 that, because of the sin of the first parents, agriculture and husbandry must be used to combat weeds and soil sterility through fencing, tilling, manuring, and draining the land. Almanac maker Nathaniel Ames in 1754 helped to justify the mechanistic science of the body in Edenic terms when he informed his readers that the Divine artificer initially had made the body of man "a machine capable of endless duration," but that, after Eve's ingestion of the forbidden apple, the living principle within had fallen into disharmony with the body, disrupting the smooth functioning of its parts.[27]

In the Chesapeake region, by the early eighteenth century, tobacco planters converted an "unjustly neglected" and "abused" Virginia into a ravishing garden of pleasure. Robert Beverley predicated Virginia's potential as a "Garden of the World," akin to Canaan, Syria, and Persia, on his countrymen's ability to overcome an "unpardonable laziness."[28] Tobacco cultivation became the means of participating in the European market, while simultaneously improving the land through labor. But the recovery was ever in danger from new lapsarian moments if people allowed themselves to indulge in laziness, narcotics, or alcohol. During the eighteenth and nineteenth centuries, migrants from the original colonies and immigrants from Europe explored, settled, and "improved" the uplands west of the Atlantic coast, the intervales of the Appalachian Mountains, and the lowlands of the Mississippi valley.

In the late 1820s and 1830s, Thomas Cole of the Hudson River school of painters depicted the American recovery narrative and the dangers of both the original and subsequent lapsarian moments. *His Expulsion from the Garden of Eden* (1827-28) contrasts the tranquil, original garden on the right with the bleak, chaotic desert on the left, while in the center God expels Adam and Eve through a gate. The garden features a meandering stream and luxuriant vegetation, while the desert comprises barren rock, hot winds, a wild cataract, an erupting volcano, and a wolf attacking a deer. *The Oxbow* (1836) portrays the possibility of recovery through re-creating the Garden on earth. The painting moves from dark wilderness on the left to an enlightened, tranquil, cultivated landscape on the right, bordering the curve of the peaceful Connecticut River. In the background, cutover scars in the forest on the hill apparently spell the Hebrew letters Noah, which when viewed upside down from a God's eye view form the word shaddai, meaning, "the Almighty." God's presence in the landscape recognizes God's covenant with Noah and anticipates the final reunion of God and the earth at the Parousia. Humans can therefore redeem the land itself as garden, even as they redeem themselves through laboring in the earth.[29]

In a series of paintings from the 1830s, Cole depicted the movement from "savagery" to "civilization" and the problem of lapsing back into the darkness of wilderness. Of an 1831 painting, *A Wild Scene*, he wrote, "The first picture must be a savage wilderness...the figures must be savage—clothed in skins & occupied in the Chase—...as though nature was just waking from chaos."[30] A subsequent series, *The Course of Empire*, followed Virgil's stages of emergence from "savagery"—*The Savage State, The Pastoral State, Consummation of Empire, Destruction of Empire*, and *Desolation*—to warn of lapsarian dangers that thwart progress and end in the ruin of civilization.

Ralph Waldo Emerson eulogized the recovered garden achieved through human dominion over nature in glowing rhetoric: "This great savage country should be furrowed by the plough, and combed by the harrow; these rough Alleganies should know their master; these foaming torrents should be bestridden by proud arches of stone; these wild prairies should be loaded with wheat; the swamps with rice; the hill-tops should pasture innumerable sheep and cattle....How much better when the whole land is a garden, and the people have grown up in the bowers of a paradise."[31] Only after intensive development of the eastern seaboard did a small number of nineteenth-century urban artists, writers, scientists, and explorers begin to deplore the effects of the "machine in the garden."[32]

Similarly, Euramericans acted out the recovery narrative in transforming the western deserts during the second half of the nineteenth century. The elements of the story again conform to the elements of Propp's heroic narrative. The land is absent of the heroes—the migrants themselves. They are transferred across inhospitable desert lands; engage in combat with hostile Indians, diseases, and starvation; receive gifts from God in the form of gold and free land; emerge victorious over nature and Indian; and liquidate the initial absence of the hero by filling and replenishing the land. In filling the land through settlement, the migrants heeded John Quincy Adams's 1846 call for expansion into Oregon: "to make the wilderness blossom as the rose, to establish laws, to increase, multiply, and subdue the earth, which we are commanded to do by the first behest of the God Almighty." They likewise heard Thomas Hart Benton's call to manifest destiny that the white race had "alone received the divine command to subdue and replenish the earth: for it is the only race that...hunts out new and distant lands, and even a New World, to subdue and replenish."[33]

With Reverend Dwinell, they commemorated the 1869 joining of the Central Pacific and Union Pacific railroads, using the Bible to sanction human alteration of the landscape. "Prepare ye the way of the Lord, make straight in the desert a highway before our God. Every valley shall be exalted, and every mountain and hill shall be made low and the crooked shall be made straight and the rough places plain." And in settling, ranching, and plowing the Great Plains, they reversed the Biblical Fall from Eden by turning the "Great American Desert" into yet another "Garden of the World." The reclamation of arid lands west of the hundredth meridian through the technologies of irrigation fulfilled the biblical mandate of making the desert blossom as the rose, while making the land productive for capitalist agriculture.[34]

At the end of the nineteenth century, Frederick Jackson Turner's essay on the closing of the frontier in American history epitomized the heroic recovery narrative. The six phases of the heroic victory are again present in Turner's narrative, although it warns of impending declension as the frontier closes. 1) The frontier is defined by the absence of settlement and civilization. "Up to and including 1880, the country had a frontier of settlement, but at present the unsettled area has been.... broken." 2) Europeans are transferred across space as the succession of frontier lines moves west, and they "adapt...to changes involved in crossing the continent." Stand at Cumberland gap and watch the procession—the buffalo following the trail to the salt lick, the trapper, the miner, the rancher, and the farmer follow each other in succession; stand at South Pass a century later and watch the same succession again. 3) The individual hero is in combat with the villain—again the wilderness, Indians, and wild beasts. "The wilderness masters the colonist." The encounter with wilderness "strips off the garments" of European civilization and "puts him in the log cabin of the Cherokee and Iroquois." 4) The heroes receive the gift of free land. But "never again," Turner warns, "will such gifts of free land offer themselves." 5) The encounter with the frontier transforms hero into victor. "Little by little he transforms the wilderness, but the outcome is not the old Europe...here is a new product that is American." 6) Democracy and American civilization "in a perennial rebirth" fill the land, liquidating the initial absence. "Democracy is born of free land."[35] With frontier expansion, temporal recovery through science and capitalism merges with spatial recovery through acquisition of private property.

INDIANS IN THE RECOVERY NARRATIVE

The heroic recovery narrative that guided settlement is notable for its treatment of Indians. Wilderness is the absence of civilization. Although many Euramericans apparently perceived Indians as the functional equivalent of wild animals, they nevertheless believed the Indian survivors possessed the potential to be "civilized" and hence to participate in the recovery as settled farmers. American officials changed the Indians' own origin stories to make them descendants of Adam and Eve; hence they were not even indigenous to America. Thomas L. McHenry, who formulated Indian policy in the 1840s, said that the whole "family of man" came from "one original and common stock" of which the Indian was one branch. "Man...was put by his creator in the garden, which was eastward in Eden, whence flowed the river which parted, and became into four heads; and that from his fruitfulness his [the Indian] species were propagated." The commissioner of Indian affairs in 1868 deemed them "capable of civilization and christianization." A successor in 1892 argued that since Indian children were "made in the image of God, being the likeness of their Creator," they had the "same possibilites of growth and development" as other children. An Indian baby could become "a cultivated refined Christian gentleman or lovely woman."[36]

Euramericans attempted to transform Indians from hunters into settled farmers by first removing them to lands west of the Mississippi, then to reservations, and later by allotting them 160 acre plots of private property. Thomas Jefferson saw them as capable of participating in the recovery narrative when he told a delegation in 1802 that he would be pleased to see them "cultivate the earth, to raise herds of useful animals and to spin and weave."[37]

With Indians largely vanquished and moved to reservations by the 1890s, twentieth-century conservationists turned "recovered" Indian homelands into parks, set aside wilderness areas as people-free reserves where "man himself is a vistor who does not remain," and managed forests for maximum yield and efficiency. With the taming of wilderness, desert, and "wild men," the recovery story reached an apparent by happy ending.[38]

But Indians, for the most part, rejected the new narrative. With some exceptions, they resisted the roles into which they were cast and the lines they were forced to speak. They objected to characterizations of their lands as wilderness or desert, calling them simply home. As Chief Luther Standing Bear put it, "We did not think of the great open plains, the beautiful rolling hills, and winding streams with tangled growth, as 'wild.' Only to the white man was nature a wilderness and only to him was the land 'infested' with 'wild' animals and 'savage' people. To us it was tame. Earth was bountiful. . . ."[39]

While adopting the Christian religion, Indians often emphasized those aspects compatible with traditional beliefs and participated in the ceremonial and celebratory aspects with greater enthusiasm than in the more austere, otherworldly practices.[40] Although taught to read and cipher, they often rejected white society's science and technology as useless for living. As Franklin satirized the colonists' effort, the Indians, when offered the opportunity to attend the College of William and Mary in Virginia, politely considered the matter before refusing:

> Several of our young people were formerly brought up at the colleges of the northern provinces; they were instructed in all your sciences; but when they came back to us they were bad runners; ignorant of every means of living in the woods; unable to bear either cold or hunger; knew neither how to build a cabin, take a deer, or kill an enemy; spoke our language imperfectly, and were therefore neither fit for hunters, warriors, or counsellors; they were totally good for nothing. We are however, none the less obliged by your kind offer, tho' we decline accepting it; and to show our grateful sense of it, if the gentlemen of Virginia will send us a dozen of their sons, we will take great care of their education, instruct them in all we know, and make men of them.[41]

FEMALE NATURE IN THE RECOVERY NARRATIVE

An account of the history of American settlement as a lapsarian and recovery narrative must also consider the crucial role of Nature conceptualized as

female in the very structure of the plot. The rhetoric of American settlement
is filled with language that casts nature as female object to be transformed and
men as the agents of change. Allusions to Eve as virgin land to be subdued,
as fallen nature to be redeemed through reclamation, and as fruitful garden to
be harvested and enjoyed are central to the particular ways in which American
lands were developed. The extraction of resources from "nature's bosom,"
the penetration of "her womb" by science and technology, and the "seduction" of female land by male agriculture reinforced capitalist expansion.[42]

Images of nature as female are deeply encoded into the texts of
American history, art, and literature and function as ideologies for settlement.
Thus Thomas Morton in praising New England as a new Canaan likened its
potential for development by "art and industry" to a "faire virgin longing to
be sped and meete her lover in a Nuptiall bed." Now, however, "her fruitfull
wombe, not being enjoyed is like a glorious tombe."[43] Male agriculturalists
saw in plow technology a way to compel female nature to produce. Calling
Bacon "the grand master of philosophy" in 1833, Massachusetts agricultural
improver Henry Colman promoted Bacon's approach to recovering the garden through agriculture. "The effort to extend the dominion of man over
nature," he wrote, "is the most healthy and most noble of all ambitions." He
characterized the earth as a female whose productivity could help to advance
the progress of the human race. "Here man exercises dominion over
nature...commands the earth on which he treads to waken her mysterious
energies...compels the inanimate earth to teem with life; and to impart sustenance and power, health and happiness to the countless multitudes who hang
on her breast and are dependent on her bounty."[44]

A graphic example of female nature succumbing to the male plow is provided by Frank Norris in his 1901 novel *The Octopus*, a story of the transformation of California by the railroad. Here the earth is female, sexual, and
alive. Norris writes,

> The great brown earth turned a huge flank to [the sky], exhaling the
> moisture of the early dew....One could not take a dozen steps upon the
> ranches without the brusque sensation that underfoot the land was
> alive,...palpitating with the desire of reproduction. Deep down there
> in the recesses of the soil, the great heart throbbed once more, thrilling
> with passion, vibrating with desire, offering itself to the caress of the
> plough, insistent, eager, imperious. Dimly one felt the deep-seated
> trouble of the earth, the uneasy agitation of its members, the hidden
> tumult of its womb, demanding to be made fruitful, to reproduce, to

disengage the eternal renascent germ of Life that stirred and struggled in its loins....[45]

In Norris's novel, the seduction of the female earth was carried out on a massive scale by thousands of men operating their plows in unison on a given day in the spring. "Everywhere throughout the great San Joaquin," he wrote, "unseen and unheard, a thousand ploughs up-stirred the land, tens of thousands of shears clutched deep into the warm, moist soil."[46] And Norris leaves no doubt that the men's technology, the plow, is also male and that the seduction becomes violent rape:

> It was the long stroking caress, vigorous, male, powerful, for which the Earth seemed panting. The heroic embrace of a multitude of iron hands, gripping deep into the brown, warm flesh of the land that quivered responsive and passionate under this rude advance, so robust as to be almost an assault, so violent as to be veritably brutal. There, under the sun and under the speckless sheen of the sky, the wooing of the Titan began, the vast primal passion, the two world-forces, the elemental Male and Female, locked in a colossal embrace, at grapples in the throes of an infinite desire, at once terrible and divine, knowing no law, untamed, savage, natural, sublime.[47]

The narrative of frontier expansion is a story of male energy subduing female nature, taming the wild, plowing the land, recreating the garden lost by Eve. American males lived the frontier myth in their everyday lives, making the land safe for capitalism and commodity production. Once tamed by men, the land was safe for women. To civilize was to bring the land out of a state of savagery and barbarism into a state of refinement and enlightenment. This state of domestication, of civility, is symbolized by woman and "womanlike" man. "The man of training, the civilizee," reported *Scribner's Monthly* in November 1880, "is less manly than the rough, the pioneer."[48]

But the taming of external nature was intimately linked to the taming of internal nature, the exploitation of nonhuman nature to the exploitation of human nature. The civilizing process not only removed wild beasts from the pastoral lands of the garden, it suppressed the wild animal in men. Crèvecoeur, in 1782, noted that on the frontier, "men appear to be no better than carnivorous animals...living on the flesh of wild animals." Those who farmed the middle settlements, on the other hand, were "like plants," purified by the "simple cultivation of the earth," becoming civilized through reading and political discourse.[49] Or, as Richard Burton put it in 1861, "The civilizee

shudders at the idea of eating wolf "[50] Just as the earth is female to the farmer
who subdues it with the plow, so wilderness is female to the male explorer, fron-
tiersman, and pioneer who tame it with the brute strength of the ax, the trap,
and the gun. Its valence, however, changes from the negative satanic forest of
William Bradford and the untamed wilderness of the pioneer (fallen Eve) to
the positive pristine Eden and mother earth of John Muir (original and Mother
Eve) and the parks of Frederick Law Olmsted. As wilderness vanishes before
advancing civilization, its remnants must be preserved as test zones for men
(epitomized by Theodore Roosevelt) to hone male strength and skills.[51]

Civilization is the final end, the telos, toward which "wild" Nature is des-
tined. The progressive narrative undoes the declension of the Fall. The "end
of nature" is civilization. Civilization is thus nature natured, *Natura
naturata*—the natural order, or nature ordered and tamed. It is no longer
nature naturing, *Natura naturans*—nature as creative force. Nature passes
from inchoate matter endowed with a formative power to a reflection of the
civilized natural order designed by God. The unruly energy of wild female
nature is suppressed and pacified. The final happy state of nature natured is
female and civilized—the restored garden of the world.[52]

John Gast depicts this ascensionist narrative in his 1872 painting,
American Progress. (Figure 2.2)[53] On the left, toward the west is *Natura naturans*, Nature active, alive, wild, dark, and savage, filled, as William Bradford
would have put it, with "wild beasts and wild men." Buffalo, wolves, and elk
flee in dark disorder accompanied by Indians with horses and *travois*. On the
right, coming from the east, advancing to the west, is *Natura naturata*, Nature
ordered, civilized, and tamed. No longer to be feared or sexually assaulted,
she floats angelically through the air in flowing white robes, emblazoned with
the star of empire. She carries telegraph wires in her left hand, symbols of the
highest level of communication—language borne through the air, the word
or logos from above. The domination of logic or pure form is repeated in the
book grasped in her right hand touching the coiled telegraph wires. She represents the city, the civil, the civic order of government—the highest order
of nature. She is pure Platonic form impressed on female matter, transforming and ordering all beneath her.[54]

Most important, however, it is American men who have prepared her
way. They have dispelled the darkness, fought the Indian, killed the bear and
buffalo. Covered wagons bearing westward pioneers, gold rush prospectors,
and the pony express precede her. Farmers plowing the soil next to their
fenced fields and rude cabins have settled and tamed the land. Stage coaches

FIG. 2.2 / JOHN GAST, *AMERICAN PROGRESS*, 1872. GENE AUTRY WESTERN
HERITAGE MUSEUM, LOS ANGELES, REPRODUCED BY PERMISSION.

and trains follow, bringing waves of additional settlers. At the far right is the
Atlantic civilization, where ships bearing the arts of the Old World arrive in
the New World. The painting itself is a lived progressive narrative. Its east to
west movement is a story of ascent and conquest.

A similar image was captured by Emanuel Leutze in his famous mural in
the U.S. Capitol, *Westward the Course of Empire Takes its Way*, painted in
1861, illustrating a line from a poem by George Berkeley (Figure 2.3). At the
center of the mural on a rock outcrop pointing west toward barren "virgin"
land is a madonna-like grouping of a pioneer with his wife and child. Below
pass men with guns mounted on horses followed by covered wagons bearing
women representing civilization. Their way is prepared by men cutting the
forest with axes and uprooting trees that lie in the party's way. Below, in the
mural's frame, is a view of San Francisco's golden gate flanked by portraits of
explorers William Clark and Daniel Boone. Like Gast's *American Progress*,
the scene is a dynamic moment in the transformation of "virgin" nature into
female civilized form through the agency of men.

A third example is the 1875 painting *Progress of America*, by Domenico
Tojetti (Figure 2.4). A female Liberty figure personifying progress drives a
chariot with a mounted American eagle pulled by two white horses. On the

FIG. 2.3 / EMANUEL LEUTZE, *WESTWARD THE COURSE OF EMPIRE TAKES ITS WAY,* MURAL STUDY, UNITED STATES CAPITOL, 1861, NATIONAL MUSEUM OF AMERICAN ART, SMITHSONIAN INSTITUTION, WASHINGTON D.C., BEQUEST OF SARA CARR UPTON. REPRODUCED BY PERMISSION.

FIG. 2.4 / DOMENICO TOJETTI, *THE PROGRESS OF AMERICA,* 1875. COLLECTION OF THE OAKLAND MUSEUM OF CALIFORNIA, THE OAKLAND MUSEUM KAHN COLLECTION, REPRODUCED BY PERMISSION.

left, American Indians and buffalo flee into darkness and disorder at the advance of civilization, while on the right, behind the Liberty icon, female figures representing agriculture, medicine, mechanics, and the arts accompany her advance. Women bearing a tablet symboling literacy follow in front of a train bringing commerce and light to a barren "virgin" landscape.

A fourth representation was that of "Civilization," painted by George Willoughby Maynard in 1893 (Figure 2.5). A white female figure dressed in white robes is seated on a throne decorated with cornucopias. She holds the book of knowledge on her lap and points to its written words as the epitome of enlightenment and education. The book represents the logos, the light or word from above. The figure's Anglo-saxon whiteness excludes the blackness of matter, darkness, and dark-skinned peoples.

All four images portray movement from dark, barren, virgin, undeveloped nature, or *Natura Naturans,* to final Platonic, civilized, ideal form, *Natura Naturata.* In the first two images, male agents effect the transformation from the undeveloped disorder of the desert to the ordered, idealized landscape. The final two paintings reveal the outcome, an enlightened world made safe for educated Euramerican men and women.

THE CITY IN THE GARDEN

The city represents the next stage of the recovery narrative—the creation of the City in the Garden (Virgil's *urbs in horto*) by means of the capitalist market. The city epitomizes the transformation of female Nature into female Civilization through the mutually reinforcing powers of male energy and interest-earning capital. Frank Norris in his second novel, *The Pit* (1903), reveals the connections.[55] In writing of Chicago and the wheat pit at the Board of Trade (a story brilliantly told in William Cronon's *Nature's Metropolis*, inspired in part by Norris's book), Norris depicts the city as female.[56] The city is the locus of power that operates in the natural world, sweeping everything towards its center. It is the bridge between civilized female form and the raw matter of the surrounding hinterlands, drawing that matter towards it, as natural resources are transformed into capitalist commodities. Chicago, writes Norris,

> the Great Grey City, brooking no rival, imposed its dominion upon a reach of country larger than many a kingdom of the Old World. For thousands of miles beyond its confines was its influence felt. Out, far out, far away in the snow and shadow of Northern Wisconsin forests, axes and saws bit the bark of century old trees, stimulated by this city's

FIG. 2.5 / GEORGE WILLOUGHBY MAYNARD, *CIVILIZATION*, 1893. NATIONAL
ACADEMY OF DESIGN, NEW YORK CITY. REPRODUCED BY PERMISSION.

energy. Just as far to the southward pick and drill leaped to the assault
of veins of anthracite moved by her central power. Her force turned
the wheels of harvester and seeder a thousand miles distant in Iowa
and Kansas. Her force spun the screws and propellers of innumerable
squadrons of lake steamers crowding the Sault Sainte Marie. For her
and because of her all the Central States, all the Great Northwest
roared with traffic and industry; sawmills screamed; factories, their
smoke blackening the sky, slashed and flamed; wheels turned, pistons
leaped in their cylinders; cog gripped cog; beltings clasped the drums
of mammoth wheels; and converters of forges belched into the clouded
air their tempest breath of molten steel.[57]

The city transforms the matter of nature in the very act of pulling it
inward. Like Plato's female soul of the world, turning herself within herself,
the city provides the source of motion that permeates and energizes the world
around it, the bridge between raw changing matter and final civilized form. In
Norris's novel, men at first seem subordinate to the city's higher force, acting
merely as agents in the preordained purpose of transforming Nature into civilization. They facilitate the change from *Natura naturans* into *Natura naturata*, from natural resource into fabricated product. Operating the steam
engines, sawmills, factories, lumber barges, grain elevators, trains, and switch-
es that make Chicago an industrial city, workers shout and signal as trains daily
debouch businessmen bringing with them trade from country to city. This
process of "civilization in the making," says Norris, is like a "great tidal
wave," an "elemental," "primordial" force, "the first verses of Genesis." It
"subdu[es] the wilderness in a single generation," through the "resistless subjugation of...the lakes and prairies."[58]

Yet behind the scenes other men, the capitalist speculators of the Chicago
Board of Trade, attempt to manipulate the very forces of Nature, pushing the
transformation faster and faster. Capitalism mystifies by converting living
nature into dead matter and by changing inert metals into living money.[59] To
the capitalist puppeteers, nature is a doll-like puppet controlled by the strings
of the wheat trade that changes money into interest-earning capital. Male
minds calculate the motions that control the inert matter below.

To Norris's capitalist, Curtis Jadwin, nature is dead. Only money is alive,
growing and swelling through the daily trade of the wheat pit. With the bulls
and bears of the marketplace the only apparent living things he encounters,
Jadwin utterly fails to account for the earth and the wheat as alive. Yet as Jadwin,
the bull trader, corners the market to obtain complete control over the bears, dri-

ving the price higher and higher, the living wheat planted by hundreds of farmers throughout the heartland rises from the soil as a gigantic irrepressible force. The capitalist's manipulation of apparently dead nature has immense environmental consequences. Jadwin, Norris writes, had "laid his puny human grasp upon Creation and the very earth herself." The "great mother...had stirred at last in her sleep and sent her omnipotence moving through the grooves of the world, to find and crush the disturber of her appointed courses."[60]

But in the late nineteenth century, as the frontier closes, forests disappear, and the land is made safe for civilization, American men begin to lament the loss of wild nature. There is an apparent need to retain wilderness as a place for men to test maleness, strength, and virility and an apparent association of men with nature.[61] Similarly, women are symbolized as the moral model that suppresses internal sexual libido. But Nature as wilderness does not *become* male, nor does civilization *become* female in a reversal of the so-called universal association of female to nature and male to culture identified by Sherry Ortner.[62] There is no real reversal of male/female valences in the closing chapters of the story of frontier expansion. In the story of American progress, males continue to be the transforming agents between active female nature and civilized female form, making the land safe for women and men alike, suppressing both unpredictable external nature *and* unruly internal nature.

Nor are nature and culture, women and men, binary opposites with universal or essential meanings. Nature, wilderness, and civilization are socially constructed concepts that change over time and serve as stage settings in the progressive narrative. So too are the concepts of male and female and the roles that men and women act out on the stage of history. The authors of such powerful narratives as *laissez-faire* capitalism, mechanistic science, manifest destiny, and the frontier story are usually privileged elites with access to power and patronage. Their words are read by persons of power who add the new stories to the older Biblical story. As such, the books become the library of Western Culture. The library, in turn, functions as ideology when ordinary people read, listen to, internalize, and act out the stories told by their elders—the ministers, entrepreneurs, newspaper editors, and professors who teach and socialize the young.

The most recent chapter of the book of the recovery narrative is the transformation of nature through biotechnology. From genetically engineered apples to Flavr-Savr tomatoes, the fruits of the original (evolved) garden are being redesigned so that the salinated irrigated desert can continue to blossom as the rose. In the recovered Garden of Eden fruits ripen faster, have fewer seeds, need less water, require fewer pesticides, contain less saturated fat, and have longer shelf lives. The human temptation to engineer nature is reaching too close to the powers of God warn the Jeremiahs, who depict the snake coiled around the Tree of the Knowledge of Good and Evil as the DNA spiral. But the progressive engineers who design the technologies that allow the recovery to accelerate see only hope in the new fabrications.

The twentieth-century Garden of Eden is the enclosed shopping mall decorated with trees, flowers, and fountains in which people can shop for nature at the Nature Company, purchase "natural" clothing at Esprit, sample organic foods and rainforest crunch in kitchen gardens, buy twenty-first-century products at Sharper Image, and play virtual reality games in which SimEve is reinvented in Cyberspace. This Garden in the City recreates the pleasures and temptations of the original garden and the Golden Age where people can peacefully harvest the fruits of earth with gold grown by the market. The mall, enclosed by the desert of the parking lots surrounding it, is covered by glass domes reaching to heaven, accessed by spiral staircases and escalators affording a vista over the whole garden of shops. The "river that went out of Eden to water the garden" is reclaimed in meandering streams lined with palm trees and filled with bright orange carp. Today's malls feature stone grottos, trellises decorated with flowers, life-sized trees, statues, birds, animals, and even indoor beaches that simulate paradigmatic nature as a cultivated, benign garden. With their engineered spaces and commodity fetishes, they epitomize consumer capitalism's vision of the recovery from the Fall.[63]

CRITIQUES OF THE RECOVERY NARRATIVE

The modern version of the recovery narrative, however, has been subjected to scathing criticism. Postmodern thinkers contest its Enlightenment assumptions, while cultural feminists and environmentalists reverse its plot, depicting a slow decline from a prior Golden Age, not a progressive ascent to a new garden on earth. The critics' plot does not move from the tragedy of the Fall to the comedy of an earthly paradise, but descends from an original state of oneness with nature to the tragedy of nature's destruction. Nevertheless, they too hope for a recovery, one rapid enough to save the earth and society by the mid-twenty-first century. The meta–narrative of recovery does not change, but the declensionist plot, into which they have cast prior history, must be radically reversed. The postmodern critique of modernism is both a deconstruction of Enlightenment thought and a set of reconstructive proposals for the creation of a better world.

The identification of modernism as a problem rather than as progress was sharply formulated by Max Horkheimer and Theodor Adorno in the opening sentences of their 1944 *Dialectic of Enlightenment*: "The fully enlightened earth radiates disaster triumphant. The program of the enlightenment was the disenchantment of the world; the dissolution of myths and the substitution of knowledge for fancy." They criticize both Francis Bacon's concept of the domination of nature and Karl Marx and Friedrich Engels' optimism that the control of nature would lead to advancement. They faulted the reduction of nature to mere number by mechanistic science and capitalism: "Number becomes the canon of the Enlightenment. The same equations dominate bourgeois justice and commodity exchange....Myth turns into enlightenment and nature into mere objectivity."[64]

Among the critics of modernism are many feminists and environmentalists who propose a reversal that will initiate a new millennium in the twenty-first century. Cultural feminists and cultural ecofeminists see the original oneness as female, the *Terra Mater* of the neolithic era, from which emerged the consciousness of differences between humans and animals, male and female, people and nature, leading to dominance and submission. The advent of patriarchy initiates a long decline in the status of women and nature. Men's plow agriculture took over women's gathering and horticultural activities, horse-mounted warriors injected violence into a largely peaceful Old European culture, and male gods replaced female earth deities in origin stories. In the proposed recovery, Eve is revisioned as the first scientist, Sophia as ultimate wisdom, and the goddess as symbol of female power and creativity. Feminist religious history redirects inquiry into the gendered nature of the original oneness as both male and female. The recovery would therefore be a feminist or an egalitarian world.[65]

Feminist science sees the original mind as having no sex, and hence accessible to male and female minds alike. It has been men, many feminists would argue, who invented the science and technology and organized the market economies that made nature the victim in the ascent of "man." For such feminists, the new narrative entails reclaiming women's roles in the history of science and asserting female power in contemporary science and technology. Hence both sexes can participate in the recovery.[66]

Environmentalism, like feminism, reverses the plot of the recovery narrative, seeing history as a slow decline, not a progressive movement that made the desert blossom as the rose. The recovery story is a false story; an original garden became a degraded desert. Pristine nature, not innocent man, has fallen. The decline from Eden was slow, rather than a precipitous lapsarian moment as in the Adam and Eve origin story. Over the millennia from the paleolithic to the present Nature has been the victim of both human hubris and social changes that overcome "the necessities of nature" through domestication, cultivation, and commodification of every aspect of an original, evolved, prehuman garden. So-called advances in science, technology, and economy actually accelerate the decline.[67]

As the twentieth century draws to a close and the second great millennium since the birth of Christ reaches its end, the environmental decline approaches a crisis. The greenhouse effect, the population explosion, the destruction of the ozone layer, the extinction of species, and the end of wilderness are all sub-plots in a grand narrative of environmental endism. Predictions of crisis, such as those of Paul Ehrlich in "Ecocatastrophe" (1969), the Club of Rome in *Limits to Growth* (1972) and of Bill McKibben in *The End of Nature* (1989), abound, as first (evolved, prehuman) nature is totally subsumed by humans and the human artifacts of second (commodified) nature.[68]

Like feminists, environmentalists want to rewrite the modern progressive story. Viewing the plot as declensionist rather than progressive, they nevertheless opt for a recovery that must be put in place by the mid-twenty-first century. "Sustainability" is a new vision of the recovered garden, one in which humanity will live in a relationship of balance and harmony with the natural world. Environmentalists who press for sustainable development see the recovery as achievable through the spread of nondegrading forms of agriculture and industry. Preservationists and deep ecologists strive to save pristine nature as wilderness before it can be destroyed by development. Restoration ecologists wish to marshal human labor to restore an already degraded nature to an earlier, pristine state. Social ecologists and green parties devise new economic and political structures that overcome the domination of human beings and nonhuman nature. Women and nature, minorities and nature, other animals and nature, will be fully included in the recovery. The regeneration of nature and people will be achieved through social and environmental justice. The End Drama envisions a postpatriarchal, socially just ecotopia for the postmillennial world of the twenty-first century.[69]

CHAOS THEORY AND PARTNERSHIP ETHICS

Seeing Western history as a recovery narrative, with feminism and environmentalism as reversals of the plot, brings up the question of the character of the plot itself. The declensionist and progressive plots that underlie the meta-narrative of recovery both gain power from their linearity. Linearity is not only conceptually easy to grasp, but it is also a property of modernity itself. Mechanistic science, progress, and capitalism all draw power from the linear functions of mathematical equations—the upward and downward slopes of straight lines and curves. To the extent that these linear slopes intersect with a real material world, they refer to a limited domain only. Chaos theory and complexity theory suggest that only the unusual domain of mechanistic science can be described by linear differential equations. The usual—that is, the domain of everyday occurrences, such as the weather, turbulence, the shapes of coastlines, the arrhythmic fibrillations of the human heart, cannot be so easily described. The world is more complex than we know or indeed can ever know. The comfortable predictability of the linear slips away into the uncertainty of the indeterminate—into discordant harmonies and disorderly order.

The appearance of chaos as an actor in science and history in the late twentieth century is not only symptomatic of the breakdown of modernism, mechanism, and, potentially, capitalism, but suggests the possibility of a new birth, a new world, a new millennium—the order out of chaos narrative of Ilya Prigogine and Isabelle Stengers. But chaos theory also fundamentally destabilizes the very concept of nature as a standard or referent. It disrupts the idea of the "balance of nature," of nature as resilient actor or mother who will repair the errors of human actors and continue as fecund garden (Eve as mother). It questions the possibility that humans as agents can control and master nature through science and technology, undermining the myth of nature as virgin female to be developed (Eve as virgin). Chaos is the reemergence of nature as power over humans, nature as active, dark, wild, turbulent, and uncontrollable (fallen Eve). Ecologists characterize "Mother Nature" as a "strange attractor" while turbulence is seen to be encoded with gendered images of masculine channels and feminine flows.[70] Moreover, in the chaotic narrative, humans lose the hubris of fallen Adam that the garden can be re-created on earth. The world is not created by a patriarchal God *ex nihilo*, but emerges out of chaos. Thus the very possibility of the recovery of a stable original garden—the plot of the recovery meta-narrative—is itself challenged.

Recognition of history as a meta-narrative raises the further question of the relativity of the histories through which we are educated and of our own lives as participants in the plots they tell. Like our nineteenth-century counterparts, we live our lives as characters in the grand narrative into which we have been socialized as children and conform as adults. That narrative is the story told to itself by the dominant society of which we are a part. We internalize narrative as ideology. Ideology is a story told by people in power. Once we identify ideology as a story—powerful and compelling, but still only a story—we realize that by rewriting the story, we can challenge the structures of power. We recognize that all stories can and should be challenged.

But can we actually step outside the story into which we are cast as characters and enter into a story with a different plot? More important, can we change the plot of the grand master narrative of modernism? Where do I as author of this text stand in relationship to it? As a product of modernism, mechanism, and capitalism, I have internalized the values of the recovery narrative I have sought to identify. I participate in the progressive recovery narrative in my daily work, my wages for intellectual labor, my aspirations for a better material life, and my enjoyment of the profits my individual achievements have wrought. Yet I also believe, despite the relativism of environmental endism, that the environmental crisis is real—that the vanishing frogs, fish, and songbirds are telling us a truth. I am also a product of linear thinking and set up this recovery narrative to reflect the very linearity of progressive history. This is history seen from a particular point of view, the view I have identified as the dominant ideology of modernism. I also believe my recovery narrative reflects a fundamental insight into how nature has been historically constructed as a gendered object.

Yet both history and nature are extremely complex, complicated, and nonlinear. What would a chaotic, nonlinear, nongendered history with a different plot look like? Would it be as compelling as the linear version, even if that linear version were extremely nuanced and complicated? A postmodern history might posit characteristics other than those identified with modernism, such as many authorial voices; a multiplicity of real actors; acausal, nonsequential events; nonessentialized symbols and meanings; dialectical action and process rather than the imposed logos of form; situated and contextualized, rather than universal knowledge. It would be a story (or multiplicity of stories) that perhaps can only be acted and lived, not written at all.

I too yearn for a recovery from environmental declension—for my own vision of a postpatriarchal, socially–just ecotopia for the third millennium. My vision entails a partnership ethic between humans (whether male or female), and between humans and nonhuman nature. For most of human history, nonhuman nature has had power over humans. People accepted fate while propitiating nature with gifts, sacrifices, and prayer (often within hierarchical human relationships). Since the seventeenth century, however, some groups of people have increasingly gained great power over nature and other human groups through the interlinked forces of science, technology, capitalism (and state socialism), politics, and religion.

A partnership ethic would bring humans and nonhuman nature into a dynamically balanced, more nearly equal relationship. Humans, as the bearers of ethics, would acknowledge nonhuman nature as an autonomous actor that cannot be predicted or controlled except in very limited domains. We would also acknowledge that we have the potential to destroy life as we currently know it through nuclear power, pesticides, toxic chemicals, and unrestrained economic development, and exercise specific restraints on that ability. We would cease to create profit for the few at the expense of the many. We would instead organize our economic and political forces to fulfill peoples' basic needs for food, clothing, shelter, and energy, and to provide security for health, jobs, education, children, and old–age. Such forms of security would rapidly reduce population growth rates since a major means of providing security would not depend on having large numbers of children, especially boys. A partnership ethic would be a relationship between a human community and a nonhuman community in a particular place, a place that recognizes its connections to the larger world through economic and ecological exchanges. It would be an ethic in which humans act to fulfill both human needs and nature's needs by restraining human hubris. Guided by a partnership ethic, people would select technologies that sustained the natural environment by becoming co-workers and partners with nonhuman nature, not dominators over it. (See Conclusion.)

A partnership ethic implies a remythicizing of the Edenic recovery narrative or the writing of a new narrative altogether. The new myth would not accept the patriarchal sequence of creation, or even the milder phrase "male and female, created he them," but might instead emphasize simultaneous creation, cooperative male/female evolution, or even an emergence out of chaos or the earth. It would not accept the idea of subduing the earth, or even dressing and keeping the garden, since both entail total domestication and control by human beings. Instead, each earthly place would be a home, or community, to be shared with other living and nonliving things. The needs of both humans and nonhumans would be dynamically balanced. If such a story can be rewritten or experienced, it would be the product of many new voices and would have a complex plot and a different ending. As in the corn mother origin story, women and the earth, along with men, would be active agents. The new ending, however, will not come about if we simply read and reread the story into which we were born. The new story can be rewritten only through action.

3

ISIS

SCIENCE AND
HISTORY

When George Sarton, founding father of the history of science, published its first journal in 1913, he named it *Isis* after the Egyptian mother goddess associated with the annual flooding of the Nile. Isis, according to Sarton in his *History of Science,* "began her foreign conquests in the seventh century, if not before. Herodotus says that...the women of Cyrene worshipped her....Temples and inscriptions to Isis and other Egyptian gods can be found in many of the Islands, even in the sacred Delos. . . ." In Greece, she was celebrated at the mysteries of Eleusis as "Demeter, the glorification of motherly love (cf. Isis)." For Sarton, Isis is symbolic of nature, and her robe conceals nature's secrets. She "says of herself," he wrote, quoting a passage from Plutarch on Isis and Osiris, "'I am everything which existed, which is now and will ever be, no mortal has ever disclosed my robe.'" Only those initiated through the mysteries (later through science) could glimpse the reality "which is now and will ever be."[1]

Sarton's own image of Isis seems to have derived from an Egyptian wall painting showing her leading Queen Nefretere to her tomb. (Figure 3.1) He refers the reader to a painting, with which "the author (Sarton) is very familiar," of Isis with Queen Nefretere. In the accompanying text, Isis is described as "clad in a sheath-like red dress with a network of beads." In contrast to Isis, Queen Nefretere "wears a flowing robe, the transparency of which is well indicated."[2]

For Sarton, the goal of positivist science was to solve the mysteries of nature by disclosing the secrets "she" harbors within.

FIG. 2.1 / ISIS CONDUCTS QUEEN NEFRETERE TO HER TOMB. FROM NINA DE GARIS DAVIES, ANCIENT EGYPTIAN PAINTINGS, SELECTED, COPIED, AND DESCRIBED, 3 VOLS. (CHICAGO: UNIVERSITY OF CHICAGO PRESS, 1936), VOL. 2, PLATE XCI. REPRODUCED BY PERMISSION.

The real meaning attached to Isis as patron of the history of science was to be found within the tradition of the conquest of nature by the "great men" of science. "I have been deeply moved time after time," he wrote, "while I was contemplating my fellow men wrestling not with other men but with nature herself, trying to solve her mysteries, to decode her message."[3]

Wrestling with nature to extract "her" secrets was the method that led to "positive knowledge" and hence to progress in understanding the natural world. Sarton formulated it as follows:

> Definition: Science is systematized positive knowledge, or what has been taken as such at different ages and at different places.

> Theorem. The acquisition and systematization of positive knowledge are the only human activities which are truly cumulative and progressive.

> Corollary. The history of science is the only history which can illustrate the progress of mankind. In fact, progress has no definite and unquestionable meaning in other fields than the field of science.[4]

The study of the history of science, he believed, was rooted in the purity of past texts. The texts were repositories of knowledge that withstood tests and trials, accumulating evidence of their validity over time and shedding the extraneous tainted clutter of particular ages.[5] The historian of science had to study the false starts of the ages in order to remain a true historian, but the task was not so much to understand the age on its own terms as to divine the process by which it shed its false consciousness and remained on the track of the truth.[6]

Writing the history of science was to construct an emerging scientific knowledge out of textual nuggets, while eliminating false pretensions to truth arising from the social context of each age. The underlying true, positive, cumulative knowledge was set free, while the messy inexact encumbrances of imperfect "men" in imperfect societies were cut off and tossed on the junk piles of the past.[7]

The image of science as positive knowledge, its construction out of atomistic textual nuggets, and the methodology of "wrestling with nature" to decode "her" secrets are all deeply imbedded in the history of Western culture. These assumptions about science, nature, and method pervade the texts of scientists and historians alike. They are challenged by new approaches to the study of science and its history put forward by critical theorists, postmodernists, and feminists.

Critical theory emerging from the Frankfurt School during the mid-twentieth century analyzes the implications of the Enlightenment for the domination of nature and human beings. Postmodernists offer approaches that deconstruct the meanings of textual representations of nature, especially those that conflate women with nature. Feminists reveal hidden biases in the science of the past, in methods of studying nature, and in the texts of scientists and historians of science. Beyond this they offer alternatives to the domination of women and nature that could lead to liberation.

AN IDEOLOGY OF OBJECTIVITY

At the level of ideology, the philosophy of nature that has guided the work of many modern scientists, as well as historians such as George Sarton, has been logical positivism. Positivism assumes that valid, verifiable, hence positive, knowledge of the world derives ultimately from experience obtained through the senses or by experiment and interpretation via the conventions and rules of mathematical language and logic. Scientific knowledge is rule-governed, context-free, and empirically verifiable and as such claims to be objective, that is, independent of the influence of particular historical times and places. Yet the positivist approach to the study of both nature and history relies on an historically associated, interlocking structure of dualities: subject and object, activity and passivity, male and female, and culture and nature.

The basic dichotomy is between subject and object; indeed objectivity, the hallmark of logical positivism, depends on it. The objectification of nature is rooted in Aristotle's locus of reality in the objects of the natural world and made explicit in Descartes's separation of mind from matter, that is, of thinking subject from external object. The dualism between activity and passivity hypothesizes an active subject—man—who receives, interprets, and reacts to sense data supplied by a passive object—nature. Nature as object, whether conceived as things (in the Aristotelian framework) or as corpuscles (in the Cartesian), is composed of dead passive matter set in motion by efficient or final causes (Aristotle) or the transfer of motion (Descartes). Stemming from the same Aristotelian roots as the ideology of objectivity is the association of passivity with femaleness and activity with maleness. As Aristotle put it, "the female, as female, is passive and the male, as male, is active, and the principle of movement comes from him."[8] The male semen contributes power and motion—the active principle—to the embryo; the female supplies the matter, or passive principle. Finally, culture is identified with the active subject and thus with the male, as a passage from the philosopher George Simmel makes clear:

> The requirement of...correctness in practical judgments and objectivity in theoretical knowledge...belong as it were in their form and their claims to humanity in general, but in their actual historical configuration they are masculine throughout. Supposing that we describe these things, viewed as absolute ideas, by the single word "objective," we find that in the history of our race the equation objective = masculine is a valid one.[9]

The Aristotelian identification of the female principle with passivity and the further association of passivity with object and the natural world have furnished the basic philosophical framework of Western culture.

Critical theorists of the Frankfurt School point out that the subject–object and attendant dualities of mainstream Western thought entail a philosophy of domination. Because an active controlling subject is separate from and dominant over a passive controlled object, the scientific rationale of objectivity can legitimate control over whatever has been assigned by culture to a lower place in the "natural" order of things. It thus maintains a hierarchical domination of subject over object, male over female, and culture over nature. In fact, this conceptual system can be used to justify the subordination of women when compounded by the separation of productive (public, male), and reproductive (private, female) spheres in modern industrialized society. Historically, nature and the female have been conflated, and cultural ideology has legitimated the domination of both. This identification appears in the science of such "fathers" of modern science as Francis Bacon, William Harvey, Thomas Hobbes, Joseph Glanvill, and Robert Boyle and has permeated the work of scientists since the scientific revolution.[10]

But feminism challenges these linkages. A feminist critique undermines the authority of modern science to make universal claims about knowledge, bodies, emotions, female "nature," and transcendent reality—claims that reinforce domination. First of all, feminists expose scientific images that gender both science and nature. Scientists, argues Londa Schiebinger, have used both male and female images to represent science to the public. A substantial number of texts from the early modern period through the 1790s depicted science as a woman, mediating between male scientists and female nature. But by the twentieth century, the image of science as female had been replaced by that of the scientist as efficient male, working in a modern laboratory, usually wearing a white laboratory coat. "Absent...are the patrons or politicians influencing his work....The fact that he is white and male is both descriptive and prescriptive; the image cultivates its own clientele," thus legitimating male domination in the sciences.[11]

Second, feminists expose the the language of dominance used by science. Ruth Bleier's *Science and Gender*, a critique of biological theories about women, uses Michel Foucault's analysis of knowledge as a discourse to argue that the very tools of scientific discourse—mathematics, observation, and experimentation—are permeated by the principle of domination. Scientists in power set the terms of the debate and determine the concepts that define reality. Scientific truth is actually produced through a gender-dichotomized social and scientific world, not revealed, as for the logical positivists, through an objective mirror. Because women have historically been excluded from power, they have not participated in the debates and discourses that defined their own "nature" as emotional, passive, and untamed. The identification of male nature as rational, active, and scientific reinforces the principle of the domination of men over both women and nature. The concept of Cartesian dualism itself therefore maintains male hegemony.[12]

Third, feminism exposes certain postmodernist approaches to the study of science and its history that entail domination. Male critics of their intellectual fathers' stories fail to deconstruct the assumptions behind their own postmodernist terms such as "master narrative," "representations," and "witnessing." The "master narratives" questioned are male stories about great men told by male historians of science.[13] The term "master narrative" is itself an example of colonizing language that looks at the "body of knowledge" from above rather than below. The narratives of the Scientific Revolution criticized are not those of women (for whom there was no revolution), blacks (for whom white Enlightenment meant enslavement), or Nature (for which the Scientific Revolution meant domination). The male reappraisals conveniently ignore feminist reappraisals, failing to challenge the ways women are dominated through narrative devices.[14]

Similarly, vision is a dominating way of knowing—a male "enlightenment" category that tells "God's stories" from a transcendent "view from above," replacing participatory (use of all the senses), oral, and tactile modes of knowing with the "perspective" of the "witness." The distancing from nature (as object) inherent in the term "representations" is made possible by sixteenth-century perspective art, the Copernican view of the earth from above, and the voyeurism inherent in scientific instruments such as the microscope, telescope, camera, and space satellite. Through the method of witnessing, Science knows Nature.[15]

Moreover, the very act of witnessing creates a gendered reality and sets standards about male and female credibility as observers. When Steven Shapin and Simon Schaffer in *Leviathan and the Airpump* (1985) establish witnessing as the key to the acceptance of scientific facts, they fail to analyze the significance of male and female witnessing of the scientific events they describe. In discussing the Duchess of Newcastle's visit, for example, they focus on male witnessing of the Duchess.[16] By contrast, Yaakov Garb has problematized the issue of male witnessing in a reading of an eighteenth–century painting by Joseph Wright of Derby (1734–1797), entitled *Experiment with the Air Pump.* Here in public space, men and women display completely different responses to the sight of a pigeon dying as an air pump evacuates its glass container. The men examine the experiment with open curiosity, staring directly at the bird trapped in the glass globe, while the women and children cry, hide their eyes, or look only at the men, viewing the result vicariously. The men "witness" a scientific truth revealed by the experiment; the women "experience" a dying dove. The male painter appropriated the power to gender both science and reality, forcing social norms about male and female intellectual and emotional responses onto nature and its study.[17]

Logical positivism, as the epitome of Enlightenment scientific method, is thus rooted in and dependent on the dualistic separation of a thinking subject from a passive object known through narrative, vision, and witnessing. This method makes possible the knowing of nature and simultaneously its domination. Positivism, as Science's way of knowing Nature, however, is codified in textual representations that are equally problematic.

THE PROBLEM OF REPRESENTATIONS

Problems of domination inherent in dualism, narrative, and witnessing at the core of positivism and Enlightenment scientific method move to a new level in the concept of representation. Nature is represented by science through written texts, illustrations, metaphors, and symbols. A feminist perspective offers a critique of interpretations about science and its history in the realm of representations of nature. A representation is a likeness, image, picture, or written text that is presented to a viewer or reader again and again. As a likeness or sign, it stands in for the object in the field of a viewer located in a different place and subsequent time from the initial act or object. A representation is a sign or narrative account intended to influence, persuade, or be interpreted by a viewer or hearer. Of particular significance are visual and written representations of Nature as female because they reveal problems in the very concept of representation itself.

Representations, such as that of Nature as female, mediate between a society's ideological structure (ideas held by a dominant social group or class) and its daily activities (its behaviors and actions) through their inscription into scientific and historical texts. The texts convey meaning to daily life through images, myths, metaphors, and descriptions. Such representations can either legitimate a dominant conceptual system or offer alternatives to the mainstream view. They play a normative role, mediating between a society's conceptual ideology and people's daily lives, reinforcing individual behaviors. Representations reveal meanings and biases in the stories Science tells about Nature.[18]

The meanings conveyed by scientific images and metaphors are tied to historical contexts. Context sheds light on verbal and visual images for a given society at a given historical moment. The verbal fabric inscribed into the text by the author is given meaning by the reader, both of whom are situated in and informed by particular kinds of social arrangements.[19] Knowledge is constructed through the power of social groups to claim privileged access to reality and that power is revealed through the rhetoric of language.

In postmodern approaches to science and its history, the traditional meaning of the text as a written document is expanded. The new texts include illustrations, photographs, films, factories, laboratories, field stations, visitors centers, museum displays, research proposals, memos, equipment, artifacts, computer messages, printouts, television programs, video tapes, advertisements, and data collections. As texts they contain a dense network of multi-leveled, coded meanings about science and society. They are studied not for their nuggets of truth or positive knowledge, but for what they reveal about relations between language, "forms of life," and the distribution of power in the world.

These texts, however, are predominantly visual. Western culture's love affair with ocularcentrism is fundamental to the power conveyed by these images. Evelyn Fox Keller and Christine Grontkowski, following Eric Havelock, point to the power of the "Mind's Eye" in the transformation from the oral culture of the Homeric era to the visual culture of Plato and beyond. The change from mythos to logos inherent in the rise of written texts and visual symbols meant that illumination, light, and seeing were associated with truth and power. Moreover, the mind's eye of cognitive, mathematical reasoning coupled with the empirical eye of observation and experimentation forms the core of the positivist scientific method. Through the centrality given to vision in Western culture, science and power fuse. But ocularcentrism comes under attack from cultures that are more participatory in their reliance on all the senses and from feminists such as Luce Irigary, Hélène Cixous, and Monique Wittig who link ocularcentrism with phallocentrism and point to the importance of touch and smell over vision in female relationships.[20]

Illustrative of the evolution of ocularcentric, voyeuristic representations of nature is the portrayal of nature as a female harboring secrets, such as George Sarton's image of Isis. As these images changed their textual meanings over time, they eventually became an integral part of the scientific method eulogized by Sarton and the positivists. The symbolism associated with Nature deified, which began with Isis' refusal to disclose her robe in the passage from Plutarch that Sarton quotes, underwent significant changes in the Middle Ages and after.

In Alain de Lille's allegory *Nature's Complaint*, (1160), *Natura* (the lower form of the Platonic world soul), laments her exposure to the view of the vulgar. Her "garments of modesty," she complains, are torn by the "unlawful assaults" of men aggressively penetrating the secrets of heaven. *Natura*, whose face is "bedewed with a shower of weeping," is questioned about her torn robe. She replies:

> As we have said before, many men have taken arms against their mother in evil and violence, they thereupon…tear apart my garments piece by piece, and…force me, stripped of dress, whom they ought to clothe with reverential honor, to come to shame like a harlot.[21]

Such imagery suggests the rape or sexual conquest of both women and nature. And just as nature aggressively investigated is depicted as a woman molested, so femininity is symbolized as an enclosure, often one associated with nature's bounty, that can be breached. Thus medieval artists depict the goddess Venus or the Virgin Mary in enclosed gardens or stone circles symbolic of the female womb and of love, fruitfulness, and pleasure. Chaucer set comic stories in enclosed gardens in which the lover in gaining access to the garden symbolically penetrates the female womb. In *The Merchant's Tale*, based on the biblical "Song of Solomon," Damyan fashions a key to unlock the circular garden and subsequently makes love to a maiden situated in a fruit-bearing tree.[22]

In the seventeenth century the disclosure of Isis is carried beyond her robe into the interior of her body as Francis Bacon advises his new "man of science" to wrest from nature the secrets harbored in her womb, to search into the bowels of nature for "the truth that lies hid in deep mines and caves" and "to shape her on the anvil." "Nature must be taken by the forelock, being bald behind," he asserted. "Nor ought a man to make scruple of entering and penetrating into these holes and corners, when the inquisition of truth is his whole object."[23]

The problems of witnessing and voyeurism are apparent in Joseph Glanvill's use of instruments such as the microscope as the means by which Science can know Nature. Nature, he said, must be "mastered" and "managed" by "searching out the depths...and intrigues of remoter nature." In this project nothing was more helpful than the microscope, for "the secrets of nature are not in the greater masses, but in those little threads and springs which are too subtle for the grossness of our unhelped senses." In the *Vanity of Dogmatizing*, Glanvill pointed out that "Nature's coarser wares" are "exposed to the transient view of every common eye; her choicer riches are locked up only for the sight of them that will buy at the expense of sweat and oil." In achieving such insights, however, true understanding is often misled by the emotions, for "the woman in us, still prosecutes a deceit, like that begun in the Garden: and our understandings are wedded to an Eve, as fatal as the mother of our miseries."[24]

By the nineteenth century nature is represented as removing her own veil and voluntarily exposing her own secrets. A sculpture by Louis Ernest Barrias, *La Nature se devoilant devant la science (Nature revealing herself to science)*, is appropriately located in the entry to the School of Medicine in Paris. In Edouard Manet's *Le Dejeuner sur l'herbe* (1863), a naked woman (based on the nymph or nature goddess in a sixteenth-century engraving) picnics on the grass with two fully clothed gentlemen.[25]

In the twentieth century we find scientists themselves fervently hoping that the veil of nature, like Isis' robe, can be lifted from matter itself (traditionally feminine) so that all may view the hidden secrets of the atom—the mysteries that Isis' robe or Nature's veil conceals. One may hope, announced the inaugural editorial from *Le Radium* in 1904, "to be able to lift a corner of the veil that conceals creation....Each of us hopes that...a sensational application of radium will completely tear away the veil and that truth will appear before everyone's eyes." "The notion of impenetrable mysteries has been dismissed," wrote Sir William Crookes in 1903; "A mystery is a thing to be solved—and 'man alone can master the impossible.'" The editors of *Harper's* (1924) applauded the "laying bare" of the atom's structure, while Hans Reichenbach in 1933 charged nuclear physicists with the task of the "unveiling of the secrets surrounding the inner structure of matter."[26]

Such textual representations are suggestive of both voyeurism and sexual assaults on nature and can be so interpreted when science and its history are placed within the context of the historical evolution of the language and metaphor of science. But they go beyond the goal that Science simply wishes to know Nature to the idea of the domination and control of nature through discovery of "her" secrets. The empirical eye of experimentation and observation coupled with the mind's eye of the disembodied calculating intellect form the basis of logical positivism as the scientific method. Positivism and ocularcentrism thus combine knowledge with power over nature.

EPISTEMOLOGIES OF GENDER AND RACE

The method of knowing nature through positivism and ocularcentric representations leads to a third problematic—the ways in which scientific knowing is linked to gender and race. George Sarton associated the progress of science, the rise of the "human race," and the fulfillment of human destiny with men:

> We have some degree of interest in every *man and woman* whom we approach near enough. Should we not be even more interested in those *men* who accomplish more fully the destiny of the race?...The same instinct which causes sport-lovers to be insatiably curious about their heroes causes the scientific humanist to ask one question after another about the *great men* to whom he owes his heritage of knowledge and culture. In order to satisfy that sound instinct it will be necessary to prepare detailed and reliable biographies of the *men* who distinguished themselves in the search for truth.[27] (Italics added)

Sarton's passage not only makes it clear that it is men who set the standards for knowing and culture, but that it is men who fulfill "the destiny of the race." While Sarton apparently means the destiny of the human race, the question arises as to the extent to which the human race and the white race are conflated in accounts of the rise of modern science. Does the history of science give undo weight to Greek and European roots and accomplishments in relation to those of other races and cultures? Just below the surface of many texts lies a Eurocentric implication that it is primarily the white race that has discovered the "truths of nature."

Although Sarton was eager to establish the pre-Hellenic roots of science among the Egyptians, Babylonians, and Hindus, he saw them as precursors to what he called the "Greek miracle." He pays tribute to specific achievements of the Egyptians and Sumerians whose work made possible Euclidean geometry and to Alexandria for keeping the Greek achievement alive after the decline of Greece. In his *History of Science*, he states, "There is no privileged "race" or community in any absolute way, but for each task and for each time some people or some nations may excel all others." Yet he goes on to note that

his concern in that volume was "with the ancient peoples whose cultural dawn
was only the prelude to the greatest achievements of the third and second millennia before Christ." And in his *Study of the History of Mathematics*, he
writes, "In reality the way for Euclidean mathematics was very gradually and
thoroughly prepared, not only by the millenary efforts of Africans and
Asiatics, but by three centuries of persistent investigations by the most gifted
people among our ancestors, the Greeks of the Golden Age."[28]

Important nevertheless is the debate about the black roots of Egyptian
science, after which Sarton named the journals and guides to the history of
science—Isis, Osiris, and Horus. His famous illustration of "Isis conducting
Queen Nefretere to her tomb," reveals that Isis herself is brown or dark yellow. Herodotus, whom Sarton cites as an authority on Isis, described the
Egyptians as having black skin and curly hair. Statues of Isis suckling her son
Horus reveal her with dark skin and black, plaited or curled hair. Historians
Danita Redd, Monica Sjöo, and Barbara Mor see such statues as prototypes of
the Black Madonnas found throughout Europe in the Christian era.[29] As his-
torian of science David Kubrin noted in 1972, "Greece is European, white;
Egypt is African, nonwhite. Yet these nonwhite roots of Western science
have been nearly completely obfuscated, at least until recently." Science in
China, India, and Egypt that preceded its development in Greece originated
with men and women whose races were other than white.[30]

The idea that the body of Nature, concealed beneath the robe of Isis,
might be brown or black raises additional questions about the "rape of
nature," as well as about science as a method for revealing Nature's secrets.
By the seventeenth century, matter at the base of the great chain of being was
associated with putrefaction, black magic, witchcraft, and black African
slaves, hence with the need for rational, scientific, and technological control
over nature.[31] At the same time Isis herself was becoming white, losing her
brown Egyptian origins. Athenasius Kircher's depiction of Isis in his *Oedipus
Aegypticus* (1652) shows her with European features and lightened skin and
hair, while his replica of the ancient Egyptian "Bembine Table of Isis," (originally made of bronze and decorated with enamal and silver) reproduced
from an ancient tablet belonging to Cardinal Bembo in 1559 retains Egyptian
features and hair design.[32]

The black or brown woman's body as the object of scientific investigation and experimentation has been exposed by feminist historians of science
in recent literature. In *Nature's Body* (1993), Londa Schiebinger investigates
theories of gender and race at the root of modern science. By the eighteenth

century, black women's bodies, especially their skulls, breasts, and genitalia, were being described by scientists and anthropologists as part of a broader "scientific" investigation of African and European anatomical and sexual differences. The prejudice that blacks were not capable of abstract thought because their skulls allegedly resembled those of apes threw into question early modern ideas held by Ambroise Paré, Galileo, and Newton that the Egyptians had invented science and mathematics. In the 1820s, Schiebinger notes, physician William Lawrence questioned the view that Egypt was a "birthplace of the arts" and asked whether the sciences, religion, and laws, could have been "discovered and framed by men with black skin, woolly hairs, and slanting forehead?" Scientists and anthropologists examined mummies, murals, and sarcophagi for evidence as to the Negro, Hindu, or Caucasian origins of the Egyptians themselves.[33] While some authorities continued to assert that the Egyptians were black or that Egypt represented a crossroads of Ethiopian, Hindu, and Caucasian cultures and that science, language, and the arts originated there, the predominant trend was to deny the black and Egyptian origins of European culture.

Martin Bernal's *Black Athena: The Afroasiatic Roots of Classical Civilization* (1987) argues that in the late eighteenth century the Egyptian origins of modern science were replaced with a white model that attributed the origins of science and civilization to the Greeks and Indo-Europeans. Bernal himself challenges this Aryan interpretation of Ancient Greece, seen as the result of an invasion from the north by Indo-Europeans who mingled with pre-Hellenic Greeks, and replaces it with a revised version of the Greeks own Ancient Model that they were colonized by Egyptians and Phoenicians around 1500 B. C. "If I am right in urging the overthrow of the Aryan Model and its replacement by the Revised Ancient one, it will be necessary not only to rethink the fundamental bases of 'Western Civilization' but also to recognize the penetration of racism and 'continental chauvinism' into all our historiography, or philosophy of writing history."[34]

Bernal accepts the ancient testimony that the Greek fertility mysteries at Eleusis featuring the grain goddess Demeter (Ceres in Rome) and her daughter Persephone (Proserpina in Rome) arose from similar Egyptian mysteries surrounding Isis and Osiris transmitted into Attica possibly as early as the fifteenth century B.C., but still celebrated in classical times. The myth of Demeter searching for her daughter Persephone in the underworld of Hades was the Greek version of Isis' search for her husband/brother Osiris, her reassembly of his dismembered body, and their son Horus' victory over Seth, his murderer. Both were celebrations by agricultural societies of the renewal of nature's fertility in the spring planting time.

Like Sarton, Bernal examines the transmission of Egyptian cultural influences into ancient Greece. But unlike Sarton, Bernal is self-consciously promoting a multicultural, multiracial account of the origins of "Western" culture and science by calling Athena "black." Neither author, however, is concerned about the racial *and* sexual implications of Isis' body as simultaneously non-white and the object of investigation of the secrets of nature. Both issues are of importance if science is to transcend its treatment of women and nature as merely experimental objects, acknowledge its debt to other cultures, and realize its potential for a liberatory, democratic future.

Sandra Harding's edited collection *The "Racial" Economy of Science* (1993) is part of a new historiography about race, gender, and science that seeks to move toward a more democratic science in the future. Its authors analyze history and historians for their privileging of concepts associated with Western and First World societies, question the roots of social hierarchy and class, and look at non-Western contributions to the theory and practice of science.[35]

CONCLUSION

Science and its history shared, and to a large extent still do share, a methodological approach to the study of nature that leads to its domination. Logical positivism, which privileges mathematical and empirically-verifiable statements as true, is reinforced by ocularcentrism, based on the supremacy of the mind's eye and the empirical eye, and by Eurocentric assumptions of the supremacy of Western science since the "Greek miracle." The three prongs taken together fuse what counts as the knowledge of nature with the power over it. These deeply held assumptions, however, have been challenged by feminists, postmodernists, and critical theorists.

The new approaches to science and its history utilize the standpoints of feminist scholars who have uncovered patriarchal and racist elements in science, postmodernists who have studied texts, contexts, and discourses as representations of nature and science, and the Frankfurt School, which has raised the problematic of ideologies of domination over society and nature. They expose universalizing tendencies in Western culture prevalent since the Enlightenment of the eighteenth century. They criticize the idea that history is linear and evolutionary and that reason reveals transcendent truths. They question whether reason can be separated from the body and from particular times and places, while challenging the authority of science to make universal claims about the body, particularly female bodies.[36]

These approaches to the history of science have (1) destabilized the assumption that Science (whether the outcome of internal or external influences), can indeed know Nature (the problem of relativism); (2) linked power and knowledge at the levels of both epistemology and practice, so that what counts as scientific knowledge necessarily reflects the relations of domination (the problem of the dominated object); (3) questioned the possibility of a scientific knowledge system independent of the culture-bound influences of sex, race, and ethnocentrism (the problem of the independence of the knowing subject); and (4) challenged the assumption that the nature behind human representations changed only through its own evolutionary and physical laws, asserting instead that human practices give rise to new objects, such as chemically-induced or genetically-engineered mutants (the question of nature as actor).

All four linkages pose problems for the historian who in the very act of writing science's history may be participating in a project of cultural domination, from which she or he seeks emancipation. While the positivist approach of Sarton generally assumed that science (whether externally or internally produced) was objective, value-free, context-free knowledge of an external world, the new history tends implicitly to accept Martin Heidegger's observation that all philosophy (including science and technology) since Descartes has been fundamentally concerned with power.[37]

The new history not only challenges the older authority of science, but also raises new problems. If reality itself is gendered by social relations, are we, either as men or women, necessarily bound to participate in the project of dominating nature, women, and underprivileged human groups? Does the social construction of science lead to a relativist historicism? Does society always mediate access to objects and processes? Is all knowledge bound by time, place, and culture?

Donna Haraway's *Primate Visions* struggles with the temptation to see science and its history through any single lens that implies that the answer to these questions is yes. Haraway lists four compelling temptations: (1) science as a social construct suggests the rejection of scientific reality; (2) Marxism suggests that social and economic institutions structure the production of knowledge about the world; (3) feminist and ethnic studies suggest that we should see science through the lens of domination; and (4) scientists suggest that organisms are real and that science can discover real relations about them. To write the history of primate science from any one position, all of which are persuasive, creates a single but false narrative.

Haraway's book tells many stories from many perspectives, each contributing its own partial mix of fact and fiction about the natural world. The resulting book is written by and about people who have emotional, political, and scientific stakes in the outcome. She writes, "I want this book to be responsible to primatologists, to historians of science, to cultural theorists, to the broad left, anti-racist, anti-colonial, and women's movements, to animals, and to lovers of serious stories. It is perhaps not always possible to be accountable to those contending audiences, but they have all made this book possible."[38]

However compelling the politics of social constructivism was in the 1980s, a synthesis between social constructivism and realism is the direction of the future. Jan Golinski points out that social constructivists have been criticized for ignoring the constraints posed by nature to the production of scientific knowledge. "Granted that observations are indeed shaped by prior expectations and by beliefs about the capacities of instruments...this does not open the way to indefinite interpretive flexibility."[39]

Feminism, postmodernism, and critical theory all suggest alternatives to totalizing histories, while attempting to move beyond problems of the domination of nature and people. Liberation entails recognizing that nature is a real autonomous actor rather than a passive object of experimentation and utility—Isis as an active bringer of the renewal of life rather than a harborer of Nature's secrets. It likewise means that women and minorities should also be accorded recognition as autonomous real beings. Finally, it means writing multilayered, sensitive, but perhaps at best partial perspectives on the past, recognizing that we too are but real bodies produced by real social relations reflecting imperfectly on a naturally and culturally constructed real world.

PART TWO

HISTORY

4

THE DEATH

OF NATURE

WOMEN AND

ECOLOGY IN THE

SCIENTIFIC

REVOLUTION

INTRODUCTION: WOMEN
AND NATURE

Women and nature have an age-old association—an affiliation that has persisted throughout culture, language, and history. Their ancient interconnections have been dramatized by the simultaneity of two recent social movements—women's liberation, symbolized in its controversial infancy by Betty Friedan's *Feminine Mystique* (1963), and the ecology movement, which built up during the 1960s and finally captured national attention on Earth Day, 1970. Common to both is an egalitarian perspective. Women are struggling to free themselves from cultural and economic constraints that have kept them subordinate to men in American society. Environmentalists, warning us of the irreversible consequences of continuing environmental exploitation, are developing an ecological ethic emphasizing the interconnectedness between people and nature. Juxtaposing the goals of the two movements can suggest new values and social structures, based not on the domination of women and nature as resources but on the full expression of both male and female talent and on the maintenance of environmental integrity.

New social concerns generate new intellectual and historical problems. Conversely, new interpretations of the past provide perspectives on the present and hence the power to change it. Today's feminist and ecological consciousness can be used to examine the historical interconnections between women and nature that developed as the modern scientific and economic world took form in the sixteenth and seventeenth centuries—a transformation that shaped and now pervades today's mainstream values and perceptions.

The ancient identity of nature as a nurturing mother links women's history with the history of the environment and ecological change. The female earth was central to the organic cosmology that was undermined by the Scientific Revolution and the rise of a market-oriented culture in early modern Europe. The ecology movement has reawakened interest in the values and concepts associated historically with the premodern organic world. The ecological model and its associated ethics make possible a fresh and critical interpretation of the rise of modern science in the crucial period when our cosmos ceased to be viewed as an organism and became instead a machine.

In investigating the roots of our current environmental dilemma and its connections to science, technology, and the economy, we must reexamine the formation of a world view and a science that, by reconceptualizing reality as a machine rather than a living organism, sanctioned the domination of both nature and women.

NATURE AS FEMALE

The world we have lost was organic. From the obscure origins of our species, human beings have lived in daily, immediate, organic relation with the natural order for their sustenance. In 1500, the daily interaction with nature was still structured for most Europeans, as it was for other peoples, by close-knit, cooperative, organic communities.

Thus it is not surprising that for sixteenth-century Europeans the root metaphor binding together the self, society, and the cosmos was that of an organism. As a projection of the way people experienced daily life, organismic theory emphasized interdependence among the parts of the human body, subordination of individual to communal purposes in family, community, and state, and vital life permeating the cosmos to the lowliest stone.

The idea of nature as a living organism had philosophical antecedents in ancient systems of thought, variations of which formed the prevailing ideological framework of the sixteenth century. The organismic metaphor, however, was immensely flexible and adaptable to varying contexts, depending on which of its presuppositions was emphasized. A spectrum of philosophical and political possibilities existed, all of which could be subsumed under the general rubric of *organic*.

Central to the organic theory was the identification of nature, especially the earth, with a nurturing mother: a kindly beneficent female who provided for the needs of mankind in an ordered, planned universe. But another opposing image of nature as female was also prevalent: wild and uncontrollable nature that could render violence, storms, droughts, and general chaos. Both were identified with the female sex and were projections of human perceptions onto the external world. The metaphor of the earth as a nurturing mother gradually vanished as a dominant image as the Scientific Revolution proceeded to mechanize and to rationalize the world view. The second image, nature as disorder, called forth an important modern idea, that of power over nature. Two new ideas, those of mechanism and of the domination and mastery of nature, became core concepts of the modern world. An organically oriented mentality in which female principles played an important role was undermined and replaced by a mechanically oriented mentality that either eliminated or used female principles in an exploitative manner. As Western culture became increasingly mechanized in the 1600s, the machine subdued the female earth and virgin earth spirit.[1]

The change in controlling imagery was directly related to changes in human attitudes and behavior toward the earth. Whereas the nurturing earth image can be viewed as a cultural constraint restricting the types of socially and morally sanctioned human actions allowable with respect to the earth, the new images of mastery and domination functioned as cultural sanctions for the denudation of nature. Society needed these new images as it continued the processes of commercialism and industrialization, which depended on activities directly altering the earth—mining, drainage, deforestation, and assarting (grubbing up stumps to clear fields). The new activities utilized new technologies—lift and force pumps, cranes, windmills, geared wheels, flap valves, chains, pistons, treadmills, under- and overshot watermills, fulling mills, flywheels, bellows, excavators, bucket chains, rollers, geared and wheeled bridges, cranks, elaborate block and tackle systems, worm, spurn, crown, and lantern gears, cams and eccentrics, ratchets, wrenches, presses, and screws in magnificent variation and combination.

These technological and commercial changes did not take place quickly; they developed gradually over the ancient and medieval eras, as did the accompanying environmental deterioration. Slowly over many centuries early Mediterranean and Greek civilization mined and quarried the mountainsides, altered the forested landscape, and overgrazed the hills. Nevertheless, technologies were low level, people considered themselves

parts of a finite cosmos, and numerous animistic, fertility cults treated nature
as sacred. Roman civilization was more pragmatic, secular, and commercial
and its environmental impact more intense. Yet Roman writers such as Ovid,
Seneca, Pliny, and the Stoic philosophers openly deplored mining as an abuse
of their mother, the earth. With the disintegration of feudalism and the expansion of Europeans into new worlds and markets, commercial society's impact
on the natural environment accelerated. By the sixteenth and seventeenth centuries, the tension between technological development in the world of action
and the controlling organic images in the world of the mind had become too
great. The old structures were incompatible with the new activities.

Both the nurturing and domination metaphors existed in philosophy,
religion, and literature. The ideas of dominion over the earth existed in
Greek philosophy and Christian religion; that of the nurturing earth, in
Greek and other pagan philosophies. But, as the economy became modern-
ized and the Scientific Revolution proceeded, the dominion metaphor spread
beyond the religious sphere and assumed ascendancy in the social and political spheres as well. These competing images and their normative associations
are evident in sixteenth-century literature, art, philosophy, and science.

The image of the earth as a living organism and nurturing mother served
as a cultural constraint restricting the actions of human beings. One does not
readily slay a mother, dig into her entrails for gold or mutilate her body,
although commercial mining would soon require that. As long as the earth
was considered to be alive and sensitive, it could be considered a breach of
human ethical behavior to carry out destructive acts against it. For most traditional cultures, minerals and metals ripened in the uterus of the Earth
Mother, mines were compared to her vagina, and metallurgy was the human
hastening of the birth of the living metal in the artificial womb of the furnace—an abortion of the metal's natural growth cycle before its time. Miners
offered propitiation to the deities of the soil and subterranean world, performed ceremonial sacrifices, and observed strict cleanliness, sexual absti-
nence, and fasting before violating the sacredness of the living earth by sink-
ing a mine. Smiths assumed an awesome responsibility in precipitating the
metal's birth through smelting, fusing, and beating it with hammer and anvil;
they were often accorded the status of shaman in tribal rituals and their tools
were thought to hold special powers.

The Renaissance image of the nurturing earth still carried with it subtle
ethical controls and restraints. Such imagery found in a culture's literature
can play a normative role within the culture. Controlling images operate as

ethical restraints or as ethical sanctions—as subtle "oughts" or "ought-nots." Thus as the descriptive metaphors and images of nature change, a behavioral restraint can be changed into a sanction. Such a change in the image and description of nature occurred during the course of the Scientific Revolution.

THE RISE OF CAPITALISM

In the sixteenth century, as the feudal states of medieval Europe were breaking up, a new dynamic force emerged that shattered premodern ways of life and the organic restraints against the exploitation of the earth. Arising in the city-states of Renaissance Italy and spreading to northern Europe was an inexorable expanding market economy, intensifying medieval tendencies toward capitalist relations of production and capitalist modes of economic behavior. As trade quickened throughout western Europe, stimulated by the European discovery and exploitation of the Americas, production for subsistence began to be replaced by more specialized production for the market. The spreading use of money provided not only a uniform medium of exchange but also a reliable store of value, facilitating open-ended accumulation. Inflation generated by the growth of population and the flood of American gold accelerated the transition from traditional economic modes to rationally maximizing modes of economic organization. The growth of cities as centers of trade and handicraft production created a new class of bourgeois entrepreneurs who supplied ambitious monarchs with the funds and expertise to build strong nation states, undercutting the power of the regionally based land owning nobility.

Whereas the medieval economy had been based on organic and renewable energy sources—wood, water, wind, and animal muscle—the emerging capitalist economy was based on nonrenewable energy—coal—and the inorganic metals—iron, copper, silver, gold, tin, and mercury—the refining and processing of which ultimately depended on and further depleted the forests. Over the course of the sixteenth century, mining operations quadrupled as the trading of metals expanded, taking immense toll as forests were cut for charcoal and the cleared lands turned into sheep pastures for the textile industry. Shipbuilding, essential to capitalist trade and national supremacy, along with glass and soap-making, also contributed to the denudation of the ancient forest cover. The new activities directly altered the earth. Not only were its forests cut down, but swamps were drained, and mine shafts were sunk.[2]

The new commercial and industrial enterprises meant that the older cultural constraints against the exploitation of the earth no longer held sway. While the organic framework was for many centuries sufficiently integrative

to override commercial development and technological innovation, the accel
eration of economic change throughout western Europe began to undermine
the organic unity of the cosmos and society. Because the needs and purposes
of society as a whole were changing with the commercial revolution, the values associated with the organic view of nature were no longer applicable;
hence the plausibility of the conceptual framework itself was slowly, but con-
tinuously, being threatened. By the sixteenth and seventeenth centuries, the
tension between the technological development in the world of action and the
controlling organic images in the world of the mind had become too great.
The old world view was incompatible with the new activities.

DOMINION OVER NATURE: FRANCIS BACON'S PHILOSOPHY

Francis Bacon (1561–1626), a celebrated "father of modern science," transformed tendencies already extant in his own society into a total program
advocating the control of nature.

Bacon has been eulogized as the originator of the concept of the modern
research institute, a philosopher of industrial science, the inspiration behind
the Royal Society (1660), and as the founder of the inductive method by
which all people can verify for themselves the truths of science by the reading of nature's book.[3] But from the perspective of nature, women, and the
lower orders of society emerges a less favorable image of Bacon and a critique of his program as ultimately benefiting the middle-class male entrepreneur. Bacon, of course, was not responsible for subsequent uses of his philosophy. But, because he was in an extremely influential social position and in
touch with the important developments of his time, his language, style,
nuance, and metaphor is a mirror reflecting his class perspective.

Sensitive to the same social transformations that had already begun to
reduce women to psychic and reproductive resources, Bacon developed the
power of language as political instrument in reducing female nature to a
resource for economic production. Female imagery became a tool in adapting
scientific knowledge and method to a new form of human power over nature.
The "controversy over women" and the inquisition of witches—both present in Bacon's social milieu—permeated his description of nature and his
metaphorical style and were instrumental in his transformation of the earth
as a nurturing mother and womb of life into a source of secrets to be extracted for economic advance.

Much of the imagery Bacon used in delineating his new scientific objectives and methods derives from the courtroom, and, because it treats nature as a female to be tortured through mechanical inventions, strongly suggests the interrogations of the witch trials and the mechanical devices used to torture witches.

The new man of science must not think that the "inquisition of nature is in any part interdicted or forbidden." Nature must be "bound into service" and made a "slave," put "in constraint" and "molded" by the mechanical arts. The "searchers and spies of nature" are to discover her plots and secrets.[4]

This method, so readily applicable when nature is denoted by the female gender, degraded and made possible the exploitation of the natural environment. As woman's womb had symbolically yielded to the forceps, so nature's womb harbored secrets that through technology could be wrested from her grasp for use in the improvement of the human condition:

> There is therefore much ground for hoping that there are still laid up in the womb of nature many secrets of excellent use having no affinity or parallelism with anything that is now known... only by the method which we are now treating can they be speedily and suddenly and simultaneously presented and anticipated.[5]

Bacon transformed the magical tradition by calling on the need to dominate nature not for the sole benefit of the individual magician but for the good of the entire human race. Through vivid metaphor, he transformed the magus from nature's servant to its exploiter, and nature from a teacher to a slave. Bacon argued that it was the magician's error to consider art (technology) a mere "assistant to nature having the power to finish what nature has begun" and therefore to despair of ever "changing, transmuting, or fundamentally altering nature."[6]

The natural magician saw himself as operating within the organic order of nature—he was a manipulator of parts within that system, bringing down heavenly powers to the earthly shrine. Agrippa explored the possibility of ascending the hierarchy to the point of cohabiting with God. Bacon extended this idea to include the recovery of the power over nature lost when Adam and Eve were expelled from paradise.

Due to the Fall from the Garden of Eden (caused by the temptation of a woman), the human race lost its "dominion over creation." Before the Fall, there was no need for power or dominion, because Adam and Eve were sovereign over all other creatures. In this state of dominion, mankind was "like unto God." While some, accepting God's punishment, obeyed the medieval strictures against searching too deeply into God's secrets, Bacon turned the constraints into sanctions. Only by "digging further and further into the mine of natural knowledge" could mankind recover that lost dominion. In this way, "the narrow limits of man's dominion over the universe" could be stretched "to their promised bounds."[7]

Although a female's inquisitiveness may have caused man's fall from his God-given dominion, the relentless interrogation of another female, nature, could be used to regain it. As he argued in the *The Masculine Birth of Time*, "I am come in very truth leading to you nature with all her children to bind her to your service and make her your slave." "We have no right," he asserted, "to expect nature to come to us." Instead, "Nature must be taken by the forelock, being bald behind." Delay and subtle argument "permit one only to clutch at nature, never to lay hold of her and capture her."[8]

Nature existed in three states—at liberty, in error, or in bondage.

> She is either free and follows her ordinary course of development as in the heavens, in the animal and vegetable creation, and in the general array of the universe; or she is driven out of her ordinary course by the perverseness, insolence, and forwardness of matter and violence of impediments, as in the case of monsters; or lastly, she is put in constraint, molded and made as it were new by art and the hand of man; as in things artificial.[9]

The first instance was the view of nature as immanent self-development, the nature naturing herself of the Aristotelians. This was the organic view of nature as a living, growing, self-actualizing being. The second state was necessary to explain the malfunctions and monstrosities that frequently appeared and that could not have been caused by God or another higher power acting on his instruction. Since monstrosities could not be explained by the action of form or spirit, they had to be the result of matter acting perversely. Matter in Plato's *Timaeus* was recalcitrant and had to be forcefully shaped by the demiurge. Bacon frequently described matter in female imagery, as a "common harlot." "Matter is not devoid of an appetite and inclination to dissolve the world and fall back into the old Chaos." It therefore must be "restrained and kept in order by the prevailing concord of things." "The vexations of art are certainly as the bonds and handcuffs of Proteus, which betray the ultimate struggles and efforts of matter."[10]

The third instance was the case of art (techné)—man operating on nature to create something new and artificial. Here "nature takes orders from man and works under his authority." Miners and smiths should become the model for the new class of natural philosophers who would interrogate and alter nature. They had developed the two most important methods of wresting nature's secrets from her, "the one searching into the bowels of nature, the other shaping nature as on an anvil." "Why should we not divide natural philosophy into two parts, the mine and the furnace?" For "the truth of nature lies hid in certain deep mines and caves," within the earth's bosom. Bacon, like some of the practically minded alchemists, would "advise the studious to sell their books and build furnaces" and "forsaking Minerva and the Muses as barren virgins, to rely upon Vulcan."[11]

The new method of interrogation was not through abstract notions, but through the instruction of the understanding "that it may in very truth dissect nature." The instruments of the mind supply suggestions, those of the hand give motion and aid the work. "By art and the hand of man," nature can then be "forced out of her natural state and squeezed and molded." In this way, "human knowledge and human power meet as one."[12]

Here, in bold sexual imagery, is the key feature of the modern experimental method—constraint of nature in the laboratory, dissection by hand and mind, and the penetration of hidden secrets—language still used today in praising a scientist's "hard facts," "penetrating mind," or the "thrust of his argument." The constraints against penetration in *Natura's* lament over her torn garments of modesty have been turned into sanctions in language that legitimate the exploitation and "rape" of nature for human good.

Scientific method, combined with mechanical technology, would create a "new organon," a new system of investigation, that unified knowledge with material power. The technological discoveries of printing, gunpowder, and the magnet in the fields of learning, warfare, and navigation "help us to think about the secrets still locked in nature's bosom." "They do not, like the old, merely exert a gentle guidance over nature's course; they have the power to conquer and subdue her, to shake her to her foundations." Under the mechanical arts, "nature betrays her secrets more fully... than when in enjoyment of her natural liberty."[13]

Mechanics, which gave man power over nature, consisted in motion; that is, in "the uniting or disuniting of natural bodies." Most useful were the arts that altered the materials of things—"agriculture, cookery, chemistry, dying, the manufacture of glass, enamel, sugar, gunpowder, artificial fires, paper, and the like." But in performing these operations, one was constrained to operate within the chain of causal connections; nature could "not be commanded except by being obeyed." Only by the study, interpretation, and observation of nature could these possibilities be uncovered; only by acting as the interpreter of nature could knowledge be turned into power. Of the three grades of human ambition, the most wholesome and noble was "to endeavor to establish and extend the power and dominion of the human race itself over the universe." In this way "the human race [could] recover that right over nature which belongs to it by divine bequest."[14]

The interrogation of witches as a symbol for the interrogation of nature, the courtroom as a model for its inquisition, and torture through mechanical devices as a tool for the subjugation of disorder were fundamental to the scientific method as power. For Bacon, sexual politics helped to structure the nature of the empirical method that would produce a new form of knowledge and a new ideology of objectivity seemingly devoid of cultural and political assumptions.

Human dominion over nature, an integral element of the Baconian program, was to be achieved through the experimental "disclosure of nature's secrets." Seventeenth-century scientists, reinforcing aggressive attitudes toward nature, spoke out in favor of "mastering" and "managing" the earth. Descartes wrote in his *Discourse on Method* (1636) that through knowing the crafts of the artisans and the forces of bodies we could "render ourselves the masters and possessors of nature."[15] Joseph Glanvill, the English philosopher who defended the Baconian program in his *Plus Ultra* of 1668, asserted that the objective of natural philosophy was to "enlarge knowledge by observation and experiment...so that nature being known, it may be mastered, managed, and used in the services of humane life." To achieve this objective, arts and instruments should be developed for "searching out the beginnings and depths of things and discovering the intrigues of remoter nature."[16] The most useful of the arts were chemistry, anatomy, and mathematics; the best instruments included the microscope, telescope, thermometer, barometer, and air pump.

The new image of nature as a female to be controlled and dissected through experiment legitimated the exploitation of natural resources. Although the image of the nurturing earth popular in the Renaissance did not vanish, it was superseded by new controlling imagery. The constraints against penetration associated with the earth-mother image were transformed into sanctions for denudation. After the Scientific Revolution, *Natura* no longer complains that her garments of modesty are being torn by the wrongful thrusts of man. She is portrayed in statues by the French sculptor Louis-

Ernest Barrias (1841–1905) coyly removing her own veil and exposing herself to science. From an active teacher and parent, she has become a mindless, submissive body. Not only did this new image function as a sanction, but the new conceptual framework of the Scientific Revolution—mechanism—carried with it norms quite different from the norms of organicism. The new mechanical order and its associated values of power and control would mandate the death of nature.

THE MECHANICAL ORDER

The fundamental social and intellectual problem for the seventeenth century was the problem of order. The perception of disorder, so important to the Baconian doctrine of dominion over nature, was also crucial to the rise of mechanism as a rational antidote to the disintegration of the organic cosmos. The new mechanical philosophy of the mid-seventeenth century achieved a reunification of the cosmos, society, and the self in terms of a new metaphor—the machine. Developed by the French thinkers Mersenne, Gassendi, and Descartes in the 1620s and 1630s and elaborated by a group of English emigrés to Paris in the 1640s and 1650s, the new mechanical theories emphasized and reinforced elements in human experience developing slowly since the late Middle Ages, but accelerating in the sixteenth century.

New forms of order and power provided a remedy for the disorder perceived to be spreading throughout culture. In the organic world, order meant the function of each part within the larger whole, as determined by its nature, while power was diffused from the top downward through the social or cosmic hierarchies. In the mechanical world, order was redefined to mean the predictable behavior of each part within a rationally determined system of laws, while power derived from active and immediate intervention in a secularized world. Order and power together constituted control. Redefining reality itself through the new machine metaphor achieved the rational control over nature, society, and self.

As the unifying model for science and society, the machine has permeated and reconstructed human consciousness so totally that today we scarcely question its validity. Nature, society, and the human body are composed of interchangeable atomized parts that can be repaired or replaced from outside. The "technological fix" mends an ecological malfunction, new human beings replace the old to maintain the smooth functioning of industry and bureaucracy, and interventionist medicine exchanges a fresh heart for a worn-out, diseased one.

The mechanical view of nature now taught in most Western schools is accepted without question as our everyday, common sense reality—matter is made up of atoms, colors occur by the reflection of light waves of differing lengths, bodies obey the law of inertia, and the sun is in the center of our solar system. None of this was common sense to our seventeenth-century counterparts. The replacement of the older, "natural" ways of thinking by a new and "unnatural" form of life—seeing, thinking, and behaving—did not occur without struggle. The submergence of the organism by the machine engaged the best minds of the times during a period fraught with anxiety, confusion, and instability in both the intellectual and social spheres.

The removal of animistic, organic assumptions about the cosmos constituted the death of nature—the most far-reaching effect of the Scientific Revolution. Because nature was now viewed as a system of dead, inert particles moved by external, rather than inherent, forces, the mechanical framework itself could legitimate the manipulation of nature. Moreover, as a conceptual framework, the mechanical order had associated with it a framework of values based on power fully compatible with the directions taken by commercial capitalism.

The mechanistic view of nature, developed by the seventeenth-century natural philosophers and based on a Western mathematical tradition going back to Plato, is still dominant in science today. This view assumes that nature can be divided into parts and that the parts can be extracted from the environmental context and rearranged according to a set of rules based on logical and mathematical operations. The results can then be tested and verified by resubmitting them to nature, the ultimate judge of their validity. Mathematical formalism provides the criterion for rationality and certainty, nature the criterion for empirical validity and acceptance or rejection of the theory.

The work of historians and philosophers of science notwithstanding, it is widely assumed by the scientific community that modern science is objective, value-free, and context-free knowledge of the external world. To the extent to which the sciences can be reduced to this mechanistic mathematical model, the more legitimate they become as sciences. Thus the reductionist hierarchy of the validity of the sciences first proposed in the nineteenth century by French positivist philosopher August, Comte is still widely assumed by intellectuals—the most mathematical and highly theoretical sciences occupying the most revered positions.

The mechanistic approach to nature is as fundamental to the twentieth-century revolution in physics as it was to classical Newtonian science, culminating in the nineteenth-century unification of mechanics, thermodynamics, and electromagnetic theory. Twentieth-century physics still views the world in terms of fundamental particles—electrons, protons, neutrons, mesons, muons, pions, taus, thetas, sigmas, pis, and so on. The search for the ultimate unifying particle, the quark, has engaged the efforts of the best theoretical physicists.

Mathematical formalism isolates the elements of a given quantum mechanical problem, places them in a lattice-like matrix, and rearranges them through a mathematical function called an *operator*. Systems theory extracts possibly relevant information bits from the environmental context and stores them in a computer memory for later use. But since it cannot store an infinite number of "facts," it must select a finite number of potentially relevant pieces of data according to a theory or set of rules governing the selection process. For any given solution, this mechanistic approach very likely excludes some potentially relevant factors.

Systems theorists claim for themselves a holistic outlook because they believe that they are taking into account the ways in which all the parts in a given system affect the whole. Yet the formalism of the calculus of probabilities excludes the possibility of mathematizing the gestalt—that is, the ways in which each part at any given instant take their meaning from the whole. The more open, adaptive, organic, and complex the system, the less successful is the formalism. It is most successful when applied to closed, artificial, precisely defined, relatively simple systems. Mechanistic assumptions about nature push us increasingly in the direction of artificial environments, the mechanized control over more and more aspects of human life, and a loss of the quality of life itself.

HOLISM

Holism was proposed as a philosophical alternative to mechanism by J.C. Smuts in his book *Holism and Evolution* (1926), in which he attempted to define the essential characteristics of holism and to differentiate it from nineteenth-century mechanism. He attempts to show that:

> Taking a plant or animal as a type of whole, we notice the fundamental holistic characters as a unity of parts which is so close and intense as to be more than a sum of its parts; which not only gives a particular conformation or structure to the parts but so relates and determines them in their synthesis that their functions are altered; the synthesis affects and determines the parts so that they function toward the "whole"; and

the whole and the parts therefore reciprocally influence and determine
each other and appear more or less to merge their individual
characters.[17]

Smuts saw a continuum of relationships among parts from simple physical mixtures and chemical compounds to organisms and minds in which the
unity among parts was affected and changed by the synthesis. "Holism is a
process of creative synthesis; the resulting wholes are not static, but dynamic, evolutionary, creative.... The explanation of nature can therefore not be
purely mechanical; and the mechanistic concept of nature has its place and
justification only in the wider setting of holism."

The most important example of holism today is provided by the science
of ecology. Although ecology is a relatively new science, its philosophy of
nature, holism, is not. Historically, holistic presuppositions about nature have
been assumed by communities of people who have succeeded in living in
equilibrium with their environments. The idea of cyclical processes, of the
interconnectedness of all things, and the assumption that nature is active and
alive are fundamental to the history of human thought. No element of an
interlocking cycle can be removed without the collapse of the cycle. The
parts themselves thus take their meaning from the whole. Each particular part
is defined by and dependent on the total context. The cycle itself is a dynamic interactive relationship of all its parts, and process is a dialectical relation
between parts and whole. Ecology necessarily must consider the complexities
and the totality. It cannot isolate the parts into simplified systems that can be
studied in a laboratory because such isolation distorts the whole.

External forces and stresses on a balanced ecosystem, whether natural or
man made, can make some parts of the cycle act faster than the systems' own
natural oscillations. Depending on the strength of the external disturbance,
the metabolic and reproductive reaction rates of the slowest parts of the
cycle, and the complexity of the system, it may or may not be able to absorb
the stresses without collapsing.[18] At various times in history, civilizations that
have put too much external stress on their environments have caused long-
term or irrevocable alterations.

CONCLUSION

By highlighting the essential role of every part of an ecosystem, that if one
part is removed the system is weakened and loses stability, ecology has moved
in the direction of the leveling of value hierarchies. Each part contributes

equal value to the healthy functioning of the whole. All living things, as integral parts of a viable ecosystem, thus have rights. The necessity of protecting the ecosystem from collapse due to the extinction of vital members was one argument for the passage of the Endangered Species Act of 1973. The movement toward egalitarianism manifested in the democratic revolutions of the eighteenth century, the extension of citizens' rights to blacks, and finally voting rights to women, was thus carried a step further. Endangered species became equal to the Army Corps of Engineers: the snail darter demanded a legal hearing before the Tellico Dam could be approved, the Furbish lousewort could block construction of the Dickey-Lincoln Dam in Maine, the red-cockaded woodpecker must be considered in Texas timber management, and the El Segundo Blue Butterfly regarded in California airport expansion.

The conjunction of conservation and ecology movements with women's rights and liberation has moved in the direction of reversing both the subjugation of nature and women. In the late nineteenth and early twentieth centuries, the strong feminist movement in the United States, begun in 1842 pressed for women's suffrage first in the individual states and then in the nation. Women activists also formed conservation committees in the many women's organizations that were a part of the Federation of Women's Clubs established in 1890. They supported the preservationists movement for national, state, and city parks and wilderness areas led by John Muir and Frederick Law Olmsted, eventually splitting away from the managerial, utilitarian wing headed by Gifford Pinchot and Theodore Roosevelt (Chapter 6).[19]

Today the conjunction of the women's movement with the ecology movement again brings the issue of liberation into focus. Mainstream women's groups such as the League of Women Voters took an early lead in studying and pressing for clean air and water legislation. Socialist-feminist and "science for the people" groups worked toward revolutionizing economic structures in a direction that would equalize female and male work options and reform a capitalist system that creates profits at the expense of nature and working people (Chapter 7).

The March 1979 accident at the Three-Mile Island nuclear reactor near Harrisburg, Pennsylvania epitomized the problems of the "death of nature" that have become apparent since the Scientific Revolution. The manipulation of nuclear processes in an effort to control and harness nature through technology backfired into disaster. The long-range economic interests and public image of the power company and the reactor's designer were set above the immediate safety of the people and the health of the earth. The hidden effects of radioactive emissions, which by concentrating in the food chain could lead to an increase in cancers over the next several years, were initially downplayed by those charged with responsibility for regulating atomic power.

Three-Mile Island is a vivid symbol of the earth's sickness caused by radioactive wastes, pesticides, plastics, photochemical smog, and fluorocarbons. The pollution "of her purest streams" has been supported since the Scientific Revolution by an ideology of "power over nature," an ontology of interchangeable atomic and human parts, and a methodology of "penetration" into her innermost secrets. The sick earth, "yea dead, yea putrefied," can probably in the long run be restored to health only by a reversal of mainstream values and a revolution in economic priorities. In this sense, the world must once again be turned upside-down.

As natural resources and energy supplies diminish in the future, it will become essential to examine alternatives of all kinds so that, by adopting new social styles, the quality of the environment can be sustained. Decentralization, non-hierarchical forms of organization, recycling of wastes, simpler living styles involving less-polluting, "soft" technologies, and labor-intensive rather than capital-intensive economic methods are possibilities only beginning to be explored.[20] The future distribution of energy and resources among communities should be based on the integration of human and natural ecosystems. Such a restructuring of priorities is crucial if people and nature are to survive.

5

FROM CORN
MOTHERS
TO MORAL
MOTHERS

CHANGING FORMS

OF EARTHCARE IN

NEW ENGLAND

Between 1600 and 1860 two major transformations in New England land and life took place. The first, a colonial ecological revolution, occurred during the seventeenth century and was externally generated. It resulted in the collapse of indigenous Indian ecologies and the incorporation of a European ecological complex of animals, plants, pathogens, and people. The colonial revolution extracted native species from their ecological contexts and shipped them overseas as commodities. It was legitimated by a set of symbols that placed cultured European humans above wild nature, other animals, and "beastlike savages." It substituted a visual for an oral consciousness and an image of nature as female and subservient to a transcendent male God for the Indians' animistic fabric of symbolic exchanges between people and nature.[1]

The second transformation, a capitalist ecological revolution, took place roughly between the American Revolution and about 1860. It was initiated by internal tensions within New England and by a dynamic market economy. Local factories imported natural resources and exported finished products. Air pollution, water pollution, and resource depletions were created as externalities outside the calculation of profits. The capitalist revolution demanded an economy of increased human labor, land management, and a legitimating mechanistic science. It split human consciousness into a disembodied analytic mind and a romantic emotional sensibility.

Ecological revolutions are processes through which different societies change their relationship to nature. They arise from tensions between production and ecology and between production and reproduction. The results are new constructions of nature, both materially and in human consciousness. Here, I focus on the changing roles women played in the New England landscape as colonialism and capitalism transformed Native American land use patterns.

CORN MOTHERS

The Indians of southern New England had been a horticultural people since approximately A.D. 1000. Extending inland from the coast, the Wammpanoag, Narraganset, Massachuset, and Nauset, the Pequot-Mohegan, the Nipmuck-Connecticut Valley tribes, the Wappinger Confederacy, and the Mahican depended on the corn, bean, and squash complex for their sustenance. Tapering off in the area between the Saco and Kennebec rivers in Maine, corn cultivation extended as far north as the Saint John's River where green or milk corn could be harvested. In contrast to the animal mythologies that focused the culture of northern gatherer-hunters, the cosmology, mythology, and rituals of New England's southern Indians centered on the cultivation of maize, supporting a system of production largely in the hands of women. The home of the corn plant and its female cultivators was a clearing in the lowland woods that gradually shifted to upland hunting forests where wood gathering and local hunting radii tapered off.

Through their cosmology and mythology, the southern New England tribes expressed their world view, translating it into daily behavior. As for other woodland cultivators along the Atlantic seaboard, their entire cosmos was alive, their mythology centered on the origins of corn, and their calendar revolved around planting rituals.[2] The animate cosmos was expressed through interlinked words of action. Father (*oosh*), mother (*ookas*), and earth (*ohke*) were all related to the verb of motion "oo": The verb "oosh-oh" was the active animate producer, meaning "he comes from him." The word "ook-as" signified a passive animate producer, while the noun "ohke" meant earth. In contrast to the northern hunters whose ancestors were animals, the Narraganset were generated from plants. When told the European creation story that Adam was made by God of red earth and Eve from Adam's rib, they related their own origin story. Kiehtan had made a man and a woman from a stone, but, not liking the result, broke them apart and made another man and woman, their ancestors, from a tree. As a result, they believed that they themselves had "sprung and grown up in that very place, like the very trees.[3]

Myths also accounted for the origin of corn. For the Massachusetts and Narraganset Bay Indians, the source of the gifts of corn and beans was their southwestern god Kiehtan. His crops grew better as one proceeded toward the southwest and more poorly toward the northeast. Roger Williams also reported the Narraganset's belief that a crow had brought a grain of corn in one ear and a bean in the other. Other Indians held that, whereas the crow had brought the bean, a blackbird deposited the first corn seed. Ritual prevented the killing of both these sacred bearers.

Another story from the Penobscot and the Saint John's River Malecite told of a woman who could produce corn from her body. She told her husband to clear land and drag her body over it after her death. Corn grew in the clearing. While legends for the Connecticut Valley Indians and other central New England tribes have not been transmitted through historical sources, we know neighboring tribes in the New York and Pennsylvania areas had Corn Mother traditions.[4]

Corn Mother mythology, sacred corn bearers, and corn ripening rituals were manifestations of a religious ethos centered on the animate vegetative world. As cultural symbols they instilled tribal survival values in those who produced the food that sustained the daily life of the tribal whole.

INDIAN WOMEN'S EARTHCARE

Women's horticulture was the major source of food, corn alone providing the Indians of southeastern New England with about 65 percent of their caloric intake. Through production practices, women had a direct impact on the environment. Most eastern woodland traditions attributed to women the major roles in planting, weeding, harvesting, and distributing the corn, beans, squash, and pumpkins.

Since horticulture was the domain of women, it is probable (although the archaeological records cannot speak with certainty) that over time women selected the seed types that would mature early in New England's short northern summers and developed the technology for cultivating the soil. The women who hoed the fields, planted seed, and weeded the plots had an intimate understanding of the labor requirements. They may well have chipped the tools they needed from the easily flaked sandstone, schist, and pegmatite, notching them for attachment to wooden handles. Little time seems to have been spent in perfecting implements or making them durable, presumably because they were not transported from site to site. Spades were pointed, straight, or convex; corn planters were long and narrow with notched sides for attachment to a stick. After the women had dug up the corn hills from the previous year with triangular stone hoes or with hoes fashioned from a large clam shell attached to a stick, they pulverized the soil with medium-sized hoes and piled it into hills.[5]

Planting time was measured both by the stars and by annual natural events. According to Verrazzano who visited Narraganset Bay from April 21 to May 6, 1524, the time for spring planting was governed by the Pleiades. The seven stars of the Pleiades, located in the head of the constellation of the large horned animal (known to Europeans as Taurus the bull) disappeared from the twilighted western horizon from early May to mid-October, their absence coinciding with the frost-free season of 153 to 163 days in southern New England.

In the Hudson River Valley just to the west, "on seeing the head of the bull...the women know how to explain that it is a horned head of a big, wild animal...and when it rises in a certain part of the heavens, at a time known to them, then is the season for planting." "The women there are the most skillful star gazers; there is scarcely one of them but can name all the stars; their rising, setting; the position of the Arctos, that is the Wain, is as well known to them as to us, and they name them by other names."[6]

When the signs were right, the women planted each hill with four grains of maize and two of pole beans that would climb and twine around them. Squash and pumpkins planted between the hills would achieve sufficient height in time to provide a broad canopy of leaves to smother late-growing weeds by reducing the light reaching the soil below. This two-tiered system allowed the corn and beans to find their place in the sun at the top of the crop system, while the spreading squash and pumpkins on the lower level formed an umbrella, shielding the soil from excessive sun and rain. Fields were probably planted over a period of several weeks, spreading out both the planting and harvesting labor and reducing the impact of late spring or early fall freezes and other climatic disasters. Some accounts indicate that the beans were planted in the "middle of May when the maize is the height of a finger or more."[7]

Pest control also required active labor. Children stationed in the fields or on the platforms of watch houses among the corn rows drove away blackbirds, crows, and chipmunks from the seed and young plants. Seed soaked previously in hellebore caused drunkenness in the marauding birds. Women and children removed cutworms from the base of the corn, a difficult task since the worms were almost invisible against the green stalk.[8]

By late May the fields required the first weeding. Early accounts praise the Indian women for their meticulous weeding, "not suffering a choking weed to advance his audacious head above their infant corn or an undermining worm to spoil his spurns." So important was weeding that an entire month of the Indian year (May) was named the "weeding month."

In July, the women hilled corn by piling earth around the base of each stalk with hoes, forcing it to grow support roots for stability against the summer winds. After this the fields required no additional attention until August, when the green or milk corn was ripe enough to begin harvesting. The main harvest took place in September while the men were away on the autumn hunt. The fresh corn was cooked with the harvested beans to produce a succotash seasoned with fish, ground nuts, and Jerusalem artichokes. The combination of corn and beans in the diet had a nutritional advantage. Maize supplied zein, the protein in corn, but lacked lysine and tryptophan which were contributed by the beans. The synergistic effect of these amino acids resulted in a highly desirable protein combination.[9]

Rogers Williams reported on the amount of the Rhode Island Indians' corn yield after it had been dried for storage: "The women of the family will commonly raise two or three heaps of twelve, fifteen, or twenty bushels a heap which they dry in round broad heaps; and if she have help of her children and friends, much more." This would mean somewhere between twenty-four and sixty bushels of shelled corn per woman for the ensuing winter and spring. These high yields of corn afforded each person in a household of five to six persons about 1,625 calories of corn per day (with a range of 1,150 to 2,900 calories), more than adequate to supply nutritional needs from grain products. The annual corn crop probably provided about 65 percent of the caloric intake of the adult Indian.[10]

Women controlled the storage and distribution of the dried shelled corn. They placed it in large grass sacks or baskets and buried it in holes dug five or six feet into the ground, "covering it from the inquisitive search of their gormandizing husbands, who would eat up both their allowed portion and reserved seed, if they knew where to find it."[11]

Indian women thus held the dominant role in horticultural production. This contrasts with the colonial division of labor between men in the fields and barn and women in the home and farmyard. The colonial ecological revolution would undercut female power, imposing European roles on Indian men and women.

THE COLLAPSE OF CORN MOTHER FARMING

Into Southern New England, the Plymouth Pilgrims (after 1620), and the Massachusetts Bay Puritans (after 1629) introduced a European ecological complex of animals, plants, pathogens, and people.

This colonial ecological revolution was externally caused and resulted in the erosion of Indian modes of relating to nature. Local ecology on which Indian gathering–hunting and agricultural production depended was disrupted by plant and animal introductions and by fur and timber extractions. Disease and war devastated the Indians' potential for biological reproduction; colonial land treaties that continually reduced tribal territories destroyed social reproduction. Radical changes in reproduction thus reinforced and further weakened forms of production. With the balance between them destroyed, the ecological core of the Indian way of life collapsed. Although many surviving Indians resisted white culture, land hunger, and settled farming, they also adapted to the new ecological conditions and, where possible used whites as allies in dealing with the now dominant English system.

Pilgrim and Puritan settlers introduced livestock and grains confined within the geometric spaces of rectangular fields outlined by fences. Their patriarchal homes were constricted domains mapped onto space as private property. Here the colonial family reproduced its own subsistence, and entrepreneurs extracted resources for the mercantile trade. But although their New World gardens were framed and farmed in an Old World image, the surveyed distances between marker trees and stone walls, needed to transmit inherited property, foreshadowed the Cartesian grids later imposed by the land survey system.

By the end of the seventeenth century, the Indians' productive–reproductive balance was undermined by the colonists' exogenous ecological introductions, their extraction of commodities for overseas trade, and a consciousness that gave precedence to European culture over "wild" nature. Indian men were forced into farming roles, undercutting female power in production, and were recognized by the colonists as the tribal decision makers, solidifying their locus of power in governance.

THE COLONISTS' EARTHMOTHER

Like the cosmos of the precolonial Indian, the eighteenth-century cosmos was alive and animate. But unlike Indian animism with its many deities within animals, plants, and rocks, the English God was transcendent, Nature acting as his vice-regent in the mundane world. Like the consciousness of the Indians, the consciousness of most rural farmers was participatory and mimetic. But unlike that of Indians, it was a participatory consciousness dominated by vision. A mix of astrological and alchemic symbols conveyed by elites through the world of print reinforced the oral culture of folk traditions.

The animate cosmos of Old England and New England, however, was not a unified fabric of ideas and symbols. In England, by the late seventeenth century, the mechanistic world view of the scientific revolution challenged Renaissance animism. Elite philosophers and scientists questioned the geocentric theory and increasingly accepted the Copernican heliocentric hypothesis. Terrestrial and celestial motions were described by mathematical laws.

In both Old and New England, two world views inherited from ancient civilizations underlay explanations for the phenomena of nature. The Egyptian and Greek views based on the circular cosmos and the eternal cycles within nature mingled with the Judaic and Christian schemes of an absolute God who produced catastrophes and dealt rewards and punishments to his earthly subjects. Both perspectives informed farmers' continuing efforts to predict weather, determine planting and harvesting dates, and maintain healthy soils.

Nature, personified as animate mother, carried out God's dictates in the phenomenal world. To the peasant and farmer, her signs and activities were often enigmatic and had to be accepted as God's will rather than challenged or analyzed. Presaged by comets, planetary conjunctions, or earthquakes, Nature inflicted God's rewards and punishments in the form of rain or drought, good harvests or crop failures, health or disease. But by understanding the celestial cycles and working within them, the land could be made to yield and the soil could be healed.

The environmental ethic of eighteenth-century New England was more benign than the wilderness subjugation ethic of the early Puritans. While the biblical imagery of dominion had been preached by seventeenth-century Puritans as a justification for taking over the land, milder pastoral imagery accompanied the eighteenth-century's extension of the Garden of Eden into the New England landscape. In both elite and popular culture, the world was the expression of a benevolent deity. A God against nature shifted toward a God who expressed his goodness through nature.[12]

Integral to the cyclical cosmos was the idea that Nature was an animate mother, subservient to God yet a powerful actress in the mundane world. New England philosopher Isaac Greenwood personified nature as a mother. Like an indulgent parent, she sometimes improved her original plan and con-

ccption on earth, while at other times she altered and dissolved her handi-
work. She was not only frugal, but active—uncertainty and mutability characterized her entire animate world. Below her surface, earthquakes, "fulmi-
nating damps," and volcanic eruptions produced continual change. Above it,
vapors from the tails of comets supplied the water, heat, and light that
restored the fluids used daily by vegetation. The air, impregnated with these
exhalations and vapors, was "the chief agent that Nature use[d] in most of her
secret processes." Respiration could produce death when the vapors were
unwholesome and pestilential, or life and health when they were refreshing.
Sometimes the cosmic exhalations destroyed vegetation, while at other times
they promoted growth and increase.[13]

Edward Taylor, poet and minister in Westfield, Massachusetts, described
"Nature's Tree" in a poem of 1705. Through her tree, she caused ore to rise
from the roots through the branches to the leaves, producing fruits. The roots
gave rise to the stones and lower metals—iron and lead. Higher up, the
warmth of the earth "hatch[ed] silver bright and gold more fine / And
sparkling gems that mock the sun and 'ts shine."[14]

Samuel Willard of Harvard believed that minerals "were at first made in
the earth, and its womb was then impregnated, and made fruitful of them."
Yale used as a textbook Benjamin Martin's *Philosophical Grammar* (1735)
which asserted that "divers mines, when emptied of stone, metal &c. have
after a while recruited again."[15]

Farmers' almanacs popularized the learning of Harvard and Oxford lecturers and European improvers in flowery, often humorous, verses that featured the cyclical nature of the seasons and the place of the farmer within the
Great Chain of Being. Nature transmitted the immutable laws of God to the
fleeting and changeable mundane world and fragile human substance. Rising
vapors, unwholesome airs, circulations, the wrack of falling elements, the
womb of chaos, the breaths and expirations of universal nature, vital airs,
pestilential heats, and gaping earthquakes characterized the annual activities
of Mother Earth in language that hearkened back to the animate cosmos of
Renaissance Europe.[16] Both almanac makers and agricultural writers
employed earth mother imagery in profusion in their discussions of agricultural methods and the relationship of the farmer to nature.

The pulsating sexuality of a laughing, vital Mother Earth and virile sun
was captured in the colorful verses and graphics heading each calendar
month. The sun's gentle heat brooded over the female Earth in dews and
rains, defending her from harm. The signs of the zodiac were personified and

assigned human needs and desires. During August, when the sun moved from the sign of Leo the Lion into that of Virgo the Virgin, Nathaniel Ames wrote:

> The Virgin lends her bosom to aswage
> And pacify Sol's burning furious Rage,
> They embrace, and down to Thetis' Bed descend
> Cool Nights arise, and all the World befriend.[17]

Almanac makers worked within the Renaissance tradition that the earth was a human being writ large with whom the farmer had an intimate, personal relationship. Ames's summer verses assumed a direct parallel between the earth's anatomy and reproductive processes and those of the farmer. In June, he wrote, man joined the "general smile of nature," as "fierce passions vex[ed] his breast." In July, mowers were cutting the humid hay as "distressful Nature pants" with "hot ascending steams." Or as John Tulley put it, "wanton Lads and Lasses do make Hay, / Which unto lewd temptation makes great way." The August verse in a 1709 Boston almanac depicted the earth's hair as needing cutting and grooming: "Terra's rich tresses that hang dangling down / Are by the bending Reapers daily mown.[18]

Colonists interpreted natural events as evidence of God's power and omniscience. Acting through nature, God could convey his pleasure or displeasure with humankind or deliver rewards and punishments. Verses warned of the wrath that Mother Earth could render—sometimes with a precaution that the lines were descriptive, not predictive:

> The Earth convulsed, her jaws are open'd wide
> Churches and all their lofty spires subside
> To Nature's Womb they sink with dreadful throws
> And on poor screaming souls the chasms close.[19]

The farmer's astrological cosmos was an integral part of a more comprehensive organic framework. Not only did the animate earth produce and recycle nitrous salts to fertilize the soil, it also gave birth to the minerals, stones, and metals beneath its surface. The animate and the inanimate, the organic and inorganic were blended into many gradations of the living.[20]

Until the introduction of agricultural improvement in the late eighteenth century, the concept of the animate cosmos formed the ethical framework for the life and labor of most farmers. The Renaissance theory that water and fertilizing salts circulated from the earth to atmosphere and back again, nourishing and restoring the health of fallow fields, legitimated a system of "naked" fallows through which the soil recovered its fertility unaided.

COLONIAL WOMEN AND THE ENVIRONMENT

Like Indian subsistence, colonial agriculture depended on the division of labor by gender. Women and men each had separate tasks and separate genderized production spaces. Male and female were equals in subsistence production, each sex being essential to the family's economic survival. The reproduction of social roles took place in these separate spaces. Girls participated in their mother's space-time zones, boys in those of their fathers.

Women's domain radiated outward from the farmhouse kitchen. Farmhouses were divided into sleeping rooms, parlor, and kitchen, all expandable as the family grew larger, with a root cellar below. Kitchens could be enlarged by adding ells or sheds with lean-to roofs. Just outside the kitchen door was the essential herb garden and beyond it, as time and labor allowed, the vegetable garden. Outbuildings provided space for butter, cheese making, poultry, and privy; at the orchard's edge, overlapping men's space, trees offered their branches for clothes drying. Beyond lay a friendly neighbor's kitchen, the village store, and the meetinghouse.[21]

But although women and men were equal partners in production, colonial relations of reproduction were patriarchal. Lineage and property rights that reproduced family power passed through the male. Almanacs repeated the Bible's anatomical justification for women's productive and reproductive roles in patriarchal society. Eve was made from Adam's side, not from his head to be his superior, nor from his feet to trample on her, "but out of his side, to be equal with him; under his arm, to be protected; and near his heart to be beloved." Man was the head of creation and, although man was made of refined dust, woman was of double-refined dust, one step farther from the earth than he. Although a partner in subsistence, under colonial patriarchy, a good wife must be submissive, humble, modest, silent, and revere her husband.[22]

But women's role in production and reproduction was far harsher than the almanacs' homilies revealed, and women's labor was intensely demanding. From tending and slaughtering chickens, cutting and cooking meat, carrying wood, milking cows and goats, to making cheese, butter, candles, and bread, growing and weeding vegetables, spinning and carding wool, often while pregnant or tending young children, she worked hard even into old age, when the farm and its management may have passed entirely into her hands. Like her husband, she engaged in trade and transactions with neighbors and townspeople (both male and female), kept notes (sometimes on the kitchen wall), and sometimes recorded her work life in her diary.[23]

Women's traditional production activities interacted directly with the environment and included care of the herb and vegetable gardens, dairying and cheese making, and poultry raising. They planted herb and vegetable gardens just outside the kitchen door with medicinal herbs that treated ailments and acted as purgatives and with culinary herbs that added flavor to routine dairy meals: tansy, peppermint, spearmint, wormwood, rue, spikenard, lovage, elecampane, pennyroyal, boneset, thyme, and sage. They weeded and manured the soil, while their free-ranging poultry kept down insect pests and added dung. During the summer as the herbs came into bloom, they gathered them into bundles to be hung in the kitchen or attic to dry. Women also planted vegetables for "green sauce" to add to stews and later as side dishes for the main meal.[24]

Eggs (the purest form of protein known), milk, cheese, poultry, vegetables, nuts, and berries all supply necessary protein and calories and constitute farm women's traditional contributions to the diet. Amelia Simmons's cookbook mentions the "frequent use" of dunghill fowl (turkeys, chickens, capons, geese, and ducks). Women's increasing skills in the preservation of root crops and the drying or pickling of fruits and vegetables extended their use beyond summer into winter and spring.[25]

Cheese and butter making were also important contributions to family subsistence and added protein in the diet. The techniques had been handed down from woman to woman since ancient times. Nineteenth-century farm journals codified ancient lore and recommended improvements. The prime cheese season was May to September. About a gallon of milk was needed to produce a pound of cheese for the family each week, two for a pound of butter.[26]

Sarah Anna Emery, who grew up in Newburyport, Massachusetts in the 1790s, recalled, as a nonagenarian, making cheese with her mother and grandmother. "During breakfast the milk for the cheese was warming over the fire, in the large brass kettle. The milk being from the ten cows, my mother made cheese four days, Aunt Sarah having the milk the remainder of the week. In this way good-sized cheeses were obtained. The curd having been broken into the basket, the dishes were washed, and unless there was washing or other extra work, the house was righted. By the time this was done the curd was ready for the press....After dinner the cheeses were turned and rubbed; then mother put me on a clean frock, and dressed herself for the afternoon."[27]

Butter making required great care and cleanliness. According to the *New England Farmer*, for best quality, the dairy house was to be as close to the spring house or icehouse as possible since carrying the milk agitated it too much. The tin pails had to be scalded and then sun or fire dried. With a wooden ladle, the woman lifted out the butter and worked it with salt until it was ready to be molded in stone pots or oak kegs.[28]

The *New England Farmer* also offered women advice on food preservation. After harvest, apples could be kept sweet and juicy by placing them in glazed jars. Grapes could be preserved until winter if enclosed in white muslin or crepe bags tied with string. Dipping eggs for a second or two in boiling water would prevent spoilage. Pickled beets could be prepared with vinegar, horseradish, onions, ginger, mace, cloves, allspice, and salt.[29]

When the *New England Farmer* published articles on cheese and butter making, it was helping to codify female empiricism and farm lore into scientific dairy farming useful to male farmers. With nineteenth-century specialization, men began to take over women's traditional areas of dairying, poultry raising, and vegetable production. The traditional dairy areas of western Massachusetts expanded as more farmers took up dairy farming and poultry raising. Agricultural specialization and farm management became significant components of the capitalist ecological revolution.

WOMEN IN CAPITALIST PRODUCTION

New England's capitalist ecological revolution began in the late eighteenth-century and was structurally complete by the 1860s. The colonial revolution had appropriated Nature's matter by transforming subjects into objects and living organisms into commodities for exchange on the market. The capitalist revolution gave back to nature "her" nutrients, but appropriated "her" labor. By transferring nature's regenerative powers to society, the land was rendered passive and manageable. No longer was it necessary to let fields lie fallow to be restored as the Sabbath restored humans. No longer must forests be left to the activity of plant succession, but species needed for human use could be planned, planted, and harvested by foresters and agronomists. The colonial mercantile exchange of commodities was transformed into a system of production units that employed wage labor on farms, in forests, and in factories. The capitalist ecological revolution was characterized by the efficient organization of land, labor, and capital, competition in the marketplace, and the emergence of large-scale control over resources.

The mechanistic philosophy developed by the natural philosophers of seventeenth-century Europe legitimated the capitalist revolution and its domination of nature. Mingled with the rhetoric of the Great Chain of Being,

Mother Earth, and the Garden of Eden that focused New England thought in the eighteenth century had been an under-current of instrumental concepts that would structure the management of nature in the nineteenth century. Mechanical metaphors and the rhetoric of manifest destiny became core concepts of a modern philosophy that saw the world as a vast machine that could be mathematically described, predicted, and controlled. A new chemical paradigm would quantify associations and dissociations of elements in soils and plants so that yields and profits could be predicted and increased. "Mother Nature" was delivered to the laboratory to undergo scientific experimentation.

The capitalist revolution split production and reproduction into two separate spheres. As male farmers began to specialize in women's traditional dairy, poultry, and vegetable production, and as textile mills took over their clothing production, woman's primary domain was redefined as reproduction. Woman's sphere still included her biological and social roles of childbearing and child rearing (although nineteenth-century family sizes dropped dramatically), but her traditional farmyard and garden production was constricted to the reproduction of daily life within the household walls. Her role as equal producer in subsistence agriculture changed to reproducer as her outdoor labor turned to indoor domesticity. With these changes the quantity of her labor did not decrease, and in most cases increased. Within the home a woman did additional putting-out work such as braiding palm leaf hats, weaving rag carpets, or making silk twist buttons or took in boarders to help support her family, especially if single or widowed. Her role as moral mother, however, emphasized the daily care of the family and the socialization of children.

The ideological split between productive and reproductive spheres was necessary for the maintenance of the market economy. Within the household, as within the larger social whole, male and female, head and heart, calculation and emotion expressed the dualities of industrial capitalism. The outward motive sphere of the male was balanced by the inward emotive sphere of the female. Man's role was to compete in the marketplace or provide labor for a male entrepreneur. Woman's role was to express superior moral virtue in setting standards of purity, piety, and nurture for her family. Woman could work for wages while single, but as wife and mother she was to use her energy on the home. For middle-class women, capitalist ideology severed woman the reproducer and homemaker from man the producer and money-maker.[30]

Journals, such as the *New England Farmer*, published numerous articles on good dairying techniques by men who had learned them from their wives, along with a few communications from women. The articles advised would-be dairymen to maintain fertile pastures and clean dairies, and suggested putting older daughters in charge of butter and cheese making.[31]

Vegetable gardening by men for the Boston and overseas markets transformed many farms in Essex and Middlesex counties in eastern Massachusetts in the 1820s, 1830s, and 1840s. Wage labor and heavy use of manures from farms and cities increased yields as well as the value of farmlands. Poultry and egg farming also became major businesses for male farmers. Rhode Island became a leader in the production of poultry, with Washington Country specializing almost entirely in the business.[32]

While poorer or more isolated farm women continued to rely on home-produced butter, eggs, and cheese, many middle-class rural wives found purchasing cheaper than production. The direction of these changes in dairying, vegetable, and poultry farming to commercial agriculture was to decrease women's direct interaction with the natural environment in the sphere of production.

Another displacement took place within women's traditional roles in household textile production. In 1810, when Albert Gallatin submitted his report on American manufactures, textiles and clothing were produced primarily in the home.[33] By the late colonial period, however, women in some areas could take their fleeces, yarn, or cloth to local spinning, carding, and fulling mills where machines could be substituted for one or two of the home operations. The new textile mills recruited young single women as labor by offering wages high enough to attract them from family farms, but below those of men. In these factories boys and girls, men and women, were all employed in a series of semiskilled to skilled and supervisory jobs.

By the 1830s, textile production had moved out of the home. Prices for finished cloth fell sixfold between 1815 and 1830, leaving women with little reason to produce their own cloth. Farm girls found employment during maidenhood in the spinning mills, but as wives and mothers they were relieved of time-consuming textile production. Instead, they could purchase the finished cloth from which to sew their families' clothing.[34]

MORAL MOTHERS: A NEW FORM OF EARTHCARE

As women's outdoor farm and indoor textile production declined, their reproductive roles were elevated. Until marriage a young farm woman might work outside the home in textile production or supervise her father's dairy, but her obligation to society was the biological reproduction that created the next generation of producers and the social reproduction that prepared her offspring to take their places in society. She must be educated in order to consciously and responsibly carry out her duties. No longer was it sufficient to learn social roles mimetically through observing the hard work, frugality, and piety of elders. a mother must actively engage herself in passing down to her children a complex of moral virtues that would redeem the amorality of the marketplace and provide a refuge from the stress of competition. Men still reproduced patriarchal society through politics, property, and production, but these were now balanced by the elevation of womanhood, motherhood, and domesticity.

The trilogy of mother, wife, and home focused the ideology of social reproduction. As mother and wife, woman embodied the moral law. Her home was the space in which she instilled morals in her husband and children. Both a morally uprighteous mother and a healthy natural environment were necessary to produce a healthy child.[35]

Farm journals especially focused on the role of nature in crating moral values. No spot on earth was freer from vice and immorality than a farm home. Shielded from urban contamination, the fresh breezes offered strength for body and soul. At the day's end, the industrious farmer could seat "himself around the hearthstone, with his affectionate wife and smiling children." Protected from the tempests of nature, the financial risks and speculations that beset the merchant, and the commotion of the politician, the farmer in his homestead remained stable and secure. "His corn ripens, his garden flourishes, and mother earth bountifully rewards him for all his toil."[36]

Female values, in combination with agricultural management, would tame and improve wild nature while simultaneously "civilizing" and elevating husbands and children. Under woman's influence on the farm, weedy pastures and fields would give way to abundant harvests and dilapidated cottages would be replaced by neatly painted farmhouses.[37]

The instrumental consciousness that manipulated nature for commercial gain found its antithesis in the romantic consciousness of personal involvement with nature. The same forests and mountains that were being exploited for lumber for the market economy were being visited, painted, and eulogized as sources of personal peace and serenity.

Middle-class women, whose direct impact on nature through production had decreased, found opportunities to influence consciousness about nature by educating themselves in the natural sciences, by writing children's books, and later by preserving nature through women's clubs. Leisure time was often used for getting in touch with the beauties of the natural world and its creator. The study of natural history became popular during the 1820s and 1830s. Women along with their husbands attended local lyceum lectures on science and religion. They deepened their appreciation of nature through the study of botany, geology, and mineralogy. Stimulated by European books such as Jean-Jacques Rousseau's *Letters on the Elements of Botany Addressed to a Lady* (London, 1785) and Priscilla Bell Wakefield's *Introduction to Botany, in a Series of Familiar Letters* (1786), plant collecting and identification gained acceptance in New England society and its burgeoning female academies as appropriate expressions of female piety. Painting flowers, describing them in travel diaries, and collecting herbarium specimens induced love of God. A growing consciousness of the value of plants, animals, rural scenery, and wilderness, coupled with the need to improve urban environments, propelled middle-class women into active work in the conservation movement toward the end of the century.[38]

Underlying the appreciation of nature was the assumption that an intimate connection between science and morals stemmed from the Deity. Hannah Gale (1818–1851) of Northborough, Massachusetts, attended the Greene Street School in Providence, Rhode Island, in 1837–1838 while preparing to become a teacher. One of her instructors was transcendentalist philosopher Margaret Fuller. Gale wrote in her diary that, in teaching her pupils "moral science," Fuller argued that ideas about duty and religion could not have arisen from the "light of nature" alone, but required revelation. According to Gale, Fuller greatly admired Socrates and "thought that no one ever had or ever could exceed the views which he formed." She emphasized a transcendent reality grasped by the mind and revealed through nature. She lectured on the transcendentalist account of the "music of nature" heard by the spiritual ear, similar to the ancients' "music of the spheres." To her pupil Hannah Gale, nature's music resembled the poetry of mathematics discovered by Isaac Newton "as he sat under the apple tree and discovered by the fall of the apple, the laws by which the world was governed." Of all the senses, sight was to her the most precious for it allowed her to "see the grand and beautiful scenes which Nature presents to us." Her greatest ambition was to be able to draw them as a constant remainder of the beauty revealed by the Deity.[39]

Also influenced by a transcendent "religion of nature" was teacher Caroline Barrett White, who recorded her responses in her diaries from 1849 when she was twenty-one until her death at eighty-seven. Born in Ashburnham, Massachusetts, she taught school there as well as in Shirley and Worcester from 1849 until her marriage in 1851. She saw an intimate connection between scientific understanding of nature and human morality. Despairing of her own capacity to avoid the sins that beset humanity, she participated in moral efforts to ameliorate social ills through the Ladies' Olive Leaf Association. Attending evening lyceum lectures and agricultural fairs educated her about the application of science to the improvement of the human condition. At the first agricultural fair held in Claremont, New Hampshire, in 1849 she was struck by the quality of the improvements in domestic animals and vegetables, and was impressed by Professor Brewster of Hanover's appeal to New Hampshire farmers to "make their profession an object of scientific investigation."

Extraordinarily sensitive to the effects of nature on her feelings, White observed nature's signs and activities as evidence of a transcendent reality created by an all-powerful Deity. The changing seasons dramatized the existential meaning of the life cycle and the transitoriness between the worlds of life and death. "This is the final day of Autumn—quickly has the summer flown, like a dream." How swiftly, she lamented, are we all hurrying on toward the land "whence no traveler returns" beyond the "vale of tears." Winter wind provoked awe and reverence for God's power. Sunsets symbolized both the separation and the connection between human and heaven, while eyes, ears, and tongue transmitted nature's emblems to the human heart.

On excursions to nearby mountains and lakes, she described nature in deeply personal terms pervaded by religious feelings and experiences of the sublime. Sunset inspired a "tumult of feeling" that subsides into a calm, making the heart swell with love of God and creation. "When I contemplate nature my heart expands with an intensity and feeling of love, of admiration, of reverence for that Being who has spread out before us the sublime works of creation and opened the boundless treadmill of knowledge for our research."[40] To these middle-class women, science offered a way to understand and express feelings about nature that were acceptable within the nineteenth-century ideology of motherhood and morality.

The capitalist revolution separated private from public life. The public sphere of marketplace and politics was dominated by men, the private sphere of home and family by women. Nature was also severed: science and technology became the instrument for economic development, spirit and emotion a counterpoint to competition. From the first perspective, land was a "virgin" to be conquered and controlled; from the second, a mother who embodied moral law.

By the mid-nineteenth century, American social and economic values had been transformed. Mainstream culture had moved beyond the values of the animate cosmos. Nature had been deeply divided into two separate realms, one subservient to economic progress, the other to the human soul. Male and female values had likewise been split into utilitarianism and romanticism. At bottom, however, they were two sides of the coin of capitalist culture.

6

PRESERVING

THE EARTH

WOMEN AND THE

PROGRESSIVE

CONSERVATION

CRUSADE

Nowhere has women's self-conscious role as protectors of the environment been better exemplified than during the progressive conservation crusade of the early twentieth century. Although that role has been rendered all but invisible by conservation historians, women transformed the crusade from an elite male enterprise into a widely based movement. In so doing, they not only brought hundreds of local natural areas under legal protection, but also promoted legislation aimed at halting pollution, reforesting watersheds, and preserving endangered species. Yet this enterprise ultimately rested on the self-interested preservation of their own middle-class lifestyles and was legitimated by the separate male/female spheres ideology of the nineteenth century aimed at conserving "true womanhood," the home, and the child.

In his book *The Fight for Conservation* (1910), Gifford Pinchot praised the women of the progressive era for their substantial contributions to conservation. He cited the conservation committee of the Daughters of the American Revolution (chaired by his mother), the Pennsylvania Forestry Association, "founded by ladies," which carried out some of the earliest work done in that state, the national forests preserved by Minnesota women, and the Calaveras Big Trees set aside by the women of California after a nine year fight.[1]

Writing his definitive history of the progressive conservation campaign in 1959, Samuel Hays also acknowledged the enthusiasm of women's organizations for conservation and their staunch support, until 1913, for Pinchot as leader of the movement. Historians Robert Welker (1955) and Stephen Fox (1981) amplified other female contributions, especially to the Audubon movement and the hiking clubs, while admitting that much remains to be learned regarding women's role in conservation.[2] Behind these brief tributes to their substantial contributions lies an untold story of immense energy, achievement, and dedication by thousands of women. Although only the most prominent women appear in recent historical studies, without the input of women in nearly every locale in the country, conservation gains in the early decades of the century would have been fewer and far less spectacular.

In the nineteenth century, women had developed interests and organizations that paved the way for their work in the conservation and reform movements of the progressive era. Literary clubs oriented toward culture drew women together for mutual improvement and shared experiences, while the women's rights and abolition movements exposed them to the political process and the public arena. Leisure time had afforded middle and upper-class women opportunities for botanizing, gardening, birdlore, and camping. Propelled by a growing consciousness of the panacea of bucolic scenery and wilderness, coupled with the need for reform of the squalor of the cities, women burst vividly into the public arena in the early twentieth century as a force in the progressive conservation crusade.[3]

Who were these women of the conservation movement? What were their accomplishments, objectives, and ideals? How did they interact with the men who promoted conservation? What ideological framework did they bring to the crusade and to the conflicts that developed within it?

FEMINIST CONSERVATION

THE GENERAL FEDERATION OF WOMEN'S CLUBS

In 1900, Mrs. Lovell White of San Francisco, (Fig. 6.1), the brilliant, dynamic founder and president of the women's California Club, took up the cause of forestry. Founded at the home of Mrs. White on a cold rainy evening in 1897 in the wake of the first and abortive California suffrage campaign—a campaign "brilliant, rich in experiences" with a "a spirit of wholesome comradeship,"—the California Club merged in January of 1900 with women's clubs throughout the state to form the California Federation of Women's Clubs. With Mrs. Robert Burdette of Pasadena as president and Mrs. White as vice-president-at-large, the first meeting was steeped in conservation ideals.[4]

Mrs. Lovell White

FIG. 6.1 / MRS. LOVELL WHITE. CALIFORNIA FEDERATION OF WOMEN'S CLUBS
CLUB LIFE, 4 NO 6 (FEB. 1906) REPRODUCED BY PERMISSION.

"The preservation of the forests of this state is a matter that should appeal to women," declared Mrs. Burdette in her opening address. "While the women of New Jersey are saving the palisades of the Hudson from utter destruction by men to whose greedy souls Mount Sinai is only a stone quarry, and the women of Colorado are saving the cliff dwellings and pueblo ruins of their state from vandal destruction, the word comes to the women of California that men whose souls are gang-saws are meditating the turning of our world-famous Sequoias into planks and fencing worth so many dollars." The forests of the state, she went on, were the source of the state's waters and together they made possible the homes and health of the people of California. "Better one living tree in California, than fifty acres of lumberyard. Preserve and replant them and the State will be blessed a thousandfold in the development of its natural resources...."[5]

In the years that followed, Mrs. White, as President of the California Club's Outdoor Art League, President of the Sempervirens Club, and later Chair of the Forestry Committee of the General Federation of Women's clubs made a national reputation "working unceasingly in behalf of forestry." "Whenever her name is associated with any project," asserted a tribute to her in 1906, "it is looked upon as a guarantee of success for the very good reason that she engineered so many undertakings by her executive strength and progressive spirit."[6]

In 1900 Mrs. White became alarmed by a report that the Calaveras Grove of Big Trees in the Stanislaus watershed of the western Sierra, discovered in 1850 and of world renown, was scheduled for cutting by an eastern lumber firm. The Big Trees, (*Sequoia gigantea*), were the largest known redwoods in existence, many measuring over 12 feet in diameter with bark up to two feet thick.[7]

In February of that year, Mrs. White asked Mrs. A.D. Sharon, a club member who was in Washington, to request the introduction of a joint resolution in Congress calling for the acquisition of the grove on behalf of the public. Success was immediate, and too good to be true! In March Mrs. White received a telegram from Mrs. Sharon: "Bill passed House Friday, Senate Monday, President signed Tuesday."[8]

Mrs. White soon realized that the bill had only authorized negotiation to purchase. No funds had been appropriated. But with cutting delayed owing to the owner's cooperation with the law, Mrs. White as president of the Outdoor Art League began a nationwide campaign for purchase of the trees as a national park.

After a bill failed to pass the house in 1904, she organized a petition drive that collected 1,500,000 signatures and was endorsed by dozens of national organizations. Upon its presentation to President Theodore Roosevelt, the first special presidential message was sent to Congress "at the request of an organization managed by women," urging preservation of the groves. In addition, Mrs. White arranged to have large photographs of the most prominent trees, named after presidents and generals of the United States, sent to key congressional committees.[9]

With Congress still refusing to act, Mrs. White embarked on a personal campaign to lobby every senator and representative in Congress. Finally in 1909 a bill was passed and signed by Roosevelt that authorized exchange of the Calaveras Groves for lands of equal value in the U.S. Forest Reserves. Hailed as a great triumph by the Women's Clubs, preservation of the Big Trees was not yet achieved. No lands satisfactory for the exchange could be found by the owner, Mr. Whiteside. The situation remained in limbo until 1926, when announcement was made of plans to cut the South Grove. At that point the fight was taken up by Mrs. Harriet West Jackson who as president of the Calaveras Grove Association determined to press for a state park in lieu of the national park originally authorized. With the assistance of the Calaveras Garden Club, the North Grove was finally set aside in 1931. But not until 1954, largely through a statewide education campaign conducted by Mrs. Owen Bradley, did the South Grove become part of the state park system.[10]

Mrs. Lovell White was also the president of the Sempervirens Club that, in cooperation with the California Federation of Women's Clubs and the Women's Club of San José succeeded in creating the Big Basin State Park that preserved large stands of California's other redwood, Sequoia sempervirens. In 1990 Mrs. Carrie Walter and Mrs. Louise Jones of the San Jose Women's Club joined a party of six other individuals, including representatives of the Sierra Club, the City of San Francisco, photographers, and nature lovers. The party spent several days in Big Basin camping in "tents on the bank of a clear stream, fringed with azaleas, and shaded by giant redwoods." Sitting around the campfire in the evening, they discussed a strategy for the preservation of the sequoias.[11]

The upshot was the formation of the Sempervirens Club (later known as the Save the Redwoods League) composed of men and women, under the guiding hand of Mrs. White, who were dedicated to saving the area from the saw. After securing an option on the land, the club conducted an education campaign through photographs, circulars, newspapers, schools, civic organizations and the women's clubs. A bill introduced into the state legislature in 1901 was bitterly opposed by business interests, lumber companies, and politicians. Finally the Assembly, convinced by public opinion, passed the bill and the Senate followed by a narrow margin. Through a statewide telegram campaign, intense pressure was put on the governor to sign in the last days of the veto period, and finally Big Basin became a state redwood park.[12]

Recognizing the need for trained men to manage and protect the state forests, the women of the California Club in 1903 drew up a bill to be introduced into the State Legislature to establish a School of Forestry at the University of California, Berkeley. At that time the only three schools of forestry in the U.S. were all on the East Coast, and West Coast forests presented special problems. In her plea to club women to use their influence to support passage of the bill, Mrs. George Law Smith, president of the forestry section of the California Federation, argued, "The need of guarding against forest fires and of lumbering the tracts, so that the industry may be permanent, necessitates the establishment of a School of Forestry where a sufficient corps of trained men may be graduated to take charge of the forests and administer them scientifically. In view of the vast and many sided interests involved your help is solicited to secure from the Legislature an appropriation to establish a school of forestry at the University of California, Berkeley."[13]

While these efforts were underway in California, across the country in Minnesota, Mrs. Lydia Phillips Williams of the Minnesota Federation was organizing a repeal of the "Dead and Down Timber Act" in order to save the Chippewa Forest Reserve from "Board Feet" lumbermen. With Mrs. Mira Lloyd Dock, a "whirlwind" on the Pennsylvania Forestry Commission and fifty other women, Mrs. Phillips chartered a steamer for an excursion into the reserve to create publicity for the repeal. Predictably, one of the two available steamers was discovered to have blown a boiler, while the other had been engaged a few hours before by a lumberman for a week. Undaunted, the women engaged the aid of a visiting boiler inspector, blacksmiths, carpenters, and plumbers, who readied the ailing steamer for departure the following noon.[14]

Soon after setting out, they discovered a number of beautiful old pines that had only been burned at the root, thereby qualifying for cutting under the act. "Not a leaf, twig, or grass blade was scorched, there was no sign of tramp or camper, but on examining the burning in the noblest tree of all the group, we discovered a small kerosene lamp almost melted down." That trophy of the expedition became the symbol of the women's campaign to save the reserve.[15]

Upon their return, women were sent to Washington to interview wavering congressmen who favored the Dead and Down Law. They told them: "'We represent the State Federation of Women's Clubs, which has a membership of between six and seven thousand and you know that six or seven thousand women represent six or seven thousand husbands and a few thousand sons who will possibly vote as their fathers vote.' Some two weeks later, having retired from the field, we dared to send a batch of petitions to this same member and received his gracious reply: ...'I desire to assure you, if I can advance the interests of the forest reserve movement in any way, command my service at any time.'"[16]

Nationally, the General Federation of Women's Clubs, founded in 1890, had been active in forestry since the turn of the century as part of a felt obligation to become informed on the most urgent political, economic, and social issues of the day. Selecting women in each state who were familiar with the principles of forestry to head the clubs' forestry committees, local members first conducted campaigns to save waste paper and clean up their towns and cities. They formed coalitions with civic organizations engaged in the beautification of yards, vacant lots, school yards, and public buildings by planting trees and shrubs. Following the example of German women, with whom they corresponded, they planted long avenues of shade trees. They also worked toward the acquisition and preservation of wooded tracts of land wherein "Nature should be left unrestrained."[17]

Local forestry committees formed study groups that emphasized both aesthetic and utilitarian aspects of forestry as the conservation of wood and water. The Forest Service provided literature and sent guest lecturers on trees and forestry to club meetings. *Century* magazine supplied them with articles on conservation, while local libraries were encouraged to acquire books on forestry. With these aids women avidly identified individual species and studied family characteristics and uses. Some, with the aid of a microscope, went on to study individual parts or to count tree rings. Others prepared topics for discussion or conducted research in the mythology and poetry associated with a given species.[18]

In addition to keeping 800,000 members informed of the conservation policies and achievements of Roosevelt and Pinchot, the General Federation's Forestry Committee played an influential role in the passage of legislation to protect forests, waters and birdlife. Under the direction of Mrs. Lydia Phillips Williams (1904–1906), who had been active in the movement to preserve Minnesota's forests, Mary Gage Peterson (1906–1908), an enthusiastic conservationist who had learned forestry at the family's Peterson Nursery in Chicago and on her numerous excursions to forests in Norway, Sweden, and Germany, Mrs. F.W. Gerard (1908–1910) from Connecticut, and Mrs. Lovell White (1910–1912), who had established a national reputation in saving the Calaveras Big Trees, the committee coordinated efforts to support such projects as the creation of national forest reserves in New Hampshire and the Southern Appalachians and passage of the Weeks Bill for protection of the watersheds of navigable streams. In 1910, 283 clubs reported that they had sent letters and petitions for state and national legislation on forest fire laws, tax remission for reforestation, and the appropriation of demonstration forests, while 250 clubs were active in the movement for bird and plant protection.[19]

The Massachusetts clubs published a *Directory of Historical Trees* that marked the location of some important historical event or were preserved for posterity as in the case of the seventy year old Avery Oak rescued from certain fate as planking for "Old Ironsides." In 1904 the women conducted a campaign to exterminate the gypsy and brown-tail moths that attacked New England trees. Men, women, children and "self-supporting undergraduates" turned out to paint gypsy moth nests with creosote and to burn brown tail nests. Clubs obtained creosote at 50¢ a gallon from dealers in Boston, along with half-pint oyster cans and brushes.[20]

In Florida, club women were instrumental in creating state forest reserves, while the women of Maine were active in setting aside Mt. Katahdin as a state forest. In Louisiana, Mrs. John Wilkinson organized a State Forestry Association to work for forestry legislation and then in 1908 went on to organize the Federation's Waterways Committee.[21]

The star of Pennsylvania's conservation efforts was Mira Lloyd Dock, the only woman to become a Pennsylvania State Forestry Commissioner. In 1897 she presented a paper on "Forestry" to the Federation of Pennsylvania Women, and an important 1904 paper became a standard reference for local forestry committees. In 1912, as vice-chairman of the Federation's Conservation Department, she presented a lengthy summation of conservation efforts in Pennsylvania that included many achievements of women.[22]

In 1886, she reported, the Pennsylvania Forestry Association was organized by "some ladies of Philadelphia." Thereafter women were active in the effort to authorize the State Forest Reserves, initial purchases for which were made in 1897. In 1911 the Pennsylvania School of Horticulture for Women was created to provide practical education in field, laboratory, and greenhouse work as well as marketing, and Dr. Caroline Rumbold, who had graduated from the University of Munich, was put in charge of a special state commission for eradication of the Chestnut tree blight with an operating budget of $275,000.[23]

The lobbying efforts of women resulted in the creation of the Pennsylvania Department of Forestry. According to a clipping in the *Journal of the American Forestry Association* in 1909, "the State of Pennsylvania never would have had that department if it had not been for the organized efforts of the women of Pennsylvania. On the morning the bill for this matter was under consideration, every desk in the House of Representatives and the State Senate was flooded with petitions from the women and their husbands. The women of the state made it impossible to kill it."[24]

In 1909, under the leadership of Mrs. John Wilkinson of Louisiana, the Federation formed a Waterways Committee to promote the development of water power, clean water, and cheaper, higher volume transportation. The rationale for women's involvement lay in the effect of waterways on every American home: pure water meant health; impure meant disease and death. Additionally, beautification of waterfronts, as had occurred in the water-towns of Europe, would lead to patriotism and love of one's country.[25]

Soon water conservation projects were underway in 39 states and 619 clubs, including the establishment of reference libraries, community plans for pure drinking water, and sanitary waterfronts. Public campaigns took place to introduce conservation education into the schools in the form of textbooks, speakers, conferences, newspaper publicity, and pamphlets. In many states such as Delaware, women held contests for school children and awarded prizes for the best essays on the waterways. They conducted public education campaigns on the importance of the conservation of natural resources and of clean water and waterfronts.[26]

Joseph Ransdell, chair of the National Rivers and Harbors Committee, speaking to the Tenth Biennial Convention of the Federation in 1910, acknowledged the important contributions of the women's clubs to conservation: "I appeal to you as a representative of the men who need and wish the help of women. We know that nothing great or good in this world ever existed without the women. We consider our movement one of the greatest and best every inaugurated in the union and we know that the women can help us."[27]

In 1910 the Federation reorganized its forestry and waterways committees under a Department of Conservation headed by Mrs. Emmons Crocker of Fitchburg, Massachusetts and added a birdlife representative, Mrs. Francis B. Hornbrooke, also of Massachusetts. This Department sent representatives to the Second National Conservation Congress in St. Paul, Minnestoa in 1910 and the National Irrigation Congress at Pueblo, Colorado.[28]

Mrs. Crocker was an exceptionally knowledgeable and dynamic individual. She addressed the Federation's Tenth Biennial Convention in 1910 on the subject of national waste and delivered a comprehensive report on the activities of the Conservation Department to the 11th Biennial in 1912.[29] At the 1912 National Conservation Congress, she was enthusiastically received when she lectured on the scientific foundation of the conservation of natural resources and its relation to life in its broadest sense.

> If we do not follow the most scientific approved methods, the most modern discoveries of how to conserve and propagate and renew wherever possible those resources which Nature in her providence has given to man for his use but not abuse, the time will come when the world will not be able to support life and then we shall have no need of conservation of health, strength, or vital force, because we must have the things to support life or else everything else is useless.[30]

The forest, she observed, provided the basic support system on which life depended—it made humus, conserved soil minerals, prevented soil and wind erosion, staved off pollution, and through the marvelous action of chlorophyll converted "carbonic acid gas" (CO_2) into pure air. Water conservation was

FIG. 6.2 / LYDIA ADAMS-WILLIAMS. A WRITER AND LECTURER ON
CONSERVATION, FORESTRY AND IRRIGATION, 14 (JUNE 1908) P. 350.
REPRODUCED BY PERMISSION

equally essential because water power conserved coal; which in turn "conserves the purity of our atmosphere." A pure water supply thus conserved human health, strength, and life. Waxing eloquent about the interconnectedness of all life, Mrs. Crocker excoriated those in her audience who downgraded the value of animal life by reducing it to a pastime for sentimentalists. Women should play a direct role in conservation by refusing to wear hats decorated with feathers, not only of the endangered egret, but less choice species as well.[31]

During the period 1907–1912, women contributed notices, news items, reports, and articles to *Forestry and Irrigation*, the journal of the American Forestry Association. They pointed out women's work to save forests in places such as Colorado, Vermont, Maine, and New York, printed lengthy summaries of progress in conservation as reported at the Federtion's biennial meetings, and announced protest actions such as that taken by Mrs. D.M. Osborne of Auburn, New York who, outraged by telephone pole workers who had mercilessly trimmed her trees without permission, "drove off the workmen and cut down the poles."[32]

Mrs. Lydia Adams-Williams, (Figure 6.2), a self-styled feminist conservation writer and member of the Women's National Press Association, was particularly vociferous in her efforts to popularize women's accomplishments. Her article "Conservation—Women's Work," (1908) in which she characterized herself as the first women lecturer and writer on conservation, complained that "man has been too busy building railroads, constructing ships, engineering great projects, and exploiting vast commercial enterprises" to consider the future. Man the moneymaker had left it to woman the moneysaver to preserve resources. She placed women's role in conservation squarely in the context of feminist history:

> To the intuition of Isabella of Spain, to her tenacious grasp of a great idea, to her foresight and her divine sympathy the world is indebted for the discovery of a great continent for the civilization we enjoy today and for the great wealth of resources. ...And as it was the intuitive foresight of a woman which brought the light of civilization to a great continent, so in great measure, will it fall to woman in her power to educate public sentiment to save from rapacious waste and complete exhaustion the resources upon which depend the welfare of the home, the children, and the children's children.[33]

In "A Million Women for Conservation" (1908), again taking liberal notice of her own accomplishments, Mrs. Adams-Williams discussed the resolutions passed by the women's clubs in support of the conservation efforts of Roosevelt, Pinchot, the Inland Waterways Commission, the Forest Service, the Geological Survey, and the American Mining Congress. The Federation in Washington, DC, of which she was a member, was the first to pass these resolutions followed by four other national women's organizations the combined membership of which totaled one million. [34]

The General Federation began to play an important role in the national conservation movement by 1908. The president of the Federation, Mrs. Sarah Platt Decker of Denver, was the only representative of a women's organization at the White House Governor's Conference on Conservation in 1908, although she was not invited to speak. Mrs. F.W. Gerard of Connecticut, chair of the Forestry Committee for the years 1908–1910, attended the Conference of the National Conservation Commission held in Washington in December of 1908 as a follow-up to the Governor's Conference.[35]

Mrs. Philip N. Moore, (Fig. 6.3), president of the Federation from 1908–1910, was a member of the executive committee of the National Conservation Congress during its first four years, was a presiding officer in 1912, and became its vice-president in 1913. Tribute was paid by the president

FIG. 6.3 / MRS. PHILIP N. MOORE, PRESIDENT OF THE GENERAL FEDERATION
OF WOMEN'S CLUBS, 1908–1910, IN MARY I, WOOD, *HISTORY OF THE GENERAL
FEDERATION OF WOMEN'S CLUBS* (NEW YORK: G.F.W.C., 1912), FACING P. IV.
REPRODUCED BY PERMISSION.

of the Congress to her "rare ability" to organize and preside over large numbers of enthusiastic women. Mrs. Moore of St. Louis, Missouri, a leader in
educational and philanthropic work, was born in Rockford, Illinois, graduated from Vassar College, and later became one of its trustees. She had been
active for many years at the local, state, and national levels of the Federation.
The voice of Mrs. Moore and dozens of other women were heard loudly and
forcefully at the National Conservation Congresses held from 1909–1912.[36]

WOMEN'S NATIONAL RIVERS AND
HARBORS CONGRESS

In 1908, seven women in Shreveport, Louisiana banded together to form the
Women's National Rivers and Harbors Congress that would cooperate with
the National Rivers and Harbors Congress then headed by Joseph E. Ransdell.
Within fourteen months, under the leadership of its president, Mrs. Hoyle
Tomkies, it had grown to 20,000 members and had held a national congress in
Washington, D.C. at which twenty states were represented. By 1910, its mem-

bership had risen to 30,000 (including a few men), represented thirty-nine states and territories, and was cooperating with other women's conservation organizations. A chapter of fifty women was formed in Honolulu, Hawaii as a result of efforts by the Women's College Club of Hawaii, the governor and his wife, and the local chapter of the Daughters of the American Revolution.[37]

On the state and national levels the Congress worked to support rivers and harbors bills on waterway development and urged passage of the bill for the preservation of Niagara Falls in the spring of 1909. It pressed for clean shores and streams, held conferences and public gatherings to educate the public, and sent lecturers to churches to preach on the "moral standpoint" of conservation. Water conservation thus joined forestry as a women's issue.[38]

On a local level the members focused on introducing conservation education into the schools, conveying to the nation's children their responsibility to save the country's natural resources. The Congress sponsored essay contests and met with teachers and clubs in an effort to create public awareness. The chapter in Honolulu worked with senior high school students to bring reforestation of the Punchbowl area of the city.

At the First Conservation Congress in 1909 in Seattle, Margaret Russell Knudsen of Hawaii, representing the Women's National Rivers and Harbors Congress, spoke of the importance of women's work in water conservation:

> It has been said that this is a woman's age and surely the signs of that fact are not wanting, for within these beautiful grounds of the Exposition are still echoing...the stirring words of eloquence and power of some of the foremost women of the world...who have journeyed not only from distant states...but from capitals of Europe to discuss the great questions of the day.[39]

As Mrs. Tomkies expressed it, "Our work is mainly to educate upon the subject. We are putting forth all the energy and influence we can muster for the cause, lest the enemy come while we are sleeping and sow in the peoples' minds the tares of 'individualism' and non-conservation."[40]

Like the General Federation, the Women's National Rivers and Harbors Congress sent articles to *Forestry and Irrigation* for the purpose of heightening the public awareness by covering "the nation with a network of information that will in time bring men and women to a full realization of our country's possibilities for permanent prosperity, and to demonstrate...the rapid and sure decadence of the country unless the national government takes the conservation of these in hand."[41] Mrs. Lydia Adams-Williams, the corre-

sponding secretary of the Congress, reported on the meeting held in
Washington, DC in December 1908 at which Gifford Pinchot praised the
women as "a power in any work they undertake." Frederick Newell "traced
the forestry movement from its inception, about twenty years ago, at a meeting with a handful of people—'mostly women, who loved trees'—to its present great proportions." Mrs. Tomkies noted that if the Women's Congress
only had more money to spend on promotion, the Congressmen of the U.S.
would have to plead, as had a Colorado legislator when he wrote to the
President of the General Federation of Women's Clubs: "Call off your
women. I'll vote for your bill."[42]

THE DAUGHTERS OF THE AMERICAN REVOLUTION

In 1909 Mrs. Mathew T. Scott was elected President General of the 77,000
member Daughters of the American Revolution. A representative of the
more liberal wing of the DAR who had recently defeated the conservatives
in a national election, Mrs. Scott was an enthusiastic conservationist who
encouraged the maintenance of a conservation committee consisting of 100
members representing every state. The chair of this committee was Mrs.
James Pinchot, mother of Gifford Pinchot, who by that token as well as her
conservation efforts was said to have "done more for the cause of conservation than any other woman."[43]

Pinchot himself addressed the 18th DAR Congress in Washington in
1909, praising the members for their efforts against "land grabbers" and suggesting certain conservation projects for further action. At the 1912 convention Pinchot thanked the women for their efforts in aiding the passage of the
Alaska coal bill, the LaFollette legislation regulating grazing, and invited
them to take up the cause of water power. The DAR Pinchot said on another occasion, "spells only another name for the highest form of conservation,
that of vital force and intellectual energy."[44]

Other conservation efforts of the DAR were directed toward the preservation of the Appalachian watersheds, the Palisades, and Niagara Falls (then
threatened by over-usage of water by power companies). In fact, as Mrs. Carl
Vrooman pointed out to the national Conservation Congress of 1911, "these
77,000 women do indeed represent a perfect Niagara of splendid ability and
force—enough, if intelligently directed, to furnish the motive power to keep
revolving all the wheels of progress in this country." In 1905–1906 women
nationwide had responded to Horace MacFarland of the American Civic

Association whose editorials in the *Ladies' Home Journal* on the preservation of Niagara Falls had produced tens of thousands of letters to Congress.[45]

DAR members worked to generate publicity and enthusiasm for conservation and forestry in their communities. The conservation committee sent letters to state governors asking advice on how they could best help each state's conservation efforts. "Most of the governors," reported Mrs. Jay Cooke Howard, "preferred to have us turn our attention to the children rather than to the men." The DAR's newsletter therefore ran a conservation column for its members' use explaining how to inculcate in children the virtues of conservation over wastefulness along with other DAR values of truth, patriotism, and obedience.[46]

The DAR's President General, Mrs. Scott, was an advocate of scientific agriculture as a branch of conservation. A widow who managed a 20,000 acre model farm in Illinois, she paid her employees' expenses to attend the state agricultural college. She also wholeheartedly supported agriculture as a profession for women.[47]

THE AUDUBON MOVEMENT

The post-Civil War resurgence of high fashion for ladies had, by the end of the century, taken an immense toll on American bird-life in the creation of exotic styles in millinery. Bird feathers and whole birds nestled atop the heads of society's upper- and middle-class women. Bonnets of "sapphire blue-velvet trimmed with flowers and a gay colored bird", hats of ruby velvet trimmed with lace, birds, and aigrette; and "coquettishly bent hat(s) of white leghorn, with...trimmings of white plumes and chiffon" were thought to lend a chic, elegant air to milady.[48]

By the decade of the 1880s, hundreds of thousands of song birds, swallows, Baltimore orioles, egrets, and terns had been sacrificed to the whims of fashion and the pockets of milliners. Editorials in *Field and Stream* during the years 1883–1884 called attention to the national tragedy and recommended laws for bird protection. Responding to the urgent need, the American Ornithologists' Union in 1886 prepared a bulletin, published as a supplement to *Science* with 100,000 copies issued separately, presenting a "Model Law" for the protection of birds and a collection of articles documenting the wholesale destruction of birds, appealing on their behalf to the ladies of the country.[49]

The first Audubon societies, organized in 1886, protested the "abominable" habit of wearing feather fashions. Growing rapidly to 30,000 mem-

born in six months and encouraged by the passage of laws in New York and Pennsylvania, the Societies' founders began publication of *Audubon Magazine* in 1887. Women who sought to educate their sisters to the peril of birds formed Audubon clubs, such as the one at Smith College where two young female students developed a plan to protect plume birds.

'Go to it,' said they. 'We will start an Audubon Society. The birds must be protected; we must persuade the girls not to wear feathers in their hats.' 'We won't say too much about the hats, though,' these plotters went on. 'We'll take the girls afield, and let them get acquainted with the birds. Then of inborn necessity they will wear feathers never more.'[50]

"Birding" rapidly caught on at Smith with early morning field trips led by luminaries such as John Burroughs, or by student observers who aroused enthusiasm for living rather than dead plumage.

This early movement, however, was doomed. It received no national press attention after 1889. *Audubon Magazine* ceased publication that year and by 1895 the A.O.U. was hopelessly discouraged by the rampant wearing of feathers.[51]

Then the tide turned. Within three years Audubon Clubs and state societies sprang spontaneously into existence in Massachusetts—where the vice-presidents included Mrs. Louis Agassiz, president of Radcliffe college, and Mrs. Julia J. Irving, president of Wellesley—in Pennsylvania, New York, New Hampshire, New Jersey, Iowa, Minnesota, Rhode Island, and the District of Columbia. In 1898 a score of ladies met in Fairfield, Connecticut to form the Audubon society of the State of Connecticut, electing as president Mrs. Mabel Osgood Wright, (Fig. 6.4), popular author of the *The Friendship of Nature* (1894), *Birdcraft* (1895), *Birds of Village and Field* (1898), numerous articles in the *New York Times* and *Evening Post*, and nature stories for children.[52]

Soon thereafter, with the publication in 1899, of the first issue of the Audubon Societies' new official journal, *Bird Lore*, Mrs. Wright took on the task of editing the magazine's Audubon section and of reporting the latest developments in the politics of bird preservation. She requested that the secretaries of the initial nineteen state societies, all but one of whom were women, send news and notes to broaden and strengthen the movement. Contributors to the journal, in addition to Mrs. Wright, included women writers such as Olive Thorne Miller, author of the popular *Bird Ways* (1885), *In Nesting Time* (1888), *Little Brothers in the Air* (1892), and *A Bird Lover in the West* (1894); Florence A. Merriam (Bailey) who wrote *Birds Through an Opera*

Glass for young people in 1889 and *A-Birding on a Bronco* (1896) modeled on Mrs. Mikller's earlier success; Neltje Blanchan (Doubleday) among whose achievements were *Bird Neighbors* (1897) and *Birds That Hunt and Are Hunted* (1898), and many other women who sent in short articles of general interest.[53]

Two sex-linked issues dominated the early years of *Bird Lore*: the protection of game birds from male hunters and nests from boy egg-thieves, and the protection of plume birds from extinction in the cause of ladies' fashions. In 1897, Julia Stockton Robbins reported that a 'hat show' conducted by the Pennsylvania Audubon Society had resulted in the establishment of Audubon Departments by many milliners. In Chicago wholesale milliners cut down on the use of egret and wild bird feathers and began using domestic ones instead. In Wisconsin the aid of both clergymen and milliners was enlisted in a broad protection campaign. At the New York State Audubon Society's second annual meeting "Madame Lilli Lehmann whose love of animals was perhaps greater than her love of music, made an eloquent appeal to women to cease from feather-wearing." In Rhode Island, according to secretary Annie Grant, an "audubonnet" display of 150 beautiful and attractive feather hats demonstrated that they could be made without the plumage of wild birds.[54]

Frank Chapman, general editor of the magazine, put the responsibility for defying fashion directly on the women themselves: "Is there no appeal from fashions' decree? Women alone can answer these questions and the case is so clear she cannot shirk the responsibility of replying."[55]

For a time the campaign seemed to be gaining ground. But in 1900 an inexplicable resurgence in fashion feathers from terns, gulls, and grebes took immense tolls along the Atlantic seaboard, and Mrs. Wright called on the members for increased action. By this time only five states had passed the A.O.U. "Model Law." Nevertheless, during the first decade of the twentieth century public consciousness over conservation and reform helped to rout the milliners and plume-hunters. By 1905, twenty-eight states had passed the "Model Law" and Audubon societies were calling for international cooperation, particularly from the British where the plume trade centered. Bird reservations, patrolled by Audubon wardens, had been created in many states and the Thayer fund was established to raise money for legislation and enforcement efforts.[56]

Still, however, the sale of white "aigrette" feathers increased at such an unprecedented rate that egrets and "snowy herons," seemed doomed to extinction. All known rookeries were continually pillaged during the breed-

FIG. 6.4 / MRS. MABEL OSGOOD WRIGHT. PRESIDENT CONNECTICUT AUDUBON
SOCIETY. BIRD-LORE 15 (1913) BY PERMISSION OF THE NATIONAL AUDUBON
SOCIETY.

ing season when the beautiful "nuptial" feathers (or aigrettes) appeared,
bringing death to the parent and certain starvation for the young. After feathers were pulled, the birds were left to die or tied up as decoys. The Audubon
Society appealed to the National Federation of Women's Clubs for help:
"The club women of America with their powerful influence should take a
strong stand against the use of wild birds' plumage, and especially against the
use of the Aigrette.... A close affiliation between this Association and the
National Federation of Women's Clubs would be mutually helpful."[57]

In 1903, an impassioned plea by women to women against the wearing of
egret feathers appeared in the California Federation of Women's Club's
newsletter. "Remember ladies, that every aigrette in your hat costs the life of
a tender mother. We see the evidence of wholesale destruction of birds in
shop windows on the street, in cars, and everywhere. In order to have the
plumage at its best, it is necessary in some instances to skin the birds alive.
With each old bird killed.... many of the young birds are still unable to care
for themselves. At least women may desist from wearing any sort of plumage
in their hats, as they have so repeatedly been urged to do."[58]

At the Conservation Congress of 1909, William Finley of the National Audubon Societies addressed the assemblage on the agricultural benefits of birds and urged that the vandalism of the plume hunters be halted. "As long as women demand these plumes, men will be found to supply them." At the close of the Congress, Miss Gillette of New York proposed a resolution, unanimously adopted, calling for forbearance in the wearing of any feathers that entailed the killing of wild birds, for the protection of nests, and for the education of children that they might learn "to love all birds of the earth."[59]

Mrs. Gerard, Chair of the General Federation of Women's Clubs' Forestry Committee appealed to the women at their 1910 Biennial Convention: "Our work for the Audubon Society is not as active as it should be. Can we logically work for conservation and expect to be listened to, while we still continue to encourage the destruction of the song birds by following the hideous fashion of wearing song birds and egrets upon our hats?... If women can raise the freight rates, because of the size of their hats, they can reduce the insect pest by changing the trimming."[60]

Speaking to the 1912 Conservation Congress, Mrs. Crocker of the GFWC's Conservation Committee asked a personal favor of the women present: "This fall when you choose your fall millinery...I beg you to choose some other decoration for your hats. You have no idea what you do when you wear these feathers until you really think deeply into it, and I am not speaking of the egret...wholly, but of the less choice feathers. There is one exception to this rule and that is the wearing of the ostrich plume which are naturally shed and can be collected without killing the birds. Will you not spread this gospel, not only to yourselves, but all the other women need to be asked to do the same thing."[61]

In October 1913, a new Tariff Act was passed that outlawed the import of wild bird feathers into the United States. It was so vigorously enforced that newspapers were filled with accounts of "the words and actions of indignant ladies who found it necessary to give up their aigrettes, paradise plumes, and other feathers upon arriving from Europe." Two days after the new law went into effect, Audubon Save the Birds Hats were being advertised in New York for $5 to $15 apiece. Congratulations poured in from all over the world for the Audubon Society's great victory.[62]

So rare as to be on the verge of extermination a few years before, by 1915 egrets in guarded rookeries in the southern United States numbered 10,580 along with 50,000 little blue herons and an equal number of ibis. Public opinion had shifted so far toward bird protection that far fewer "bad bird laws" were being introduced into state legislatures. The work of a decade and a half had begun to show results.[63]

CONSERVATION IDEOLOGY

THE CONSERVATION TRILOGY

Although the women of the organizations represented at the National Conservation Congress were public activists in their local communities, they nevertheless accepted the traditional sex roles assigned to them by late nineteenth century American society as caretakers of the nation's homes, husbands, and offspring, supporting rather than challenging the two spheres ideology of the nineteenth century.

At the national Congresses, women repeatedly called on the traditions assigned them by society in justifying the public demands they were making. Unwilling and unable to break out of these social roles, and supported by the men of the Congress, they drew on a trilogy of slogans—conservation of womanhood, the home, and the child.

THE CONSERVATION OF TRUE WOMANHOOD

The "conservation of true womanhood" was a subject repeatedly stressed by women at the Conservation Congresses. Mrs. Scott of the DAR pleaded "as the representative of a great National organization of the women of the land, for the exalting, for the lifting up in special honor, of the Holy Grail of Womanhood."[64]

Speaking to the Conservation Congress of 1909, Mrs. Overton Ellis of the General Federation of Women's Clubs called conservation "the surest weapon with which women might win success." Centuries of turning last night's roast into hash, remaking last year's dress, and controlling the home's resources had given women a heightened sense of the power of the conservation idea in creating true womanhood. "Conservation in its material and ethical sense is the basic principle in the life of woman...."[65]

In her presidential address to the General Federation's Tenth Biennial Meeting in 1910, Mrs. Philip N. Moore set conservation in its context for women as "no new word, no new idea," but a unifying theme for the contributions of women to society as the conservers of life.[66]

Mrs. Carl Vrooman, also of the DAR, emphasized the ideal woman's subservience to the man in conservation. "We may not, it is true, formulate any new policies for you, or launch any issues, or make any very original contributions to your program, but there is one thing women can bring to a movement of this kind—an atmosphere that makes ideas sprout and grow, and ideals expand and develop and take deeper root in the subsoil of the masculine mind."[67]

THE CONSERVATION OF THE HOME

The home as the domain of true womanhood became the second theme in the conservation trilogy. The National Congress of Mothers, represented by Mrs. Orville Bright of Chicago, dedicated itself to conservation of natural resources for "the use, comfort, and benefit of the homes of the people." Mrs. Bright adopted the utilitarian philosophy of the progressives in stressing that conservation primarily benefitted human life rather than other organisms, since the fare of forests, land, waters, minerals, or food would be of little consequence were there "no men, women and children to use and enjoy them."[68]

Margaret Russell Knudsen of Hawaii, of the Women's National Rivers and Harbors Congress, argued at the 1909 Conservation Congress that conservation of the home was the special mission of woman. The "mark of civilization was the arrival of woman on the scene. In no national movement has there been such a spontaneous and universal response from women as in this great question of conservation. Women from Maine to the most Western shore of the Hawaiian Islands are alive to the situation because the home is woman's domain. She is the conserver of the race."[69]

CONSERVATION OF THE CHILD

Third in the trilogy was the link between the conservation of natural resources and the conservation of the children and future generations of the United States. According to Mrs. John Walker, a member of the Kansas City chapter of Daughters of the American Revolution, woman's role in conservation was dedicated to the preservation of life, while man's role was the conservation of material needs. "Woman, the transmitter of life" must therefore care for the product of life—future generations. The children of the nation should not be sacrificed to "factories, mills, and mines," but must be allowed "to enjoy the freedom of the bird and the butterfly...and all that the sweet breast of Nature offers so freely."[70]

Mrs. Overton Ellis of the General Federation of Women's Clubs promoted the conservation of children's lives at the 1909 Congress: "Women's supreme function as mother of the race gives her special claim to protection not so much individually as for unborn generations."[71] Mrs. Welch, also of the General Federation, asserted that what conservation really meant was conservation of child life. Because the unscrupulous use of child labor in the name of money. "the god of greed," was claiming the lives of children by the scores, without the conservation of children's health and well-being the conservation of natural resources had no real meaning. The Federation was dedicated to "the enactment of laws which shall tend to the conservation of the vital forces represented in the mothers of the race and the children who are the country's future citizens."[72]

WOMEN'S SUFFRAGE AND THE CONSERVATION MOVEMENT

Although the women who attended the National Conservation Congresses were speaking out on public affairs of interest to the nation's welfare, they were limited in their influence on legislation through lack of the vote. By the time of the conservation congresses, several states (Colorado, Idaho, Wyoming, and Utah) had given women the vote and a nationwide women's suffrage campaign was underway. Mrs. Scott of the DAR noted the possibility that women might sometime in the future "undertake, in addition to their other duties, they heavy responsibilities of the voter and political worker."[73] While women representatives at the congresses did not have a platform that related suffrage to conservation, nevertheless, the issue was frequently mentioned.[74]

Although the General Federation of Women's Clubs did not take an official position on the extension of the vote to females until late in the suffrage movement, the issue was raised at the Federation's Tenth Biennial (1910). In her speech on "Equal Suffrage," Miss Kate N. Gordon, Vice-President of the National American Woman Suffrage Association, cited the census of 1900 that had revealed that 117,632 more women than men in the United States were literate with the ratio constantly increasing owing to the vast influx of illiterate male immigrants. Women, she argued, should have the right to express an opinion through suffrage on matters of vital importance to their lives. Taxes, the milk supply, public health, education, and moral conditions were all issues that directly affected the sphere of the home, which through the female vote would be represented in the Legislatures. "We have never had a democracy," she asserted, "we have only had a sex oligarchy and...there are some men and women who are not satisfied with existing conditions resulting from a sex oligarchy. We don't want a man-made world; we don't want a woman-made world, but we want a world where the opinions of men and women rate equally and then, and not till then, will we have a true democracy."[75]

The anti-suffragists, however, also drew on conservation rhetoric—"the watchword of the hour"—in arguing against the extension of the vote to women. Suffrage was not a "natural" right bestowed on human beings at birth, proclaimed Alice Chittendon of Brooklyn. On the contrary "in opposing the extension of suffrage to women, we are seeking to conserve woman's natural forces for the great work Nature has given her to do. The conservation of energy strengthens one's forces, while diffusion weakens them." Scientific and biological evidence, she said, indicated that the "welfare of the State and Race" would suffer if the burden of suffrage were added to all the other responsibilities of womanhood. As civilization grew out of its savage state wherein women had had more power (as, for example, among the Iroquois, Lycians, and Saxons) to its present level of development, the "law of intended differentiation of sex activity" took effect. "Each sex should have its own work to do... in the social and intellectual world," she asserted, quoting a "recent writer."[76] She concluded:

> A diffused energy cannot be a vitalizing one.... If woman must now
> assume the responsibilities and duties of political life — if she must do
> man's work in addition to her own natural powers and energies, and we
> shall have deterioration and not progress...I would have woman seri-
> ously consider whether she may not better serve her day and generation
> by conserving her God-given powers for her own great work as a
> Home-maker, rather than diffuse her forces by seeking to do man's
> work also.[77]

DENOUEMENT

The Fifth National Conservation Congress opened in Washington, D.C. on November 18, 1913. It proceeded for three days. Its own vice-president, Mrs. Philip N. Moore of the General Federation of Women's Clubs, did not speak.

Nor did any other woman from the Federation, the DAR, the Country Women's Clubs, or the Women's National Rivers and Harbors Congress. The sole female voice heard was Miss Mabel Boardman from the American Red Cross who lectured on "Conservation of Life in the Lumber Camps."[78]

American Forestry (the new name of the journal of the American Forestry Association) carried a full report on the meeting in its November issue. Descriptions of the activities of the Congress were accompanied by the portraits of fifty men who had chaired and worked on the committees. A photograph taken the night of the Forestry Banquet on November 19 showed some 160 men seated at round tables before a speakers' platform. Mrs. Philip N. Moore was not among them.[79]

A brief note in the Forestry Committee's report to the Congress seems to provide the explanation for the absence of women:

> The desirability of...an organization (to represent the mutual forestry and lumbering interests) was emphasized by the presence at (the Fourth National Congress in) Indianapolis (1912) of a number of men who were no longer in need of the general educational propaganda relative to the conservation of natural resources, but attended the Congress for the purpose of meeting progressive men in their own and related lines and securing specific information helpful in the solution of their own problems.

> The need for a working organization and a rallying point, where mutual and more or less technical problems may be discussed is felt particularly by the forestry and timber interests....The active workers desired an opportunity to exchange views on technical problems....[80]

Conservation and forestry had come of age as technical professions. As such they were no longer accessible to women. After 1912 the American Forestry Association ceased to print articles or news items on the work of women in forestry. Lydia Adams-Williams disappeared from the scene.[81]

A second explanation for the disappearance of women also seems plausible. That same year the popular nationwide struggle for the preservation of Hetch Hetchy Valley, a part of California's Yosemite National Park, reached its conclusion. With the passage of the Raker Act by Congress in 1913, the City of San Francisco won its long battle for a public water supply. The women of the conservation crusade had worked hard to preserve the valley as an integral part of the park.

Gifford Pinchot, the women's early inspiration and supporter in conservation efforts, had taken the opposing side, recommending at the congressional hearings that a dam be constructed across the valley to serve the interests of thousands of city people rather than accommodate the needs of the few who camped and hiked in the area. The women's clubs, unable to support or understand Pinchot's position, openly split with his approach to conservation. From 1908 until 1913 they worked for preservation of the valley.[82]

Soon after a City of San Francisco referendum in November 1908 favored construction of the dam, John Muir had taken the Hetch Hetchy issue to the nation. Many in the conservation movement rallied to support its preservation through letters and telegrams to the House Committee on Public Lands which held hearings in January 1909. Among them were women who had camped in the valley, who were members of the Sierra Club or Appalachian Mountain Club, and who were opposed to the commercial use of such a scenic wonderland.[83]

Martha Walker of Los Angeles pointed out that "it would be a glittering example of our 'commercial spirit' were we to lose Hetch Hetchy." She had spent all her summers in the Sierras and was confident that soon easterners would "come to know the wonders of these high Sierra hillsides, with their gardens of beautiful flowers and great trees."[84]

Eva Channing of Boston, who visited California in the summer of 1908, was a firm believer "in national parks and the right of people to have them safeguarded." Martha Haskell, also of Boston, who had camped there and wanted to preserve it for the people, pointed out that the cost to the nation was far greater than for San Francisco to seek water elsewhere. Grace Esther Dattle of San Jose, who had visited the valley, knew that it would one day be needed as an overflow for visitors to Yosemite.[85]

Others represented women's organizations or spoke on the basis of professional experience. Mrs. William Hanson of the Forestry Committee of the Florida Federation of Women's Clubs wrote that those "imbued with the forestry spirit" were anxious to conserve remaining woodlands. Mary Worstell of New York City had lectured more than 150 times for the New York Board of Education on Yosemite National Park and her extensive travels in the Sierras. From Virginia City, Nevada came a telegram from Laura McDermott who was outraged that "America's greatest gift from the Creator is about to be sacrificed at the feet of Mammon." "I am a graduate of the University of California, a botanist and hope to be a protector of nature's wilds," she concluded.[86]

Prominent among those testifying at the Senate hearings on February 10 was Harriet Monroe, Sierra Club enthusiast, editor of *Poetry Magazine*, and representative of 500 members of the Chicago Geographical Society and 5,000 members of the Saturday Walking Club. Her brief argued that irreparable injury would be done to the beauty of the valley:

> United States Army engineers and others have reported that
> San Francisco is exceptionally well placed for water supplies;
> that the present source may be developed to three times the present
> consumption; and that no less than 14 other sources are easily
> available. Why then should she be permitted like some ruthless
> Cleopatra, to dissolve this pearl without price in the cup she lifts
> to her lips?"[87]

After the House committee voted by only 8 to 7 in favor of the dam construction with a strong dissenting minority report, and the Senate failed to report the bill out of committee, the resolution was temporarily withdrawn. But the battle lines were only beginning to form.[88]

By December of 1909 Muir had begun to bombard the popular magazines with articles and photographs describing the scenic wonders of the valley. The *Federation Courier*, official organ of the California Women's Clubs, ran his "Brief Statement of the Hetch Hetchy Question" in December announcing that the bill would soon come before Congress. As president of the Society for the Preservation of National Parks (formed because the San Francisco based Sierra Club was divided 589 to 161 against the dam), Muir had collected the endorsement of the General Federation of Women's Clubs, the California Federation, and many other State Federations who all adopted resolutions protesting the scheme. On the east coast the same article was carried in the Federation's *Woman of Today*, published in Boston. By the end of 1910, 150 women's clubs throughout the country were actively engaged in the campaign to preserve Hetch Hetchy Valley.[89]

The women's support for preservation was viewed dimly by the men of the opposition. Marsden Manson, San Francisco's city engineer who supervised the surveys and plans for the dam, believed that his opponents consisted largely of "short-haired women and long-haired men" who were members of the "so-called nature-loving societies like the Appalachian [sic] Club of Boston, the Saturday Evening Walking Club of Chicago, et id genus omne." He maintained a "list of names and addresses of people objecting to (the) use of Hetch Hetchy," that included numerous women and believed it

necessary to dispel fallacies perpetrated by "individuals and corporations acting behind the screen of well meaning and innocent nature lovers."[90]

Manson found an ally, however, in Caroline K. Sherman of Chicago who
had met him on a visit to Yosemite and told the Forestry Department of the
Chicago Federation of Women's Clubs of his "intimate acquaintance with
every tree, shrub, and herb," of his "close study of the sequoias," and of his
ancestor, John Clayton, "whom we all knew as the botanist for whom
Claytonia was named." Assuring the club that he was not a "cold-blooded
engineer, ignorant of forestry, and indifferent to beauty," while Muir
although a poet and artist "could not speak with the authority of a sanitary
engineer," she argued that health should come first and "then as much beauty as possible." She was convinced that she had "carried her audience completely," conveying to the women Manson's view that "monopolists profess-
ing to be interested in 'conservation'" were using the "holy word 'conservation' for conserving their own private interests."[91]

Because President Taft, who followed Roosevelt to the White House, and
his secretary of the Interior Richard Ballinger were at odds with Pinchot, a
decision on the question was temporarily postponed. But by the first year of
the Wilson administration in 1913 the fate of the valley was sealed. With the
new Secretary of the Interior Franklin Lane, a San Francisco attorney, favor-
ing the project, the House rapidly scheduled hearings for which the preservationists were unable to marshal forces. In September when the House passed
the bill 183 to 43, preservationists nationwide threw themselves into the fray.[92]

The National Committee for the Preservation of Yosemite National Park,
headed by Robert Underwood Johnson, editor of *The Century*, and Charles
Eliot, president of the First Conservation Congress, circulated brochures on
"The Hetch Hetchy Grab" and "The Invasion of Yosemite National Park."
Among prominent citizens listed as preservationists for the park were Mrs.
Emmons Crocker, chair of the Conservation Committee of the General
Federation of Women's Clubs. On the committee, which represented most of
the states of the union, were twenty-five women, some of whom, like Mrs.
Philip N. Moore, were General Federation leaders now openly opposed to
Pinchot. In fact the stance taken by women prompted William Kent, congres-
sional representative from the San Francisco Bay Area, to write to Pinchot that
the conspiracy against the dam was "engineered by misinformed nature lovers
and power interests working through the women's clubs."[93]

Although preservationists lost the battle over Hetch Hetchy in
December 1913, they had aroused the nation. The passage of the National

Parks Act in 1916 that established an administration in the Department of the Interior for the numerous parks created since 1872 gave them some compensation for its loss. Increasingly women availed themselves of opportunities to visit the National Parks and meet the challenges of wilderness outings.

The Sierra Club afforded women expanded opportunities for wilderness and on many club trips, female members began to outnumber males. More women than men had become members of the National Parks Association by 1929.[94]

On a national level the conservation movement slackened during the second decade of the twentieth century, with the erosion of government backing, the narrowing of support for Gifford Pinchot, and the professionalization of forestry and water-power engineering. Although women were not active in the professions or as visible on the national level as they had been at the height of the conservation crusade, their interest in the creation of parks, gardens, and bird preserves did not vanish with the decline of organized conservation. The General Federation of Women's Clubs continued to maintain a Conservation Committee, and the Audubon societies provided women with avenues for leadership as secretaries and presidents of local chapters. Constituting approximately 35% of the Audubon national membership in 1905, the number of women had risen to slightly over 50% by 1915.[95]

During the decade and a half that introduced the century, women's organizations had helped the nation to achieve enormous gains in the conservation of natural resources and the preservation of scenic landscapes. Yet the platform for promoting these objectives had been a mixed one. Working closely with the men of the movement, women frequently saw themselves as ideologically opposed to what they perceived as commercial and material values. Feminist and progressive in their role as activists for the public interest, they were nevertheless predominately conservative in their desire to uphold traditional values and middle-class life styles rooted in these same material interests. These contradictions within the women's conservation movement, however, were in reality manifestations of the similar mixture of progressive and conservative tendencies that characterized the progressive era itself.

PART THREE

PRACTICE

7

EARTHCARE

WOMEN AND THE

AMERICAN

ENVIRONMENTAL

MOVEMENT

The word ecology derives from the Greek word "oikos," meaning house. Ecology, then, is the science of the household—the Earth's household. The connection between the Earth and the house has historically been mediated by women.

The 1960s and 1970s witnessed the rise of both the environmental and women's movements. Not surprisingly many persons explored the connections and implications of the identities between nature and women and between ecology and feminism. Both movements have been liberatory and democratic in their outlook and reformist or revolutionary in their politics. Yet, however positive and hopeful these connections may be, they also pose the threat of reinforcing traditional forms of oppression.

Well before the current linking of feminist and environmental concerns, the connection between home and environment had been established by a 19th century woman ecologist. Ellen Swallow [Richards], upon graduating from Vassar College in 1871, became the first woman to enter the Massachusetts Institute of Technology. Upon completion of her studies as a special chemistry student, she continued on at M.I.T. as an instructor in the fields of sanitary chemistry and nutrition. She set up a laboratory where women could conduct experiments and was an enthusiastic supporter of women students. In 1892 she developed a science of environmental quality which she called "oekology." She envisioned it as a science concerned with industrial health, water and air quality, transportation, and nutrition. Soon it became known as "home ecology" and then "home economics."

Her research and published work helped to establish the principles of the ecology of earth and home through books such as *Air, Water, and Food; Euthenics, the Science of Controllable Environment; Sanitation in Daily Life; The Cost of Cleanliness; Home Sanitation;* and *The Chemistry of Cooking and Cleaning.* Clean air, safe water, and good food were the requirements of a healthy human life. Fresh, clean air, free of the pollutants of offensive factories, was necessary to human health; fouling a stream caused injury to one's neighbor below; and fertile soil was required to grow nutritious food. Any individual who selfishly used these life-sustaining elements squandered the human inheritance. Each family and city were points in the Earth's larger cycles of water flow and vaporization, of soil dissolution and deposit, and of plant scavenging, cleansing, and purification.[1]

Seventy years after Ellen Swallow founded the science of ecology, another woman environmentalist, Rachel Carson, made the question of the care of the Earth a public issue. Her book *Silent Spring* (1962) focused attention on the death-producing effects of the chemical insecticides accumulating in the soil and in the tissues of living organisms. Together with the possibility of nuclear war, pesticides posed an insidious, hidden threat to the future of life on Earth. DDT, chlorinated hydrocarbons (such as aldrin, dieldrin, chlordane, and heptachlor), and organophosphates (such as parathion and malathion) were deadly elixirs, bombarding human beings from the moment of conception to the moment of death. As residues in the soil, distributed through surface and underground waters, they concentrated in the food chain, progressively contaminating and poisoning all life. The genetic resistance of some insects to particular pesticides and the extreme sensitivity of some of the natural enemies of these insects to the new chemicals frequently brought about ecological imbalances in which one pest was simply traded for another. "We stand now," Carson concluded, "where two roads diverge." The "less traveled" fork—the road of biological control by natural enemies and of alternative control technologies—"offers our last, our only chance to reach a destination that assures the preservation of our earth."[2]

The following year, Betty Friedan's controversial *Feminine Mystique* hit the grocery stores. Friedan attacked the post-World War II mystique that had sent women back from the factories into the home to have babies, chauffeur children, bake gourmet meals, and entertain their husband's business associates. The suburban housewife and mother had become the model of female fulfillment.

A decade passed before the confusion and anomie associated with the "I'm just a housewife" mystique began to surface for middle-class women. The "problem that had no name" could not be solved by psychoanalysis, sex therapy, love, diet, or waxing the kitchen floor. "The trapped housewife" burst from the home and into the public arena.

Despite reassurances from homemakers like Phyllis (*Sixpense in her Shoe*) McGinley that cookies and dust mops could be creative adventures, the women's movement began to grow. The demand for equity in the workplace, in education, and in the bedroom spawned the liberal feminist phase of the movement. Friedan argued that inner growth and development, self-assertion, autonomy, and, above all, education would be the keys that would transform a deadened, dependent, forfeited female into a vigorous, creative woman with a plan for a fulfilling new life.[3]

WOMEN AND NATURE

Although the environmental and women's liberation movements emerged simultaneously in the 1960s and many women participated in both, the systematic interconnections between the two were developed by the feminists of the 1970s. Feminist theory analyzed the woman–nature connection from several perspectives.

Some feminists, such as Mary Daly, Sherry Ortner, and Susan Griffin, operated on the assumption that recent cultures are all fundamentally patriarchal and denigrate women in significant ways by identifying them with nature. Others, such as Merlin Stone, Dolores LaChapelle, and Adrienne Rich, argued that in an earlier prehistoric past, when mother goddesses and the Earth Mother were widely worshipped, women seem to have had a higher status. Women today, they suggested, could perhaps recapture this earlier age of nature worship through ceremonies, rituals, poetry, and a new language and thereby reinstate the ancient ideal. A revolution in symbol structures could help to transform the patriarchal–technological culture that brought about the separation of people from nature and the lower status of women. In a new age of consciousness, the Earth as symbol of life, beauty, and spiritual fulfillment could regenerate respect for nature and reunify all human beings with other organisms and the planet.[4]

One of the most popular writers on woman and nature, Susan Griffin, has beautifully expressed the power of the symbolic fusion of women with earth:

I know I am made from this earth, as my mother's hands were made from this earth, as her dreams came from this earth and all that I know, I know in this earth...all that I know speaks to me through this earth and I long to tell you, you who are earth too, and listen as we speak to each other of what we know: the light is in us.[5]

The importance of symbol in generating the emotional response that can lead the way to a new ethic and to new behavior patterns toward the Earth and toward women is undeniable. A revolution in root metaphors away from "The Machine," which has guided industrial society since the 17th century, is now taking place in American culture. From Earth Day 1970, *The Whole Earth Catalog*, and Friends of the Earth, to *Mother Earth News*, *New Woman, New Earth*, the "Minding the Earth" radio series, and "Spaceship Earth," the new symbolism is pervasive. *Only One Earth, The Wooing of Earth*, and "A Theology of the Earth," all titles of works by René Dubos, reflect a new unitary outlook binding together the people and other organisms of the planet.[6]

But this symbolism can be double-edged. The identification of women and nature implicit in phrases like "virgin lands," "man's war on Mother Nature," "penetrating the secret springs of Nature," and "wrestling with Nature herself to decode her messages" are suggestive of sexual assaults that render both women and nature passive and submissive. Science and philosophy from Aristotle and Francis Bacon to sociobiology and nuclear physics have used language and symbol to devalue women through identifying them with nature. Sociobiologists write of "rape" by mallard ducks, "lesbianism" in kittiwakes, and "homosexuality" in roundworms. Members of the Department of Energy have reputedly called solar energy effeminate, while a geologist who was asked about Mount St. Helens' next eruption replied: "We don't know her intentions.... We haven't been able to probe her deeply enough with our instruments."[7]

Despite the obvious need for new symbols and a new language, many feminists also recognized that without a simultaneous revolution in the social, sexual, and economic structures that exploit both women and Nature, the symbolic revolution cannot succeed.

The psychological approach to the woman–nature question elaborated by writers such as Dorothy Dinnerstein, Evelyn Fox Keller, and Nancy Chodorow locates the origins of female subordination in biological functionalism. Woman's primary role as reproducer places her in intimate contact with

FIG. 7.1 / THE MOTHER'S DAY MARCH IN WASHINGTON, D.C., MAY 10, 1981.
SPONSORED BY THE MOTHER'S DAY COALITION, THE DEMONSTRATION WAS A
PROTEST AGAINST BOTH NUCLEAR WARFARE AND NUCLEAR POWER.
PHOTOGRAPH BY PAT PATRICK, REPRODUCED BY PERMISSION.

her offspring during most of their childhood. The female child identifies with her mother and emulates her social role, defining herself through the self of her mother. She thus achieves adulthood through a merging of her self with that of another female, a process of fusion. In contrast, the male child, in attaining adulthood, develops in antithesis to his mother, seeing her as "other" rather than as self, and achieves manhood through a process of separation.

The result is a dual psychology, with the female psyche rooted in fusion, empathy, identification, and wholeness and the male psyche based on separation, distinction, division, antithesis, and dualism. Because child-rearing by the mother seems to be a nearly universal phenomenon, households and cultures are founded on dualities that result in patriarchy, the separation of mind from body, of people from nature, subject from object, and the domination of woman and nature as "other."[8] (Figure 7.1)

One possible solution is to alter the early childhood household arrangements so that men participate in child-rearing. Blurring, fusing, and sharing of roles in both workplace and home could result in an increasing number of nurturing males, and hence in a culture with a manifest concern for the welfare of nature, children, and future generations.

Another approach advocated by feminists such as Shulamith Firestone is the liberation of woman through reproductive technology. This approach includes a spectrum of possibilities that would give women the right to choose when and if they wish to bear and raise children: male and female contraceptive devices, voluntary vasectomies and tubal ligations, amniocentesis and genetic counseling, and, ultimately, test-tube reproduction and cloning.[9]

Science and technology are here viewed as potentially liberating and progressive, yet these approaches also raise a host of difficult ethical questions about the nature of control over life itself. For example, amniocentesis allows the woman to know the sex of her unborn child and thus to decide whether or not to abort the fetus. If, through contraceptive and genetic technology, families decide to have one or two children and to make the first child a male, then an increase in the proportion of males in society could result. If the psychological approach to the woman–nature question is valid, and if first children tend to be more highly motivated, aggressive, and domineering than second children, then the outcome could be an increase in dominating males, with negative implications for women and nature.

The social–economic analysis of the woman–nature question accepts many of the insights of the foregoing feminists but is critical of the idea of universal sex oppression and of the dichotomies "public–private" and "self–other" as explanatory categories. Rather than postulating a separate sex/gender system as the framework of analysis, this approach examines the historical context of male and female gender roles in different systems of economic production.

Anthropologists such as Eleanor Leacock, Patricia Draper, and Mina Caulfield argue that many hunter–gatherer societies seem to exhibit relatively egalitarian relations between men and women. Moreover, many of these groups establish ritual behaviors that maintain a dynamic equilibrium between population and resources. Here nature and culture are not separate dichotomies in which nature is devalued and culture elevated. The nonhuman world is alive, sensitive, intelligent, and on a par with the human portion. In some cultures animals are members of separate societies governed by special spirits, particular rocks and trees are sacred, and the Earth is a living nurturing mother. Women and men perform different tasks and have different roles, but each is essential to the survival of the group as a whole and neither is devalued. The society is geared to the production of use values (food, clothing, heating, shelter, etc.) as the material basis for sustaining life.[10]

In the precapitalist household mode of production that prevailed in much of colonial America, although a patriarchical culture was transported across the Atlantic, the sexual division of labor functioned as a family survival strategy in which the labor of both males and females was equally important to the household and the village community. In this system of production, nature appears as a resource, but is not yet the basis for commodity consumerism.

Early capitalist societies, on the other hand, have tended to exploit middle and upper–class women in the private sphere as reproducers and psychic resources, while lower-class women may bear, in addition, the burden of working as wage laborers in the public or productive sphere. Likewise, nature is exploited as a free resource, making it possible for a privileged class to reap large profits at the expense of the Earth.[11] As Karl Marx put it: "Natural elements entering as agents into production, and which cost nothing no matter what role they play in production, do not enter as components of capital, but as a free gift of Nature to Capital."[12]

For the advocates of the social-economic approach, women, wage laborers, minorities, and nature must all be liberated through a revolution in modes of production and a simultaneous sexual revolution. Political action on both fronts must be undertaken in concert and with mutual support.

FEMINISM AND ECOLOGY

The simultaneous emergence of the women's and environmental movements over the past three decades raises additional questions about the relationships between feminism and ecology. Is there a set of assumptions basic to the science of ecology that also holds implications for the status of women? Is there an ecological ethic that is also a feminist ethic?

The structures and functions of the natural world and of human society interact through a language common to both. Ethics in the form of description, symbol, religion, and myth help to mediate between humans and their world. Choices are implied in the words used to describe nature: choices of ways in which to view the world and ethical choices that influence human behavior toward it. Ecology and feminism have interacting languages that imply certain common policy goals. These linkages might be described as follows:

1. *All parts of a system have equal value.*

Ecology assigns equal importance to all organic and inorganic components in the structure of an ecosystem. Healthy air, water, and soil—
the abiotic components of the system—are as essential as the entire
diverse range of biotic parts—plants, animals, and bacteria and fungi.
Without each element in the structure, the system as a whole cannot
function properly. Remove an element, reduce the number of individuals or species, and erratic oscillations may appear in the larger system.

Similarly, feminism asserts the equality of men and women. Intellectual
differences are human differences rather than gender- or race-specific.
The lower position of women stems from culture rather than nature.
Thus policy goals should be directed toward achieving educational,
economic, and political equity for all.

Ecologists and feminists alike will therefore assign value to all parts of
the human–nature system and take care to examine the long- and short-
range consequences of decisions affecting an individual, group, or
species. In cases of ethical conflict, each case must be discussed from
the perspective of the interconnectedness of all parts and the good of
the whole.

2. *The Earth is a home.*

The Earth is a habitat for living organisms; houses are habitats for
groups of humans. Each ecological niche is a position in a community,
a hole in the energy continuum through which materials and energy
enter and leave. Ecology is the study of the Earth's household. Human
houses, whether sod houses, igloos, or bungalows, are structures in an
environment. Most are places wherein life is sustained—shelters where
food is prepared, clothes are repaired, and human beings cared for.

For ecologists and feminists the Earth's house and the human house are
habitats to be cherished. Energy flows in and out; molecules and atoms
enter and leave. Some chemicals and forms of energy are life-sustaining;
others are life-defeating. Those that lead to sickness on the planet or in
the home cannot be tolerated. Radioactive wastes or potential radioac-

tive hazards are present in some people's environments. Hazardous chemicals permeate some backyards and basements. Microwaves, nitrite preservatives, and cleaning chemicals have invaded the kitchen.

The home, where in fact women and children spend much of their time, is no longer a haven. The soil over which the house is built or the rocks used in its construction may emit radon (a radio-active decay product of radium), potentially a source of lung cancer. The walls, furniture, floor coverings, and insulation may contain urea formaldehyde, a nasal, throat, and eye irritant. Leaky gas stoves and furnaces can produce nitrogen dioxide and carbon monoxide, resulting in nausea, headaches, and respiratory illnesses. An underground garage in an apartment build- ing can be an additional source of indoor carbon monoxide. The home's faucets may be piping in carcinogenic drinking water, formed by the action of chlorine on organic compounds in reservoir supplies.[13]

Disinfectants sprayed where people eat or children play may contain phenols, cresols, or ammonium chlorides that can produce toxic effects on the lungs, liver, and kidneys, or act as nervous system depressants. Oven cleaners may contain caustic alkalis.[14]

The bathroom and bedroom may feature cosmetics and shampoos that can produce headaches, eye-makeup contaminated by bacteria and fungi, deodorants laced with hexachlorophene, and hair dyes contain- ing aromatic amines that have been linked to cancer.[15]

The kitchen may have a microwave oven and the living room a color television emitting low-level radiation when in use. The refrigerator may be stocked with food containing nitrite preservatives, food dyes, and saccharin-filled "low-cal" drinks, suspected as potential carcino- gens. In the cupboards pewter pitchers or dishes containing lead glazes can slowly contribute to lead poisoning, especially when in contact with acidic foods. The indoor atmosphere may be filled with cigarette, cigar, or tobacco smoke containing particles that remain in the air and accu- mulate even in the lungs of non-smokers.[16] For ecologists and feminists alike, the goal must be the reversal of these life-defeating intrusions and the restoration of healthy indoor and outdoor environments.

3. Process is primary.

The first law of thermodynamics, which is also the first law of ecology, asserts the conservation of energy in an ecosystem as energy is changed and exchanged in its continual flow through the interconnected parts. The total amount of energy entering and leaving the Earth is the same. The science of ecology studies the energy flow through the system of living and non-living parts of the Earth. All components are parts of a steady-state process of growth and development, death and decay. The world is active and dynamic; its natural processes are cyclical, balanced by cybernetic, stabilizing, feedback mechanisms.

The stress on dynamic processes in nature has implications for change and process in human societies. The exchange and flow of information through the human community is the basis for decision making. Open discussion of all alternatives in which ecologists and technologists, lawyers and workers, women and men participate as equals is an appropriate goal for both environmentalists and feminists. Each individual has experience and knowledge that is of value to the human–nature community.

4. There is no free lunch.

"No free lunch" is the essence of the laws of thermodynamics. To produce organized matter, energy in the form of work is needed. But each step up the ladder of organized life, each material object produced, each commodity manufactured increases entropy in its surroundings, and hence increases the reservoir of energy unavailable for work.

Although underpaid environmentalists are said to accept free lunches, nature cannot continue to provide free goods and services for profit-hungry humans, because the ultimate costs are too great. Thus, whenever and wherever possible, that which is taken from nature must be given back through the recycling of goods and the sharing of services.

For feminists, reciprocity and cooperation rather than free lunches and household services are a desirable goal. Housewives frequently spend much of their waking time struggling to undo the effects of the second law of thermodynamics. Continually trying to create order out of disorder is energy consumptive and spiritually costly. Thus the dualism of sep-

FIG. 7.2 / DIANE VANLANDINGHAM (LEFT) AND PATTI HARKEY OF THE
OKLAHOMA SOLAR ENERGY ASSOCIATION DEMONSTRATE THE USE OF THEIR
"SOLAR CLOTHES DRYER." PHOTOGRAPH BY KAY AHAUS. REPRODUCED BY
PERMISSION.

arate public and private spheres should be severed and male and female
roles in both the household and the workplace merged. Cooperation
between men and women in each specific context—childrearing, day-care
centers, household work, productive work, sexual relations, etc.—rather
than separate gender roles could create emotional rewards. Men and
women would engage together in the production of use-values and would
work together to scale down the production of commodities that are costly to nature. Technologies appropriate to the task, technologies having a
low impact on the environment, would be chosen whenever possible.
(Figure 7.2)

WOMEN AND THE ENVIRONMENT

An attempt to synthesize the foregoing theoretical approaches to nature and
women with a program of environmental action for the 1980s was made by
conferences such as the "Women and Life on Earth: Ecofeminism in the '80s"
conference held at the University of Massachusetts, Amherst, in March 1980.
Over a three-day period 500 women explored the meaning of ecofeminism as
a force for the future. They concluded that, as mothers, nurturers, and caretakers, women should direct their creative energies to heal the plant, bringing

to the public sphere the care and concern of women for all of life, and that, as feminists, women should work to transform the institutions of modern society that discriminate against women and minorities.[17]

A West Coast eco-feminist conference was held at Sonoma State University in April 1981. The women–nature connection was also prominently featured at a "Women and Appropriate Technology" conference in Missoula, Montana, in April 1979, and at the "Future, Women, and Technology" conference at San Diego State University in March 1981, attended by 750 women. A "Women in Solar Energy" (WISE) conference preceded the "Fifth National Passive Solar" conference in Amherst, Massachusetts, in the fall of 1980. In 1987, the twenty-fifth anniversary of Rachel Carson's *Silent Spring* was celebrated with an "Ecofeminist Perspectives" conference at the University of Southern California in Los Angles, followed by another at the University of Dayton in 1995.

In addition to conferences, college courses have focused attention on the feminism–ecology connection, such as the ongoing summer institute on "Ecology and Feminism" initiated at Goddard College in Plainfield, Vermont in the summer of 1980 in conjunction with the Institute for Social Ecology. A student-generated class, "Women and Nature," took place at the University of California Berkeley in the fall of 1980 and a course designed by Jane Yett was taught at U.C. Santa Cruz in 1981. Courses on ecofeminism ensued, throughout the country in the 1980s and '90s.

Resistance to a feminist–environmental coalition came from both movements. Environmentalists reacted negatively to the intrusion of feminist issues that seemed to them to muddy and complicate an already difficult struggle. At anti-nuclear rallies and solar technology conferences, the presence of lesbian feminists challenging male control of technology seemed particularly galling.[18]

Feminists likewise expressed dismay at the untimely desertion of many women who joined the "anti-nuke" movement just when issues such as the ratification of the Equal Rights Amendment, anti-abortion legislation, and child care costs loomed large. Women who worked to bridge this gap by negotiating time and energy trades between local organizations reported reluctance to reciprocate when the other group needed help.

Just as feminists had to contend with anti-abortionists such as Phyllis Schlafely who wanted women to revert to the old values of home and hearth, many women environmentalists found themselves in marked disagreement with pro-nuclear advocates such as Dixie Lee Ray, former head of the Atomic Energy Commission, and "anti-environmentalists" such as Anne Gorsuch, President Ronald Reagan's appointed head of the Environmental Protection Agency.[19]

Yet, in the same way that environmental hazards in the workplace and their long-term implications for human health helped to forge an environmental–labor coalition, so environmental issues that particularly affect women have contributed to the building of a feminist–environmental coalition. Questions of reproductive health, the health of children and loved ones, the future of subsequent generations on Earth, and the implications of technology have caused women to take active stands against the spread of nuclear weapons and nuclear power, radioactive wastes, hazardous wastes, pesticides and herbicides, and to join the appropriate technology movement. Through organizations, the media, pamphlets, public conferences, street theater art, art and poetry, they have attempted to arouse public interest and opinion and to influence government policy. The participation of thousands of women around the country and around the world in such activities illustrates the depth of their concern and the power of their activism.

Women also play important roles on the editorial boards and advisory panels of prominent environmental magazines and are highly visible in local, state, and national environmental, research, and lobbying organizations. In the 1980s Louise Dunlap founded and directed the Environmental Policy Center, a large Washington environmental lobby, and its affiliated Environmental Policy Institute. Bambi Batts Young, a biochemist with a Ph.D. from the Massachusetts Institute of Technology directed a research unit on human behavior and toxicity in the environment at the Center for Science in the Public Interest in Washington. Elizabeth Anderson directed the Cancer Assessment Group of the Environmental Protection Agency. Pat Hynes, who wrote *The Recurring Silent Spring* in 1989, was an environmental engineer in the EPA.

NUCLEAR TECHNOLOGY

In the 1970s and '80s the level of participation of women in the environmental movement was highest on nuclear issues. A much larger percentage of women than men considered themselves definitely or somewhat anti-nuclear (58 percent to 41 percent), while equal numbers of women and men characterized themselves as being definitely or somewhat interested in environmental issues (72 percent to 72 percent). The National Organization of Women adopted a resolution in October 1980 "against the use of nuclear power in favor of safer energy methods, including solar power, wind power, organic conversion, hydroelectric power and coal mined safely and burned cleanly." The League of Women Voters maintained an active role in disseminating public information on nuclear as well as other environmental issues.[20]

On November 17, 1980, hundred of women gathered in Washington, D.C., to take part in Women's Pentagon Action, a movement organized in opposition to nuclear power plants, nuclear weapons, the neutron bomb, and the MX missile as violent weapons, damaging to human life, reproductive health, and the natural environment. They also called for freedom from violence on the streets, equal pay for work of equal value, an end to the oppression of lesbians, and freedom of choice in bearing children.[21] Over the rest of the country women formed anti-nuclear alliances, engaged in nuclear power-plant protests, and published anti-nuclear pamphlets and articles. (Figure 7.3)

Women in the anti-nuclear movement found a martyr in Karen Silkwood, killed November 13, 1974, in an apparent automobile accident on her way to release notes to a *New York Times* reporter and a Washington official of the Oil, Chemical, and Atomic Workers International Union, alleging unsafe occupational health and safety standards at the Kerr McGee Corporation's plutonium plant in Crescent, Oklahoma. Since November 13, 1978, the anniversary of her death has been commemorated as Karen Silkwood Day by women activists. A play, "Silkwood," produced by Union Sisters, Inc., of Washington, D.C., commemorating her heroism, toured the country during 1981.[22]

The movement also found a visionary prophet in Dr. Helen Caldicott, Australian-born pediatrician at Children's Hospital Medical Center in Boston and author of *Nuclear Madness*, who argued for a direct connection between women's concern for life and the deadly effects of nuclear technology. An outspoken activist against nuclear war and a member of Physicians for Social Responsibility, she held that the most potent moral issue was that, in the event of nuclear war, targeted areas would be demolished within 20 minutes, and within 30 days, 90 percent of all Americans would be dead. Because of massive damage to the ozone layer all birds and mammals would die, leaving a few insect species better able to withstand radiation than other living organisms. Wilderness would vanish (Figure 7.4).[23]

FIG. 7.3 / ANTI-NUCLEAR DEMONSTRATION. WOMEN ANTINUCLEAR PROTES-
TORS AT THE EARTH DAY DEMONSTRATION ON WALL STREET, APRIL 23, 1990.
(PHOTO BY CINDY REIMAN, IMPACT VISUALS)

FIG. 7.4 / DR. HELEN CALDICOTT, A PEDIATRICIAN AND AUTHOR OF *NUCLEAR
MADNESS*. (PHOTO USED BY PERMISSION)

The life of the Earth has been a particularly poignant issue for her. "I think I've come to terms with my death," she states. "So it's not even 'I'd rather be here and alive.' I worship this Earth. I just worship nature."[24]

> I've actually adjusted to the fact that we may not survive. And I wake up every morning and thank God that we're still here and look at the beautiful trees and flowers. And as I go on, my perception and love of nature is heightened: A rose is so beautiful to me now, a gardenia, a tree, or even a blade of grass or an ant. It's so precious....I'm much more conscious of the world.[25]

Caldicott believes that women have a special responsibility to mobilize men and the whole human race against nuclear weapons. Even the men who negotiated the test-ban treaties are "wringing their hands" and "saying that it is the women who will stop it."[26]

Men's distrust of emotions, Caldicott believes, derive from our scientific era in which emotions are held to bias the interpretation of data. This led to a death-producing thanatophoric paralysis of the emotions.

> What women must do is go in there and be absolutely passionate because if we are not passionate we will almost certainly destroy ourselves. Because of the women's liberation movement, women have discovered their power in the positive masculine principle that we use now. We have to combine this with our positive feminine feeling and passion. We have to take over and take the lead.[27]

The perspective of many Third World women on nuclear technology and nuclear weapons was presented at the 1980 "Women and Life on Earth Conference" in a paper by Catherine Georgia Carlotti entitled, "W.A.R.S.: Women Against Racism and Sexism." First used against Asian peoples, nuclear weaponry represents for many simply the latest stage in the history of U.S. policies of black enslavement, Native American destruction, and the ideology of manifest destiny that asserts the superiority of whites over peoples of black, red, brown and yellow colors. Carlotti, director of Fight Back for Children in New York City, asserted that these policies affect minorities, women, and children for whom "racism is a real condition in United States society.... The outcome of our struggle against the people who continue to push nuclear technology hinges upon our capacity to bridge the racist division."[28]

Petra K. Kelly, a founder of the German Greens, who worked with the Economic and Social Committee of the World Congress on Alternatives and

Environment, was also concerned about the diversion of funds and natural resources to the arms race. Noting that 40 to 70 percent of all Third World agricultural labor is provided by women, who plant, tend animals, and haul water, she extended a "plea to all women to join their sisters who have risen up—who have helped to shape the ecological revolution."[29]

RADIOACTIVE WASTES

In 1980 water, on the Pine Ridge Indian Reservation near Edgemont, South Dakota, was found to have an alarmingly high level of radiation from uranium tailings washing into the Cheyenne River. A high rate of birth defects and cancerous deaths was reported at the Pine Ridge Hospital.

Lorelei Means, one of the founders of Women of All Red Nations, WARN, raised the alarm about aborted and deformed babies, leukemia victims, and the high rate of sterilization of women on Indian reservations. Another member of the organization, Winona LaDuke, urged women to try to stop nuclear development: "When we take uranium out of the ground it affects the women first, through the fetuses, and our children."[30] (Figure 7.5)

WARN was organized in 1977 to discuss the erosion of the family, forced sterilization, and the shrinkage of reservation lands. Not a separatist or women's liberation movement, Native American women characterized themselves as powerful spiritual leaders in their communities and as supporters of all Native peoples.

The summer of 1980 Survival Gathering of Native American People in the Black Hills of South Dakota issued a "Declaration of Dependence on the Land"—Mother Earth:

> We call for the recognition of our responsibility to be stewards of the land, to treat with respect and love our Mother Earth who is a source of our physical nourishment and our spiritual strength.

> We are people of the land. We believe that the land is not to be owned but to be shared. We believe that we are guardians of the land.[31]

CHEMICAL WASTES

Lois Gibbs of the Love Canal Homeowner's Association in Niagara Falls, New York, played a critical organizational role in raising public consciousness about the effects of hazardous waste disposal by Hooker Chemicals and Plastics Corporation in her neighborhood of 1,200 homes.

FIG. 7.5 / NATIVE AMERICAN ANTI-NUCLEAR PROTEST. CARLYLE RANDALL

A Native American Vietnam War veteran speaks at a rally near the main gate of the Nevada Test Site on November 10, 1991. She is giving the international hand sign meaning, "I bear no weapons." The Veteran's Day Witness was in protest of nuclear weapons testing done underground at the test site. (Photo by Dana Schuerholz, Impact Visuals)

Love Canal, an area partially excavated by William T. Love in 1892 as a link between the upper and lower Niagara River, was purchased by Hooker Chemical and used as a chemical waste dump between 1942 and 1953. Sold to the city of Niagara Falls for one dollar, the site was used by the Board of Education for a school building in 1954. Then in 1978 the New York State Department of Health began investigating numerous complaints from residents in the area.

Lois Gibbs, whose son had experienced health problems since attending the local elementary school, conducted a neighborhood campaign to close the school. She found many people willing to talk to her about their families' health problems.

A much higher than normal rate of miscarriages, birth defects, and stillbirths was found in the neighborhood. A local study conducted by the women themselves on women who had become pregnant during a period of construction, when dust contamination was higher than normal, revealed that out of 15 pregnancies only one normal baby was born. Additionally, many women in the neighborhood were found to have breast or uterine cancer, and a twelve-year old girl had to have a hysterectomy.

In August 1978 the New York State Health Department recommended that the school be closed; that week Gibbs organized the Love Canal Homeowners Association to pressure for redress from Hooker Chemical. Governor Hugh Carey, who was running for reelection, agreed to have the state buy the homes at fair market value and some 710 families were initially declared eligible to move.[32]

Because much of the blue-collar male population of the Love Canal area found it difficult to accept the fact that they were unable to protect or provide adequately for their families, the women assumed a leadership role in bringing the issue to public attention.[33] Love Canal is the story of how lower-middle-class women who had never been environmental activists became politicized by the life and death issues directly affecting their children and their homes. The women of Love Canal, said Gibbs, "are no longer at home tending their homes and gardens.... Women who at one time looked down at people picketing, being arrested and acting somewhat radical are now doing those very things. Now in many households dinner is not ready at 5 o'clock, laundry is not quite done, and the neighbor is taxiing the children around."[34]

Women researchers also assumed responsibility for conducting studies of the problem. Adeline Levine, a sociologist at SUNY, Buffalo, who interviewed residents, concluded that the psychological stress resulting from government indecision over relocation and aid, as well as failure to supply information on health effects, was as important a health factor as the negative physiological effects themselves.[35]

Beverly Paigan, a molecular biologist at Roswell Park Memorial Institute, made a preliminary survey of health effects among the residents. Her results caused a panel of epidemiologists from the Environmental Protection Agency to recommend further scientific investigation. But a committee appointed by Governor Hugh Carey and chaired by Lewis Thomas, head of the Sloan-Kettering Cancer Center, criticized her survey as not presenting "sound epidemiological research." Paigan, in turn, questioned the lack of data introduced to substantiate the conclusions of Thomas's committee as well as the committee's failure to use documented cases of acute health effects. She and other critics pointed to a possible conflict of interest inasmuch as the Thomas report criticized all but the work of the current New York State Health Department, an institution that had extensive powers over state medical facilities, where all but one of the panel members were administrators.[36]

In Martinez, California, children who attended Las Juntas Elementary School were only 1,000 yards away from two hazardous waste dumps operated by IT Corporation and Acme Fill. Seventy-five percent of the trucking trips on the residential street on which the school was located were waste related. Children exposed to odors while walking to the school had been coming home ill. Dorothy Sakazaki, who lived in the area, attempted to get an environmental impact report on the problem in 1980:

> We still can't get the road to those dumps out of this community. We're poor people but we still have pride. Trucks have tipped over on the road. We can't even make the place safe for our children.[37]

The same year, Chambier Bechtel, a mother and graduate of the University of California, Berkeley, led a movement to clean up the highly toxic chemical PCB (poly-chlorinated bibphenyl) after a PCB spill was discovered in a children's play yard in Sonoma, California. "Black oily stuff was everywhere—on the trees hanging over the creek, on the sidewalk and the ground." With Allen Simontacchi, a lineman for the Pacific Gas and Electric Company, Bechtel visited a school bus stop where, a year earlier, a PCB-filled capacitor on a utility pole had leaked into a water-filled ditch in which children collected tadpoles. Here samples showed 29,000 parts per million (ppm) even after the first cleanup, far in excess of the federally mandated limit of 50 ppm. Soon PG&E workers and their families began calling Bechtel, reporting more spills, exposures, and health problems. Despite fines levied by the EPA on PG&E and a new policy of reporting spills to local homeowners, the PCB problem continued to gain local and national attention.[38]

PESTICIDES AND HERBICIDES

In September 1979 the Bureau of Land Management (BLM) began a scheduled spraying of the controversial herbicide 2,4-D on timberland near Grant's Pass, Oregon. While the U.S. Environmental Protection Agency had banned most uses of the defoliant 2,4,5-T on the grounds of a high incidence of miscarriages and birth defects among a group of women near Oregon's Suislaw National Forest,[39] concern remained that 2,4-D, which is chemically similar to 2,4,5-T, was also dangerous, especially to pregnant women. Joann Rosall of Wolf Creek, Oregon and 100 demonstrators, including pregnant women, conducted sit-ins near the scheduled spray sites.[40] At the time, Rosall told reporters:

> We've been camped here since Monday morning...and they're either going to stop or they're going to spray those chemicals right on top of us. If the BLM calls the police to try and move us out, we'll handcuff ourselves to the trees. And we're not bluffing. We've got the cuffs.[41]

A BLM spokesperson said that the pregnant women would not be sprayed and might "die of starvation before we [get] to their unit."[42] The handcuffing action was not necessary but the area was occupied until the spraying season ended in October. Protests over types of chemicals, spraying methods, and adequate notification of intent to spray continued.

On November 25, 1979, in a municipal court in Modesto, California, attorney Joyce Carillo of California Rural Legal Assistance represented 14 migrant worker's children who had been exposed to pesticides. The pesticides were dusted on bean and tomato fields from airplanes flying near a summer school, and several children became ill. The chemicals, toxaphene and orthene, both organophosphate pesticides, were suspected of causing health problems. Several compounds in toxaphene were found to be mutagens and thus potentially carcinogenic, while orthene metabolizes to the toxic chemical *monitor*, which can eventually affect the nervous system.[43]

In Berkeley, California, Mary Shinoff of the Berkeley Community Health Advisory Board and her colleague Sharon Ann Miller reported on the use of 13 different pesticides in Berkeley parks. They found that the Cedar-Rose neighborhood park and playground had been sprayed with oryzalin, a chemical suspected of causing birth defects, and urged the adoption of a comprehensive city-wide plan to eliminate lack of coordination among agencies using sprays.[44] Such actions by women led to stricter regulation.

APPROPRIATE TECHNOLOGY

For many women who became aware of environmental hazards and nuclear technologies through environmentalism and became conscious of sexism through feminism, the appropriate technology movement presented an appealing alternative. Here the hands-on skills necessary for personal survival and control over one's own life were revered and disseminated. Renewable energy sources, energy and food self-reliance, and low-environmental-impact technologies became the movement's hall-marks.

Nevertheless, the appropriate technology movement had its own ways of reinforcing traditional sex roles. Activist Judy Smith pointed out that in work situations it was usually the men who directed construction, made decisions, and did the work requiring technical skills, while women disseminated information, educated the public, and performed the more menial hands-on tasks. Moreover, what was defined as appropriate technology varied according to sex. The solar oven and the organic garden may actually have served to reinforce women's traditional time-consuming role in the kitchen.

Women involved in the appropriate technology movement, however, found great satisfaction in building bridges, solar collectors, greenhouses, and doing home repairs themselves, without resorting to high-cost contractors. Carpentry and plumbing skills taught to groups of women by other women rather than male "experts" became popular forms of education.[45]

THE ANTITOXICS MOVEMENT

During the 1980s, an environmental justice movement oriented toward improving the urban environment and the status of minorities emerged in the United States. The grassroots antitoxics movement is dominated by women. Women of color—especially Native Americans, blacks, Hispanics, Pacific Islanders, and Asian Americans—along with white women, comprise 80-85 percent of the local activists.[46] The movement took off in 1982 with protests from a community that was 60 percent African American and 4 percent Native American over a proposed PCB (polychlorinated biphenyls) disposal site in Warren County; North Carolina. It was spearheaded by black activist Cora Tucker who founded a local chapter of Citizens for a Better America.[47]

The antitoxics campaign was galvanized by the United Church of Christ's 1987 report on "Toxic Wastes and Race in the United States," documenting that fifty-eight percent of the country's blacks and 53 percent of its Hispanics live in communities where the dumping of hazardous wastes is uncontrolled.[48] The movement attempts to reverse injustices disproportionately experienced by minorities, such as the siting of landfills, toxic waste sites, and incinerators in inner cities, poor rural areas, and on American Indian reservations. Righting the inequities of the past requires new laws, regulations, compensation, removal, and reversal of the causes of injustice. Long term goals include the redistribution of wealth and environmental goods and services.[49] (Figure 7.6)

Environmental equity is an ecofeminist issue. The body, home, and community are sites of women's local experience and local contestation. Women experience the results of toxic dumping on their own bodies (sites of reproduction of the species), in their own homes (sites of the reproduction of daily life), and in their communities and schools (sites of social reproduction). Women's leadership and organizing skills gained in grassroots struggles empower them to change society and themselves. (Figure 7.7)

Women fighting hazardous waste landfills and incinerators in their communities have forged multiracial coalitions. According to Sue Greer, of People Against Hazardous Landfill Sites (PAHLS) in Wheeler, Indiana, "If you want to win a local environmental fight in a multi-racial community, it is essential to actively recruit and welcome people of color into your group.... In the long run, what is the future of the Grassroots Movement for environmental justice, if it is not a broad-based multi-racial movement?"[50] Kay Kiker of Alabamans for a Clean Environment (ACE), reports that "ACE has about 350 members, and we are biracial. That was one mountain we had to climb. A lot of people left ACE because we decided to be a biracial group, but we've gotten beyond that."[51]

When women began protesting toxic wastes, male officials ignored them and criticized them for being overemotional. They labeled them "little old ladies in tennis shoes" and "hysterical housewives." Blue collar women appropriated the labels and turned them into empowerment. Said Cora Tucker, "When they first called me a hysterical housewife I used to get very

FIG. 7.6 / WOMEN OF WEST HARLEM ENVIRONMENTAL ACTION.

Women of West Harlem Environmental Action join with other groups to pro-test the potentially health threatening emission caused by the North River Sewage Treatment Plant in Harlem and the scaling down of the state park planned for the area. The March 31, 1990 acion was part of New York Public interest research Group's (NYPIRG) "1,000 Points of Blight" campaign. (Photo by David Vita, Impact Visuals)

FIG. 7.7 / EL PUENTE, EARTH SPIRIT, PROTESTS INCINERATOR.

Students from El Puente's Earth Spirit protest the proposed Brooklyn Navy Yard incinerator. El Puente Ojo Cafe (Brown Eyed Bridge), formerly known as Toxic Avengers joined with other groups in the January 14, 1993 action. (Photo by Catherine D. Smith, Impact Visuals)

upset and go home and cry... I learned that's a tactic men use to keep us in our place. When they started the stuff on toxic wastes...a guy got up and says, 'We have a whole room full of hysterical housewives today, so men we need to get prepared.' I said, 'You're exactly right. We're hysterical and when it comes to matters of life and death, especially mine, I get hysterical.... If men don't get hysterical there's something wrong with them.' They stopped calling us hysterical."[52]

In 1988, a multi-racial protest by 1000 women and men was led by Mothers of East Los Angeles (MELA) against the city of Los Angeles' plan to locate a hazardous waste incinerator in their neighborhood. MELA, a coalition organized initially by Latino women to protest a prison slated for construction in east Los Angeles, put pressure on the local Air Quality Management District, the California Department of Health Services, and the Environmental Protection Agency to halt the project. In 1991, after lawsuits threatened to drive up costs, the project was withdrawn.[53]

Another protest over a state-of-the-art hazardous waste incinerator in California was led by Hispanic women farm-workers. As Esperanza Maya recalls, "My nightmare began in 1987," when she first attended a public meeting in Avenal, twenty miles from her home in Kettleman City; in California's Central Valley, where Chemical Waste Management Corporation was proposing to build an hazardous waste incinerator.[54] After learning that the lights she saw every evening in the hills above her community came, not from bikers' campsites, but from an already existing CWM landfill, she cried all the way home. The experience propelled her to co-found El Pueblo para el Aire y Agua Limpio (People for Clean Air and Water) in Kettleman City, a community where 1200 Spanish speaking farm-workers reside. On January 25, 1988 she received a call from Bradley Angel of Greenpeace, who told her there would be a public input meeting the next day in Kettleman City. When she arrived at the meeting with four friends and found it packed with employees of Chemical Waste Management, she spoke out, asking why her community had not been informed of the meeting. She was told that a notice had appeared in English in the classified advertisement section of the Hamford Centennial Newspaper, forty miles away. She then asked why the Environmental Protection Agency had not informed them when the permits would be issued. Finally, she demanded that translations of the documents and simultaneous translations of the meetings be available to the Hispanic community.

With the support from others in her community—Lois Gibbs' Clearinghouse for Hazardous Wastes, Ralph Nader, Jessie Jackson, and Los Angeles Congresswoman Maxine Waters—she inspected chemical dump sites in other states, organized marches, and uncovered records of the company's past fines and violations. El Pueblo insisted that the entire 1000 page EPA Envirnomental Impact Report (EIR) be translated into Spanish and took the case to court. When the state Supreme Court ruled that the EIR was inadequate, Chemical Waste Management withdrew its proposal and construction of the incinerator was halted.

On the Sioux Indian reservation in Yankton, South Dakota, Native American women stood up in community meetings to protest hazardous waste dumping on their lands. Charon Asetoyer, Executive Director of the Native American Women's Health Education Resource Center, who began a resource center in the basement of her home and held meetings at the kitchen table, says the environment is a women's issue.[55] Cancer and birth defects resulting from radioactive mining tailings and hazardous waste dumps on native lands awakened her community to problems faced by women and children, along with their husbands and brothers. When Waste Management and Monsanto Chemical companies proposed a waste dump for nuclear and chemical wastes on their reservation with promises of employment and safety, the women forged liaisons with the Karen Silkwood Association and the Citizen's Clearing House for Hazardous Wastes. They built awareness and confidence in their community by filling baskets with Easter eggs and talking to the grandmothers in each family about their relationship to Mother Earth. Finally, the plan was aborted.

The ultimate solution to such problems is not more and more Superfund cleanup moneys, but reduction of production. Industries must (1) reduce production of unneeded, especially toxic-producing commodities and focus on the fulfillment of basic needs, (2) reduce and eliminate waste output, (3) recycle, reuse, and exchange waste and energy that cannot be eliminated, and (4) treat and destroy non recyclable waste at the site of production instead of releasing it to the environment. Only through a total reorientation of the goals of production toward the fulfillment of basic needs, security, and healthy reproduction can problems of environmental and social inequity be reversed.

CONCLUSION

Juxtaposing the goals of the women's and ecology movements leads to important conclusions regarding the future of life on Earth. Unless the home is liberated from its status as "women's sphere" to that of "human habitat," the feminist movement cannot succeed. Unless the Earth is liberated from the overkill of certain kinds of high technologies and renovated with low-impact "appropriate" technologies, the environmental movement cannot succeed. Environmental, technological, social, and linguistic revolutions must all take place simultaneously. In this way perhaps the future of life on Earth may be sustained.

8

PEACE WITH

THE EARTH

WOMEN AND THE

SWEDISH

ENVIRONMENT

With Abby Peterson

"It is beginning to dawn on women that they must assume the responsibility for house-keeping nature." These words that so succinctly state the connection between women and *oikos*, the Greek work for "house" from which the science of ecology derives its meaning, were written not by a feminist of the 1980s, but in 1941 by the Swedish critic and reformer Elin Wägner (1882–1949). The insights in her book, *Alarmclock*, still ring out to women active in the global environmental movement today as they struggle to restore the partnership between humans and nature that is essential for the renewal and continuance of life on earth. In Sweden, as in the United States, the women's movement for care of the earth has been explored from both symbolic and political perspectives. Individual women active in the movement identify with a range of potential strategies and issues.[1]

WOMEN AND NATURE

Wägner's alarm was intended to awaken women to the destruction of their heritage by the mechanization of production that used plants and animals as if they were machines, wasted resources, and polluted the earth. Anticipating the argument of Rachel Carson's *Silent Spring* (1962) by more than twenty years, she saw that war and chemical pesticides were death-producing technologies aimed at destroying all of life itself. "Soldiers spray the largest 'enemies' with bullets, agriculturalists spray the smallest 'enemies' with their chemical solutions....Spray an enemy people's soldiers to death and an indispensable part of the human family has been subjected to a treatment the consequences of which no one can estimate. Spray the parasites of the grapevines and one destroys the life in the earth under them without which the grapevine cannot live." To make "peace with the earth" (as she entitled an essay of 1940), workers and soldiers alike must stop putting all their energy into machines that destroy the world and alter matter itself.[2]

Women, she believed, must recapture their ancient tradition of caring for the land by bursting out of the confines of their homes and extending their housekeeping to the whole globe. "In agreement with matriarchy's understanding and methods, the proper way to treat nature is with caution, housekeeping, and care." The matriarchal heritage that influenced Elin Wägner derived from the age of prehistory portrayed in Johann Bachofen's *Mother Right* (1861) and Robert Briffault's *The Mothers* (1920). In her book *A Thousand Years in Småland* (1939) she recounted the old religion of nature in southern Sweden where the giant woman Ana fought the male God of Christianity.[3]

In 1933 Wägner met the dynamic and practical Flory Gate (b. 1904) and the two women began working together to rediscover the wisdom of matriarchy expressed in the traditions of peasant farm women. (Figure 8.1) Three years later they visited Vienna's "Women's Organization for World Order," a group that opposed the disorder brought about by men's system of monocultures in farming and forestry, advocating instead diversification modeled on the principles of nature. Here they came in contact with the Swiss farmer Mina Hofstetter who combined hoe cultivation with organic planting, using vegetable rather than animal fertilizers. To Wägner, this rough-hewn farm woman, who in her long skirts and heavy boots spoke of her own health and the soil's health in one breath, became Mother Earth herself.[4]

With Elizabeth Tamm, Wägner wrote *Peace with the Earth* in 1940, arguing for cooperation with nature and its life-giving layer of soil. If humankind was to survive, they asserted, nature's health and self-regulation must come first. Reacting to the massive wind erosion in the Dust Bowl in the United States and water erosion from overgrazing and deforestation in Italy's Appennine mountains, they argued that modern technology had provided the means to disturb the equilibrium of nature. Human use of the topsoil must not interrupt the delicate balance of the humus layer's self-renewal. To achieve this, they proposed agricultural methods based on the use of varied compost, "cover" cultivation, and shallow plowing.[5]

FIG. 8.1 / FLORY GATE AND ELIN WÄGNER: 'DAUGHTERS OF MOTHER EARTH.'
FROM ULLA ISAKSSON AND ERIK HIJALMAR LINDER, 1980. ELIN WÄGNER:
DOTTER AV MODERJORD, 1922-1949, P. 273. BONNIERS, STOCKHOLM. FEMALE
HISTORICAL COLLECTIONS, UNIVERSITY OF GOTHENBURG, SWEDEN.

Flory Gate, who took up farming in 1944, set out to build on older farming methods that had been successful for centuries. Although farming
intrudes on nature, she believed it could be done carefully by having many
crops and fields. Using a seven field rotation system and natural rather than
artificial manures to protect the soil's bacteria, she cultivated oats, potatoes,
beets, peas, and rye. With the wool from the farm's sheep, she and Elin
Wägner wove clothing and blankets. They milked their cows by hand, rather
than with milking machines, sieved and separated the cream, and made butter and cheese. By the age of 80, Flory Gate had given up active farming, but
retained her conviction that nature must be healed. Although women, nature,
and the soil have all suffered from degradation, women can use the science of
ecology to liberate both themselves and the land.[6]

The connection between war and herbicides that Wägner had criticized
has been injected with new meaning by one of Sweden's most outspoken contemporary critics—political writer, novelist, and winner of the 1980 Nordic
Council's Prize in Literature, Sara Lidman. The product of a matrifocal

farming tradition in northern Sweden where women's power in the home was absolute, Lidman returned to her roots to write a series of five epic novels in the region's dialect that portray successive changes in human relationships to the land. In an area of long dark winters where "cold is like a burning knife, death is always very close." Survival depends on the strength of human fiber. Here women provided the family with food and clothing from cows, pigs, and sheep, and in the winters men took teams of horses upcountry to cut lumber for charcoal, firewood, homes, and barns and a surplus for tax payments. Impact on the forest was relatively low and it grew back rapidly.[7]

Lidman complained that the lumber companies treated the forest as something to be erased from the earth. Large areas were stripped bald (kalhygge) and then declared euphemistically to be "young" again (föryngringsyta). Fast-growing Canadian pines (*Pinus contorta*) were introduced and treated with fertilizers while other species were kept down with herbicides. As in Vietnam, where during the war years she reported on the effects of defoliation, chemicals such as 2,4,5-T and 2,4-D (now outlawed) produced a higher than average incidence of cancer among local workers.

Her collection of newspaper articles spanning the decade from 1970–1980, entitled *Each Leaf is an Eye*, captured the perception of the Vietnamese people that herbicides were poisons thrown into the eyes of their grandmothers. The Vietnamese view that nature is animate, expressed in the saying "Each step I walk on this ground, I walk in the intestines of my ancestors," bears similarities to Lidman's own ancestor's belief in Vittran, the female force in nature that must be propitiated, lest she retaliate by inflicting cows, horses, and humans with sickness.[8]

Elin Wägner's critique of the mechanistic treatment of the environment and her matriarchal perspective on nature were extended by another of Sweden's women writers, Uppsala poet, artist, and philosopher Elisabet Hermodsson (b. 1927) who has explored the connections between woman and nature in her paintings and poems. As a philosophy student during the 1950s, Hermodsson was an early critic of the positivist school of thinking that then dominated Swedish universities. The positivists attempted to remove value judgments from science by admitting as truth only two kinds of statements, those based on mathematics and those based on experiment; language, like nature, was constructed from atom-like elements that when added together produced a sum. This way of thinking, she argued, separated ethics from science and made research vulnerable to exploitation. In modern society, science took the place of patriarchal religion.[9]

As an artist and poet, she wanted to open the water-tight compartments between science, religion, and art to new ways of seeking knowledge about reality. She saw values embedded in both scientific descriptions and in artistic creations. Concern for the earth as a mother could lead to the reassertion of spiritual connections to nature. For example, in a poem of multileveled meanings, written while on the island of Crete, the locale of Bachofen's matriarchal age, she saw her own intimate relationship to the earth and to women of the past.

and my roots
burst ever deeper
from the heat
down in the earth of iron chippings
and red clay

Pondering that "the universe was once born as woman," she wrote of God as a woman and of the wisdom that men, trapped in the patriarchal age of Saint John, can learn from women.[10]

Another critic of the positivist view of nature was Eva Moberg, writer and columnist for Sweden's major newspaper (*Dagens Nyheter*). She wrote of the need for a symbolic understanding of reality as part of a dynamic development not limited by the static view that produced positivism. She defended the study of ancient traditions as a search for a step forwards, not backwards. But in the search for a new paradigm, the new physics was overemphasized. The insights which came from mythology, archeology, and anthropology, she believed, were far more explosive.

To Moberg, peace and environmental issues are women's questions and are integral to the goals of women's liberation. The struggle for a more peaceful society in a cooperative balance with nature is a struggle between the sexes directed towards eliminating the female monopoly on nurturance and love and the male monopoly on aggression and dominance. Because men's domination of technology and industrial production has led the world to the brink of disaster, women's experiences of nurturing are needed to reevaluate and reformulate society's goals. A vision of a life-giving future must stem from changes in the male psyche.[11]

Extending the woman–nature connection from written language to art, a group of women in Gothenburg prepared an art exhibition in the fall of 1983 that centered around a tree trunk found in the forest in the shape of a woman with legs, arms, and breasts reminiscent of the ancient mother goddesses preserved in the sculpture of stone age Europe (Figure 8.2). The catalogue for

FIG. 8.2 / TREE, REMINISCENT OF NERTHUS, BRONZE-AGE GODDESS OF
NORTHERN EUROPE, WITH EARTH MOON GODDESSES BY BENEDICTE
BERGMANN. FROM WITCHPOWER EXHIBITION, GOTHENBURG, FALL 1983,
(PHOTO BY MONICA ENGLAND, GOTHENBURG). REPRODUCED BY PERMISSION.

the exhibition was entitled "Witchpower," symbolizing the knowledge of
nature and women's healing powers that were systematically obliterated in
the witch hunts of the Renaissance. The parallel between the witch hunts and
comtemporary threats to future generations is exemplified by the possibility
of nuclear war. The Gothenburg women expressed solidarity with the
women's peace action at Greenham Common in England set up to protest the
installation of cruise missiles by the United States. To these women, the peace
camps made visible the connections between the death-producing missiles
and the alternative of life without violence.[12]

Common to the writings of these Swedish women was a reaction to the
technological conquest of nature in modern industrial society. Their approach
stresses the need for a reunification with nature that derives from a vision of
balance between human needs and respect for the earth. Like the American radical feminists Susan Griffin in *Woman and Nature* (1978), Mary Daly in
Gyn/Ecology (1978), and Carol Christ in "Why Women Need the Goddess"
(1982), they emphasized an experiential immersion in the symbols, language,
and rituals of women's connection to agriculture, the ancient deities of nature,
and the procreation of life. These symbolic connections "empower" women to

unified actions to preserve the earth, from which all life flows. But more broad-
ly, these women attempted to reassert values necessary to today's society, to
support nature's own "right" to exist free of human intervention, and to initiate change at the ideological or symbolic level of society. Such goals were common to both the Nordic and American women's movements.[13]

THE WOMAN'S MOVEMENT AND THE
ENVIRONMENTAL MOVEMENT

In her book *Alarmclock*, Elin Wägner had explicitly stated the connection
between women's liberation and the liberation of the earth: "Men's struggle
for dominance over nature has been fought side by side with their struggle for
domination over women. The victory over domination must be a double victory if it is to be complete." To many Swedish women this expression of the
political rather than the spiritual dimension of Elin Wägner's thought was
uppermost. Changing the symbolic structures of the understanding, however important, did not change the power structures of society that produced
the domination of women and nature. The struggle to change society must
thus be waged on both the ideological and the material levels.[14]

In 1979 a heated debate in Sweden's largest morning newspaper over the
political implications of Wägner's book took place. To some women her
ideas represented a naive form of matriarchal spiritualism that glorified
women's oppression in the family and could never be the basis for political
action. To others, who distanced themselves from the spiritual elements of
her thought, the concept of women's work in the family generated a politics
of liberation and suggested alternatives for social change and an ecologically
balanced society.[15]

The debate reflected a shift in the politics of the radical wing of the
women's movement around 1977 away from a strategy of infiltration of
women into the male-dominated spheres of production and the state towards
a new politics grounded in the concept of "women's culture." Based on
women's common potential for child-bearing and the realities of their common household work in contemporary Swedish society, "women's culture"
attempted to offer a ground for a unification of women that cut across class
lines. In Sweden today, women usually carry the major burden of childcare
and housework even when both partners in a marriage work full-time.
(Eighty-one percent of all Swedish women are in paid employment and half
of these hold full-time jobs.) According to Louise Waldén, "women's culture," based on women's shared experiences of nurturance as well as oppres-

sion, "created a system of values at odds with that prevailing in society." These values intersected with those of the environmental movement to create a rationale for social change.[16]

THE POLITICS OF REPRODUCTION

In developing strategies for change that would lead to a healthy future, women have been politicized by and most active in issues that affect reproduction and that proceed from women's role in the maintenance of everyday life. By taking the "round stomach's conception of the world" seriously, says Eva-Lena Neiman, "women can inject the environmental movement with new blood and new working methods" based on "women's experience of birth, care, and nurturing of children, plants, and animals."[17]

Such strategies and actions fit a theory of the "politics of reproduction" through which the implications of women's engagement with environmental issues can be better understood. The "politics of reproduction" is a taxonomy of potential political issues that has its theoretical basis in the societal division of labor between the sexes.[18]

In Sweden's patriarchal–capitalist society, women bear the responsibility for reproductive labor. Their role as reproducers includes both the biological (intergenerational) reproduction of the species and the (intragenerational) reproduction of the workforce through unpaid labor in the family and paid labor in the welfare state. In Swedish society 81 percent of working age women hold regular jobs, but of working women, 40 percent work part-time and most women are employed in low paying jobs with little opportunity for advancement. Men dominate both the production of exchange commodities and the women responsible for reproduction. Not only women, but even the interests of reproduction, are subordinate to men and the interests of production. The division of labor between the sexes, then, generates different, and often opposing, sets of political interests. Thus while economic growth is characteristic of men's community of interests, environmental balance is characteristic of women's community of interests.[18]

Women's political actions can be located along an ideological axis ranging from acceptance of women's role as nurturant social mother and of existing social relations to strategies designed to change the distribution of patriarchal and capitalist power. As a theoretical tool, the "politics of reproduction" consists of four categories that help to characterize women's political and environmental interests and to explain the context for their environmental actions.

1. Biological (intergenerational) Reproduction

Biological reproduction involves the intergenerational reproduction of the species. Women's shared experiences of, and potential for, child-birth unify women in their concern for the quality of life for future generations and for the survival of humankind. Here two political issues are paramount: ecological and nuclear issues.[19]

The ecological issues of industrial and agricultural pollution have motivated more women than men. In a protest in the northern coastal town of Sundsvall against air pollution from an aluminum factory, women were far more concerned about the problem than men. According to a poll taken by the National Institute of Environmental Medicine, 59% of the female respondents were concerned with the potential health risks as opposed to 36% of the men. The protest was successful in forcing the company to adhere to the legally allowed levels for discharge and stopped a planned expansion in the area.[20]

A national referendum on nuclear power, held in 1980, involved thousands of workers, mostly women, in a campaign that resulted in a compromise allowing the construction of no more than 12 reactors all of which must be shut down in 25 years. Analysis of the voting patterns reveals that 43% of Swedish women in contrast to 21% of Swedish men opposed the use of nuclear power.[21]

After the referendum, protest actions focused on the location of nuclear disposal sites. Birgitta Ohlsson organized a group of women and men in central Sweden called "Save the Voxna Region" that successfully challenged government-sponsored test drilling for nuclear waste disposal. Arguing that the community's water and air would be endangered by the proposed burial method, the citizens first patrolled the region and then blocked traffic to the site. Their actions aroused a massive objection to locating the site in the area and the plan was dropped. "One thinks of children and grandchildren and the earth and all kinds of other things and one must begin to struggle...," said Ohlsson.[22]

Women's concern about life-threatening nuclear technology focused on the possibility of global nuclear war and the disposal of radioactive by-products of nuclear reactors. The "Women's Culture Association," formed in 1977, initiated the formation in 1979 of the organizations of

"Women's Struggle for Peace" and "Women Against Nuclear Power" that opposed the spread of nuclear technology and the arms race. As Ulla Torpe of the Swedish Women's Leftist Association put it, "Military violence and violence against nature both have their basis in the same type of violence, in other words, technological violence." The struggle for peace, she asserted, must be accompanied by the struggle for nature and the preservation of the environment.[23] (Figure 8.3)

2. Family (intragenerational) Reproduction

Women's function as reproducers of the future labor force through unpaid labor in the home gives rise to a set of interests involving the basic needs of food, clothing, and shelter for the family.

The effects of pesticides on the quality of food initiated a nationwide protest by women. Marit Paulsson of Ytter Malung in central Sweden and a group of women invited members of the executive branch of the Swedish government to taste preserves made from raspberries sprayed with herbicides by the forest industry. The officials, who were filmed on national television, refused. Taking their preserves to spokesmen for all of Sweden's political parties, the women raised massive public opinion against the herbicides. As a result, a law was passed in 1979 prohibiting the use of herbicides in all forests (although local authorities may make exceptions).[24]

Swedish women have been instrumental in organizing neighborhood associations to improve badly-planned apartment complexes. The associations attempt to make the neighborhood environment more "living" and more suitable for children. Thus cement has been torn up and replaced with flowers, grass, and vegetable gardens, and social activities for adults and children have been promoted.[25]

While such actions strive to make homes and food healthier and safer in existing Swedish society, other actions have as their objective the ultimate transformation of society. The Swedish Women's Leftist Association devoted a double issue of its journal *Vi mänskor* in 1980 to the question of a future based on self-supporting local societies. Such alternatives must be built on women's "lost" knowledge of agricultural production and their common experience of nurture.[26]

FIG. 8.3 / FOR LIFE—FOR PEACE.' WOMEN'S PEACE RALLY IN UMEÅ, SWEDEN,
ORGANIZED BY 'WOMEN FOR PEACE,' IN 1983. (PHOTO BY INGER HARNESK,
UMEÅ.) REPRODUCED BY PERMISSION.

Exemplifying such a vision of the future, a group of forty women from
Ekerö, outside Stockholm, who met through the women's movement,
organized Tant Grön (Auntie Green), a biodynamic food cooperative
that meets the needs of its members. For these women, the cooperative
was "one step on the path towards an ecologically balanced society."
Their objective was to build alternative systems alongside the larger
system in the struggle against helplessness.[27]

In a related example, Birgit Ward started Food Front in Stockholm in
1974, giving rise to a movement that encompassed stores throughout
Sweden. The stores sold fruits, vegetables, preserves, and other biodynamic products grown and processed without the use of chemicals and
run on a collective basis.[28] Women also initiated a movement to produce
and preserve organically-grown food and to promote solidarity with the
Third World through conscientious purchase of foodstuffs. Malin
Dahlgren started MUDI-MUMS (MUDI: Food without animal industries, MUMS: Food not from multi-national companies).[29]

3. The Welfare State: Intragenerational Reproduction in the Public Sector

In Sweden's advanced welfare state some of women's traditional reproductive functions of childcare and healthcare have been transferred to the state, which in turn has employed women to carry them out. As one of Europe's most sex-segregated labor markets, jobs for Swedish women are mostly found in healthcare, social work, education, and service (e.g. cleaning and clerical). Here women have challenged the quality of the work environment offered by the state and protested the centralization and consolidation of services.[30]

For example, the introduction of video-display terminals into offices raised concern over their effects on health. In Gothenburg the trade union made an agreement with the county government that hospital and clerical workers be assigned other work during periods of pregnancy. The Swedish government asked its Workers Protection Committee (Arbetarskyddsstyrelsen) to conduct an investigation on the effects of video-display terminals on pregnancy. Trade unions representing workers in private industries also discussed the problem and some unions asked for a daily schedule of two-hour rotations on and off VDT's in order to reduce the effects of muscular and eye strain.[31]

Women also protested state trends toward centralization when a local maternity hospital was scheduled for shutdown. To avoid being sent to the regional hospital in Örebro, women in Karlskoga circulated and submitted a petition containing 14,000 signatures. Their attempt to save their services, however, was unsuccessful.[32]

4. The Liberation of Women as Reproduction Workers

While the first three categories of the politics of reproduction articulate a political struggle directed toward the interests of "others," the fourth category directs the struggle towards the self-interests of women as reproduction workers in a sex-segregated society. Here we find the equality politics of the traditional branches of the women's movement as well as the politics of women's liberation.

In the environmental professions, equality politics focuses on bringing women into male-dominated fields in the environmental sciences, such as ecology, forestry, entomology, and plant pathology. For ecologists such as Ingrid Stjernquist of Lund, who studies agroecosystems from the perspective of natural ecology, and Sif Johansson, an animal ecologist in Stockholm who entered the field because of concern over the environment, scientific ecology is a means for reversing the devaluation of both women and nature.[33]

The liberatory direction attempts to provide alternative ways of organizing production and reproduction, production and consumption, technology and nature as models for women's liberation and for an ecologically balanced society. By restructuring production on the basis of the needs of reproduction, alternatives are sought to ecologically abusive and women-oppressive private industries.

Putting this theory into practice was Algots North, Sweden's first large-scale worker-owned women's company based on a philosophy of production for use and need, not for consumerism and profit. Seamstresses from the defunct state-owned garment industry in Skellefteå joined together to produce sensible, functional work clothes, leisure clothes, and "basic" clothes of high quality. By interviewing workers and patients about their needs, the women designed new types of garments. Production was collectively organized in groups, not in assembly lines, and the products were distributed through the women's movement and the environmental movement.[34]

WOMEN AS ENVIRONMENTAL ACTIVISTS

As activists in Sweden's major environmental organizations, women have worked jointly with men to achieve environmental balance. Yet many of the activities undertaken by women through these organizations are also congruent with the foregoing "reproduction politics."

The Swedish chapter of the international organization Friends of the Earth (Jordens Vänner) was formed in 1971 by a group of four women (Erika Daléus, Birgitta McAllister, Ingrid Bengtsson, and Kerstin Frejdling) and two men (Lennart Daléus and Robert McAllister). More women than men have served on the ten-member board and women's concerns are taken very seriously. According to Erika Daléus, women have been the core of FOE. Over the years men have come from and gone back to their careers, but the women have remained. "The work is so important to us, we can't leave," she says. Women in FOE organized ecology projects supporting organic farming and taught children a global philosophy of Sweden's role in world food and clothing production and consumption.[35]

Women have also been very active in the Swedish organization, Future in Our Hands (Framtiden i Våra Händer), and have traditionally constituted more than half of the local contact persons. They have been predominant on the editorial board of the organization's magazine *New Lifestyle* oriented toward a just distribution of world resources. The organization supported women's tree planting and protection movements in Kenya and India—the "Green Belt Movement" in Kenya and the "Tree Hugging Movement" in the Indian province of Uttar Pradesh—thereby expressing support for ecological balance outside Swedish borders.[36]

In the coalition of environmental groups known as Miljöförbundet, the goal has been to have women comprise at least half of the board. But this has been difficult to achieve as women are reluctant to assume the time-consuming posts. A women's group within the organization has held discussions on the role and problems women experience working in the environmental movement.[37]

The oldest environmental group, the Swedish Conservation Association (SNF, or Svenska Naturskyddsföreningen), founded in 1909 as a professional organization, has grown from 3,000 in its early years to 80,000 or more as amateurs, including many women, have become active members. But because its regional boards, which set policy, arrange debates, and organize field excursions are composed of professionals, women work to amplify their role in the formal organizational structure. Girls and women play active roles in SNF's youth organization and youth magazine.[38]

Within the formal political structure, women's environmental concerns and activism have found expression primarily through the Center and Environmental parties.

The Swedish parliamentary system is characterized by a conglomerate of six parties arranged within two blocs: the non-socialist or "bourgeois" bloc consisting of the Moderate Party (Moderata Samlingspartiet), the Center Party (Centerpartiet), and the Liberal Party (Folkpartiet) and the socialist bloc consisting of the Social Democrats (Socialdemokratiska Arbetarepartiet), who have governed Sweden's parliament for all but seven years of the past six decades, and the Left Party Communists (Vänsterpartiet Kommunisterna). The Environmental Party (Miljöpartiet), a recent contender for parliamentary representation, is modelled after the German Green Party. In 1994, women held approximately 41 percent of all parliamentary seats, a world record.[39]

The Center Party is the traditional spokesperson for environmental issues in parliament and their party program stresses ecology: "Our work builds upon an ecological holistic view—of man's role on earth." Support for their environmental proposals is traditionally sought across bloc boundaries. On matters concerning the environment, the Center Party and the Left Party Communists are political allies. The Social Democratic Party, intimately tied to the labor movement in Sweden, aligns itself with the Moderate and Liberal Parties on environmental issues as its policy of full employment often comes into conflict with environmental concerns.[40]

Birgitta Lindblom Hambraeus, a representative of the Center Party since 1971, has introduced a wide range of motions in Parliament that would promote an ecologically balanced society. An advocate of philosopher Martin Buber's I-thou environmental ethic, Hambraeus believes that personal relations are the basis for moral decisions. Accordingly, in international relations and trade, she argues, Sweden should demand the same moral standards for preventing environmental destruction as it does internally.[41]

Her continuing concern for energy as an issue caused her to question the benevolence of nuclear power by initiating a 1973 motion in parliament concerning the environmental and security risks of nuclear development, and she became a central figure in parliament in the debates that led up to the nuclear referendum of 1980. Her goal has been to propose legislation that would help resolve energy problems without destroying nature.[42]

Inspired by Germany's Green Party, Sweden formed its own Environmental Party—the Greens in 1981. The party won numerous local offices and achieved national parliamentary representation in the elections of 1988. They lost that representation in the 1991 elections when Swedish voters opted for a conservative government, although they retained their positions in most local governments. They regained their parliamentary representation with 21 seats in the September 1994 elections as the Social Democrats obtained sufficient votes to form a minority government. In the 1994 parliament, women comprised 44 percent of the Greens, 48 percent of the Social Democrats, and 45 percent of Left Party. [43]

The Environmental Party's platform reflects many of the goals of the women's movement. It works to attain a balance with nature through the abolition of nuclear power, the development of new energy sources, the decentralization of living and working environments, the reduction of dependence on automobiles through increased public transit, the manufacture of products that satisfy basic human needs, and self-sufficient agriculture without the use of chemicals.[44]

To achieve these goals the party has set up 29 issue-oriented committees. Women are most active on those concerned with peace, housing, schools, children, medical care, agriculture, and culture. Men are dominant on those that deal with the economy, energy, science, labor, and international issues. The other committees have a more even division of representation. The party hopes to maintain paid positions for at least one man and one women on its main political committee. As the party representing the goals of the alternative movement, it began publishing its magazine, *Alternativet,* in September 1981. In realizing its objectives, the party is dependent on the work and support of local *ad hoc* groups dealing with the environment, alternatives, and women's issues.[45]

While women are active in party politics, and in 1994 held seven of 19 cabinet positions, they are less visible among the governmental administrators and bureaucrats who implement policy and who are employed in such agencies as the ministry of agriculture that supervises the National Environment Protection Board and the National Franchise Board for Environment Protection.[46]

CONCLUSION

The foregoing discussion reveals that women in the Swedish environmental movement have been most motivated by issues stemming from their identification with reproduction and motherhood. At the symbolic level, they have been inspired by cultural and historical alternatives in which women seem to have had more powerful positions in the home and production and in which nature was a freer and more powerful force, less subdued and bound by the warp of science and technology. At the political level, they have been most active in environmental issues that negatively affect the reproduction of the species and their own reproductive labor.

These actions in defense of nature must be evaluated in the context of the ultimate goals of the women's and environmental movements. The connections made so visible by their work contain an inherent contradiction. The type of modern westernized society experienced and named by women today

TABLE 3 / A TYPOLOGY OF WOMEN'S POLITICAL IDEOLOGIES IN SWEDEN

	Equality goals	Women's culture politics	Organizational strategies
A political strategy based on sexual politics and politicization of personal relationships	(1) A faction within the 'Frederika Bremer Association'	(2) Isolated women active eithin the peace and environmental movements	men and women
	(3) Factions within the 'women's liberation movement	(4) Factions within the 'women's liberation' and the women's peace movements	only women
A political strategy based on a rejection of sexual politics	(5) A faction within the Fredrika Bremer Association	(6) Most women engaged within the peace and environmental movements	men and women
	(7) The party political women's auxiliaries	(8) A faction within 'Women for Peace.' and the 'National Association of Housewives.'	only women

* The 'Fredrika Bremer Association' is the major non-socialist women's (men are included) organization devoted to equality between the sexes

as capitalist–patriarchy is the result of a historical separation between two spheres of life. Women are identified with the home, reproduction, and nature, men with public life, production, and culture. That women so consciously and dramatically have come to the defense of nature by joining the environmental movement would seem to reinforce their historical identification with nature and to work against their hopes for liberation. Similarly, the feminist movement's emphasis on women's role in the family and on women's common culture would seem to simply cement their oppression in the private sphere.[47]

The problem posed by these inherent contradictions is not only endemic to the history of feminism, but symptomatic of a deep and critical division in strategies within the women's movement today. Should women, recognizing the realities of a sex-segregated society, use women's values as the basis for

change? Or should they reject this historically constructed separation altogether and push for total equality? (Table 3.)

Strategies that would liberate both women and nature offer promise as well
as problems. Equality politics advocates the liberation of women by injecting
culture with new values as women become equals with men in the production
process. Through infiltration it is hoped that the goals of production can be
changed in directions less destructive to nature. But what will be the practical
basis for such social changes? How will changes actually be brought about by
women's infiltration into male-dominated centers of power?

Women's-culture politics uses the values and needs of reproduction as
the basis for an alternative to the double oppression of women and nature.
This strategy would reduce the work time spent in production and would
bring men into the sphere of reproduction through increasing their participation in nurturing and household work. As men learn and absorb these values, nature will also be nurtured. But how can men be convinced to use their
increased time for care of the home and family rather than for leisure?

Alternative "green" politics supports the revolutionary potential of
small-scale alternatives in work and private life that have both environmental
balance and reproductive needs as goals. Although this approach must also
confront entrenched power structures, it incorporates the values of the first
two strategies. Through experimentation with alternative modes such as producing and distributing organic food on a collective basis, developing new
energy sources that have minimal environmental impact, conservation and
recycling of energy and wastes, decentralized and communal living arrangements, neighborhood healthcare facilities, and worker-owned production
systems oriented towards human needs rather than consumerism, models for
the future can be constructed within the larger society.

As Elin Wägner stated in *Peace with the Earth*: "Against the ideals of the
day—mechanization, specialization, and speed—we consciously put up the
ideals we think will be tomorrow's—self-activity, diversity, and patience." A
new way of life thus germinates in the womb of the old.[48]

9

THE

ECOLOGICAL

SELF

WOMEN AND THE

ENVIRONMENT IN

AUSTRALIA

"Ecofeminism is the third wave of the feminist revolution. It says that the feminine values of non-violence, cooperation, and nurturing will help to connect us with nature and prevent 'ecocatastrophe.'" So wrote essayist Virginia Westbury in the May 1991 Australian edition of the fashion magazine *Elle*. Ecofeminism in Australia, she asserts, is widespread, multifaceted, and controversial. It concerns both saving the earth and making life better for women.[1]

Ecofeminist Freya Mathews holds that both nature and individuals comprise interrelated communities of ecological selves. The idea of nature as an ecological self causes us to act on behalf of other creatures and the whole of creation. Nature is like a community of interconnected individuals. Just as a human community is compassionate and caring, so Nature deserves human care and should not be abused. Our human capacity for caregiving forms the ground for defending nature. Ecofeminism, which is based on interconnectedness and compassion, deepens the idea of the cosmos as an ecological self deserving of moral consideration. An ecofeminist ethic of earthcare is the outcome.[2]

In her 1991 book, *The Ecological Self*, Mathews argues that just as the individual is a self so the cosmos as a whole is a self. Through inanimate stars, rocks, and animate beings, the cosmos realizes itself. Each part of the whole matters to it; each part possesses a value. Individual selves have intrinsic value, hence a claim to moral consideration. Individual selves value themselves and are ends in themselves. So too the cosmos as a self-writ-large has intrinsic value, and human beings are morally obligated to treat it as such.[3]

From a scientific viewpoint, as well, Mathews believes, the cosmos has intrinsic value. The cosmos as a whole is a self-maintaining system, just as individuals are self-maintaining. As selves, individuals maintain their own structures and identities over time by importing energy from the environment and excreting waste. Individual selves are not merely anatomical or physiological; they are ecological entities connected to the environment. They reproduce themselves over time in particular ways through food and other forms of energy. A self's intrinsic value is a result of its ability to maintain and renew itself and its dependence on and connectedness to other selves. But all species have equal value with respect to the whole. Thus an individual whale has a greater power to maintain itself than does its food, an individual krill, but neither has higher value as a species. Species diversity is thus a requirement for the self-realization of the cosmos.[4]

From an indigenous people's point of view, Mathews argues, the cosmos also has value as a self-writ-large. Primal peoples treat the land as sacred. The earth is a source or womb of life. It is a great Mother, a body that gives rise to all life and on which life itself depends. Aboriginal communities relate to nature as if it were an ecological self that has intrinsic value. This approach likewise entails an ethic of care and compassion. Compatible with ecofeminism.[5]

In this chapter, I show how women in Australia are providing leadership in reversing ecological damage and in developing an ecofeminist ethic of earthcare. In so doing they are leading an ecological revolution to save their land. I use a model of human interactions with the environment based on the concepts of ecology, production, reproduction, and consciousness (see Table 1, introduction) and illustrate them through the Australian example.

Australia, an island continent roughly the size of the continental United States, with a population of approximately 17 million people (of which 250,000 are aboriginal), has a capitalist economy and a democratic parliamentary form of government. Its population is largely concentrated along the eastern, southeastern, and western coasts with vast stretches of desert lands in the interior. Colonized by the British beginning in 1787, Australian lands had been the home of aboriginal peoples for upwards of 40,000 years. Australia went through a long period of colonial, extractive development followed in recent decades by the growth of an industrial capitalist economy. Both types of economic transformation can be viewed as ecological revolutions attended by problems of ecological deterioration, depletion, and pollution.[6] Today Australia's own ecological problems are intimately connected to multinational capitalism, the global environmental crisis, and ecological revolution.

It is my thesis that the global ecological crisis that has become visible in the late twentieth century is the product of two contradictions. The first contradiction results from the assaults of capitalist production on ecology (see Table 1, inner sphere). Its symptoms include the greenhouse effect (from increased carbon dioxide and other greenhouse gases emitted from industry and automobiles), ozone depletion (from industrial products such as styrofoam and refrigerants that emit chloroflurocarbons), deforestation (from widespread global clearcutting of forests), pollution (from agricultural pesticides, fertilizers, industrial toxins, nuclear wastes, and particulate emissions), and species extinctions. The effects of such forms of resource depletion and pollution are circulated through the biogeochemical cycles by means of energy exchanges and, as a result, alter local ecologies such as those in Australia.[7]

The second contradiction results from the assaults of production on biological and social reproduction (see Table 1, middle sphere). One symptom is experienced in biological reproduction in the form of increased human populations in developing countries as colonized peoples are pushed onto marginal lands by an inexorably expanding global capitalist market-system. People respond by increasing their reproductive rates to provide labor and old age security, while nonhuman indigenous species respond with declining reproductive rates. In developed countries, such as Australia, where birth rates are near replacement levels, industrial toxins assault human and nonhuman reproduction through increased birth defects, miscarriages, and leukemias. A second symptom is the increased flow of industrial products into homes in the form of consumer goods that generate attendant wastes and indoor pollution, affecting the quality of daily life and resulting in increased health problems. A third symptom is manifested in social reproduction through social dislocation, crime, and the breakdown of education and community as resources are shifted away from community infrastructures and into industrial production. A fourth symptom, also within social reproduction, is the increasing inability of governments to deal with problems of resource depletion and pollution through standard regulatory and legislative methods, approaches that seem to many people to be merely bandaids covering gaping wounds between human and nonhuman nature.

These two deepening contradictions, the first between production and ecology, the second between production and reproduction, also affect the realm of human consciousness. The efficacy of the Western worldview and its basis in mechanistic science, liberalism, and individualistic (egocentric) ethics that has been dominant for the past three hundred years is undermined. Consciousness includes the ways in which humans represent the physical world to themselves through science, religion, philosophy, art, and language and the ways they translate those representations through ethical belief systems into behaviors (see Table 1, outer sphere). Australia offers examples.

An increasing awareness of the global ecological crisis as manifested by these deepening contradictions and failing confidence in the dominant western worldview has led many thinkers and activists toward a radical revisioning of all three spheres of interaction between humans and nonhuman nature—production, reproduction, and consciousness. Rethinking and restructuring these relationships in fundamental ways over the next several decades could result in a global ecological revolution to a sustainable way of life on the planet. Women are not only active participants in such a revolution but, in the view of many, are at its forefront. Australian women are leading the transformation in a multitude of ways that are helping to resolve the contradictions and to formulate new forms of consciousness about nature. Women's activism stems from two historically constructed differences from men—first, women's environmental attitudes and second, their economic and social situations. How are women leading Australia's revolution?

The first factor behind women's environmental leadership is their differing attitudes toward the environment from those of men. For example, a survey taken in Queensland shows that on a variety of environmental issues in which support by gender varied, "females appear[ed] to have greater support for every environmental and political issue covered by the survey." These issues included ending uranium mining, logging on Fraser Island, World Heritage rainforest protection, concern that the government was not doing enough to protect the environment, voting as influenced by environmental policy, and voting for Green Party candidates if available. On one issue, the construction of a space base on the Cape York peninsula, men expressed greater support than women, and on two issues (initiating oil shipping controls along the Great Barrier Reef and instituting constitutional power to protect the environment) there was no significant difference by gender. The study concluded that "Queensland females were almost twice as likely to have high environmental scores than males. This gender-based attitudinal variation is quite marked and is highly statistically significant."[8]

Nationwide, more Australian women than men belong to environmental and conservation organizations. Surveys taken at the national level of individuals under fifty years of age, indicate that women are more concerned than men about environmental issues (54 to 46 percent on pollution, 53 to 47 percent on nature conservation, and 42 percent to 29 percent on social and environmental issues), while men are more concerned about economic issues than women (61 percent to 48 percent).[9]

The second factor behind Australian women's activism is their differing economic and social situations from those of men. Women occupy different economic niches than do men, and their relationship to both society and nature reflects different experiences of nature and differing approaches to resolving environmental problems. Their work is heavily concentrated in caregiving, service, and volunteer activity. In 1991, women comprised 97 percent of all nurses, 75 percent of the health industry, 66 percent of all educators outside of universities, and 65 percent of all service industry employees. Of the unpaid workforce two-thirds was female, with women constituting 96 percent of those engaged in fulltime childcare, 70 percent of those in the home workforce, and 67 percent of all volunteers.[10]

In their 1991 report on "Women and Ecologically Sustainable Development," prepared for the Prime Minister and Cabinet in conjunction with a national task force on sustainable development, Valerie Brown and Margaret Switzer state: "The interaction between Australian women and men and their respective physical and social environments diverges sufficiently to suggest that, to an ecologist observing the human species, they would represent different habitats, and different uses of the same environmental niche."[11]

Women make up 70 percent of those with incomes below the poverty line, and these women are the first to experience the effects of environmental pollution and depletion on their lives and health. Aboriginal and Torres Strait Islander women as a group have higher levels of poverty, poorer health, and higher mortality rates than do other Australian women and men. They are also faced with deteriorating environmental conditions that undermine traditional relationships to the land and the health of their communities. Brown and Switzer conclude, "A national Ecologically Sustainable Development strategy cannot be effectively implemented without the informed participation of women. Women and men contribute to maintaining environmental, economic, and social sustainability in distinctive ways."[12]

I shall argue that, consistent with women's high levels of environmental awareness and values, their different economic and social experiences from those of men, their high representation in service and caregiving work, and Mathews' concept of an ecofeminist ethic of care and compassion, Australian women have become active, effective agents on behalf of the environment. This work has taken place at all levels of society's relationship to the environment—in production, reproduction, and environmental consciousness. Through helping to reverse the deepening contradictions between production and ecology, between production and reproduction, and by helping to craft a new ecological consciousness, Australian women are central players in bringing about an ecological revolution to save the planet. Their achievements are infused with an ethic of earthcare.

PRODUCTION

In Australia's highly agricultural, resource-extractive economy, an accumulating degradation of the land has occured over the past two centuries. Through production (extraction, processing, and marketing), animals, plants, and minerals are transformed from integral parts of ecological systems into natural resources and then into capitalist commodities. Here humans have their most immediate impact on the land, and under capitalist production, which uses resources primarily to create profits, ecological impacts are far greater than when land is used for subsistence purposes alone. Australia's extractive industries comprise mining, sheep and cattle ranching, lumbering, and intensive, irrigated agriculture. Impacts include deforestation, soil erosion, salinity buildup, pesticide and toxic pollutants, water pollution, and declining air quality.

Women have contributed to reversing these assaults of production on the land, particularly in agriculture and forestry. Christine Sharp, a "Green" appointee to Western Australia's Environmental Protection Authority, founded the Small Tree Farm in Western Australia to promote green development that would achieve a production system that works with nature, not against it. She writes,

> The majority of people today live in urban areas, or work for tertiary industry, or both. Their direct experience is removed from the produc-

tion system which is providing for their material needs....The production system needs a period of rapid change, to avert environmental catastrophe, to the point where our industry is based on an earth-care philosophy....When those who understand the fundamental necessity of earth-care join with those who grasp the essential need for production, we shall together unlock a vast creative potential for a new future of social and environmental harmony.[13]

Sharp's earthcare test for production requires that economic activity should uphold or improve biological complexity and genetic integrity; conserve energy and resources; fulfill genuine human needs; and promote self-management by those working in the production process. Production methods that fulfill these objectives include organic farming; farm forestry through shelter woodlands; permaculture and agroforestry using tree crops and fodder tree systems; the use of unemployed and volunteer workers in collective earthcare conservation works; and restructuring the timber industry as earthcare forestry through selective logging in jarrah forests, longer rotations, selective uses of timbers, and flexible, skilled sawmilling.[14]

Women have played a prominent role in the Federal government's 1990s "Decade of Landcare." In Western Australia, CREST, the Centre for Rural Environmental Studies and Technology, located in Wongan Hills, sponsors workshops for rural women who are isolated from access to technical education, but who are concerned about future impacts of soil degradation and deforestation. Beginning in the early 1990s, landcare consultants organized workshops for women living throughout the wheatbelt who either worked alone or with their husbands. The workshops were taught by and for women by such consultants and professionals as Jennie Brett, a private landcare consultant, Jenny Berry, a soils expert with the Department of Agriculture, Faye Lewis, a Department of Agriculture hydrologist, and Louise Duxbury of the Greenhouse Corps.

The overall goal of the Landcare workshops has been to balance conservation with farm production so that production could be raised while simultaneously preserving soils and vegetation. The topics covered include: 1. Whole farm planning (reading aerial maps and photographs to develop watershed perspectives). 2. Reading soil maps, testing soils, and understanding land formation history. 3. Studying water movements above and below the surface and reversing degradation through tree planting and improved groundwater pumping practices. 4. Communication and community organizing to improve women's roles in decision-making. The women who organized and participated in the workshops expressed a deep concern about the state of the environment for future generations and believed that if there were more women in decision-making roles, there would be fewer problems with soil degradation.[15]

In Victoria, Landcare was started by the Victorian labor government as a gender-neutral project headed by Marion Pinique. But women then continued to initiate and maintain high profile landcare groups. They wished to create a covenant on the land for the sake of the future, as opposed to using the land for profit. They obtained grants from the Victorian government to plant trees on degraded, eroded, salinated soil. The women formed tree groups, obtained seedlings from rural areas, nurtured and cared for them, and then replanted them in rural areas. Volunteers planted thousands of trees throughout the state. The women saw their work as a way to reverse damage from chemicals, to improve soils and yields, and to save farms. A "Women on Farms" gathering, held in Warragul, Victoria, was attended by 110 women. Yet not all women in Victoria were in support of this approach. In opposition to the environmental movement and in support of continued timber harvesting, Dominique LaFontaine organized timber workers' wives to protest cutbacks in the forest production industries.

Aboriginal women have also played an active role in saving the Australian land for their own traditional means of production. Nganyinytja, as the sole heir of her father, is the principal custodian of land at Angatja, 600 kilometers southwest of Alice Springs in the central Australian desert. Women's subsistence activities provided 80 percent of her people's daily food. Women, she says, have respect and power in the traditional tribal way of life. Her concern is to save her lands from degradation and mining. She says, "Let your heart and mind be as open as the land. The earth belongs to everyone, black and white. We all need to care for our environment with this kind of love and respect if we are to survive."[16]

Her goal, as part of the "Back to the Homelands" movement, has been to save her people and their children from the consequences for aboriginal people of the problems associated with modern living, such as loss of tradition, lack of meaningful work, and drug and alcohol abuse. In part to educate tribal members in their own traditions, she founded the "College in the Desert" at Angatja in the Musgrave Ranges. She became an ambassador for her people on behalf of traditional land rights in the federal capital in Canberra and the state capitals. With the assistance of a lawyer, she was able to win freehold title to her lands. She and other women traveled to Adelaide, the capital of South Australia, to demonstrate. They took a group of politicians to their lands to describe their problems, presenting their arguments through song and dance, painting their bodies, and tying red bands of authority into their hair.

REPRODUCTION

Women's efforts on behalf of the environment also work toward reversing the contradiction between production and reproduction. Through reproduction, human societies maintain themselves over time both biologically and socially. Through intergenerational reproduction, both human and nonhuman organisms produce offspring that must survive to reproductive age when they can reproduce the next generation. In order to do this, they must reproduce themselves intragenerationally from day to day and moment to moment by ingesting energy in the form of food and conserving energy through adequate clothing, shelter, and fuel. These two aspects of biological reproduction are augmented in human societies by two forms of social reproduction—methods of first socializing the young into becoming productive adults, and second, maintaining the social order through law and governance. In any given society, such as that in Australia, reproduction over time exists in a dialectical interaction with production. If production systems result in waste products that threaten biological reproduction and social problems that weaken the social whole, an ecological and social crisis occurs. A contradiction opens between production and reproduction. Today, a movement toward ecological sustainability, guided by an ethic of earthcare, seeks to resolve this contradiction. Australian women have been at the forefront of healing the rift by transforming all four aspects of reproduction. Following are some examples.

BIOLOGICAL REPRODUCTION

The first example is drawn from the impacts of production on intergenerational biological reproduction. The release of toxic substances from production processes threatens the reproduction of healthy life, both human and nonhuman. In Sydney, the Total Environment Centre investigates problems of toxics for human health. Kate Short works with the Centre's projects through its Toxic Chemicals Committee. She points out that women comprise 85-90 percent of the Australian Toxics Network. Humans, she argues, are part of an uncontrolled experiment on the impacts of toxics on non-tar-

get species. Pesticide and petrochemical industries are among the most capital-intensive industries in the world. Yet the effort cleanup is borne by volunteer women. "Why do women do it?" she asks. Because they bear children
and they and their children bear the consequences. Their wombs and breast
milk are contaminated with pesticides such as DDT, benzene, and dieldrin.
They are exposed to chemicals in cleansers, detergents, and polluted water.
Their homes are treated for termites, and their washing is exposed to air pollution from pesticides and crop dusting.[17]

Cancer "hot spot" clusters exist throughout Australia. Women become
active when they themselves have miscarriages or cancers and when they
bury their children from leukemia. According to Short, women from all over
Australia have fought for a clean environment—from the tobacco and fruit
growing areas of North East Victoria, from suburban Perth and Sydney, from
the central and northern coasts of New South Wales, to rural Tasmania and
northern Queensland. In Western Australia, Naomi Segal, of Householders
for Safe Pesticide Use, fought a seven-year battle against the widespread use
of chlorinated hydrocarbons, such as aldrin, dieldrin, chlordane and heptachlor, which were still being imported into Australia. Pat Jackson, a former
kangaroo shooter in Mungindi in northern New South Wales, had cancer and
her daughters were unable to conceive children. After becoming ill she began
to question the safety of the chemicals sprayed on cotton crops in her area.
Goats and trees had died, and she could smell chemicals on her skin. She had
little formal education, but learned to read Environmental Protection
Authority documents, contacted the Total Environment Centre in Sydney,
and ultimately made pesticide spraying an issue on national television, resulting in an industry audit. The story was made into a television docu-drama
entitled "Act of Necessity," released in May 1991.[18]

Grace Bartram, a champion glider pilot, journalist, and author of several books, together with Lorraine Wright, both of Coff's Harbour in northern
New South Wales, found a high level of birth defects after a child was born
in the area with a cleft palatte. They kept statistics on miscarriages and birth
defects, attributing the problems to aerial spraying of pesticides, which
Bartram knew from her experiences as a glider pilot could be distributed
through wind thermals, inversions, and air pollution. Eventually aerial spraying was halted in the area.[19]

THE REPRODUCTION OF DAILY LIFE IN THE HOME

A second area of activism concerns the impact of production on the reproduction of daily life in the home. In Australia's capitalist patriarchal society,
unpaid household labor has been estimated as constituting up to 62 percent of
the Gross Domestic Product, of which women's contribution is two-thirds.
Women make up 96 percent of fulltime home-carers. The home is a locus
through which products such as food, clothing, and fuel that are essential to
daily life enter and out of which waste products flow. Much responsibility for
the way and rate by which resources and energy are used and chemicals and
wastes are disposed of is in the hands of women. Yet women and children are
also at risk, inasmuch as no indoor air quality standards exist and household
chemicals are not regulated separately from industrial standards.[20]

Women have established environmental networks that deal with the prob-
lem of the assaults of production on the reproduction of daily life in the home.
Nationwide, over 200 local groups have formed to deal with household envi-
ronmental management. In Victoria, the group Householder's Options to
Protect the Environment (HOPE), was formed in 1989 on June 5, World
Environment Day, by Janet Mackenzie, in Mansfield, a town in northeast
Victoria. It grew out of children's play group gatherings in women's homes.
Women expressed their concerns about the environment and asked how to
change home consumption patterns and hence society. They began to substi-
tute nontoxic cleansers such as sodium bicarbonate and vinegar for commercial
cleansers. They then went on to question the role and use of garbage disposal
sites. The initial workshop in 1989 soon spawned groups all over Victoria. The
groups undertook campaigns to make information widely available on environmental problems, energy, recycling, use of paper instead of plastics, home-
made cosmetics, food purchasing, and reuse of waste materials.[21]

Another group, the Women's Home Environment Network (WHEN)
was started by Mina Sirianni, who was involved in the wider organization while
living in Vancouver. She returned to Australia from Canada, and in April of
1990 organized the first meeting of the Australian chapter of WHEN in Kew,
an eastern suburb of Melbourne. Thirty middle-class women attended. They
were concerned about garbage, consumption, and purchasing. Sirianni "found
alternative outlets with understanding storekeepers, where I could satisfy my
needs for reusing containers, reducing packaging, and purchasing environmentally safe products....Our goal of one small bin of garbage per month

[that which could not be recycled] was soon attained." The group's efforts were publicized and supported on public radio by environmental commentator David Suzuki. As a result, new satellite groups were formed. WHEN's objectives are to encourage conservation, recycling, shopping locally, buying organic food, composting and mulching, making their households toxic free, creating no garbage, protecting trees, preferring vegetarian meals, using cloth diapers, using environmentally friendly means of transportation, and protecting the rights of indigenous people. Its approach can be summed up as "Think of your home as a microcosm of the planet."[22]

In 1987, the Rural Women's Network was organized by Jenny Mitchell of Victoria's Department of Agriculture and Rural Affairs. The network joins together women in isolated rural areas to share information on a variety of domestic and farm related issues such as farm chemicals, water, pests, wastes, chicken raising, and other issues including rural domestic violence and to promote "women on farms" gatherings. In 1990, acting on the suggestion of Kay Sectches, Minister for Conservation, Forests, and Lands, the Department of Conservation and Environment of the State of Victoria began the Women's Conservation and Environment Network. It was coordinated by Mary Dykes. The purpose was to try to make the Department more responsive to women, especially in rural and forest areas.[23]

In New South Wales, State Parliamentary Leader Elisabeth Kirkby of the Australian Democrats sees the home as a nodal point in a system of inputs and outputs. Whatever is taken into the home will flow through it and back out again into the waste stream. The home is connected to and at the center of a multitude of environmental problems including the greenhouse effect, deforestation, ozone depletion, and water and air pollution. Women can help by developing green consumption habits guided by a list of do's and don'ts regarding purchasing, packaging, recycling, and disposal of food, cleaners, clothing, toiletries, and plastics; the management of energy, water, toxins, and wastes; and the use of environmentally-sound transportion methods. Although Kirkby's analysis sees the home as part of an environmental system, she does not challenge the role of production in that system, focusing instead on the responsibility of the individual consumer. "Its very easy to give up or to blame industry," she asserts. "But ultimately industry sells to the public....Change starts with the individual and at an everyday level. Women are particularly well-placed to help protect the environment because they are still the ones most responsible for the economics of the home."[24]

A critique of "green housework," however, has been made by Lesley Instone of the Royal Melbourne Institute of Technology. She analyzes green housework manuals, such as John Elkington and Julie Hailes' *Green Consumer Guide* (1989); *The Green Cleaner* by Barbara Lord, a best selling nonfiction book in 1990; *Greenhousehold Gardens*; and *A Consumer's Guide to Cleaning and Greening Actions*. Household ecology asks women to do green housework. But environmental work is divided along gender lines, and women are being asked to tidy up the effects, not remove the causes, of the unecological home. Cleaning and maintenance increase for women. Most men do not participate in domestic labor. They do not wash clothes, shop, do the dishes, clean toilets, and so on.[25]

The post-World War II industrialized world saw the decline of women's work in production and the shift to consumption and the rise of suburbia and household work. Instone observes that women are now expected to become green consumers, to take care of the environment, and to please the family. The woman shopper must read all the labels and evaluate their claims as to shades of greenness. But it is men as producers who are structuring and controlling consumption. Single mothers and lower-class and full-time working women have no time to be green cleaners. Moreover, green products are more expensive. The middle-class housewife is the target of the new green-clean industry. Yet the home is not the major source of pollution. From the perspective of gender roles and the historical trend to "more work for mother," "greenhouse" literature individualizes, feminizes, and locates solutions to the environmental crisis in the home.

SOCIAL REPRODUCTION IN THE COMMUNITY

A third area in which women have worked to reverse the assaults of production on reproduction is in social reproduction. Reproduction of the dominant social system occurs in schools, churches, and the community, as young people are socialized into the norms of adult society and as adults continue their own educations and community involvement. In Australia, women provide 66 percent of community services and constitute 64 percent of the primary and secondary education workforce. "Social development is the accumulation of values and rules of behaviour which go to make up a culture and social system....[But] Western democratic models...tend to be characterised by expert-oriented, patriarchal, and hierarchical social systems which can generate problems as well as solutions for ecologically sustainable development."[26]

Women provide a primary vehicle for transmitting social values to the next generation. Australian women are particularly active in devising environmental curricula that challenge the dominant systems' exploitation of nature, and instead instill concern for the environment and an appreciation for nature in children both in and outside of schools. At the Centre for Environmental Studies at the University of Tasmania, Hobart, Tania Stadler coordinated a course on Landcare for primary and secondary school teachers. To teach children about soil and water conservation and land management, teachers developed local examples and materials on soil ecology, soil conservation, water, vegetation, and landcare ethics. The teachers, who came from all over the state to participate in the course, taught a variety of subjects from mathematics, science, geography, English, and art, and created projects and case studies that could be used in their own subjects to teach Landcare principles. Of the intial class of 39 secondary school teachers, 23 were women.

Nel Smit, curriculum officer of the Department of Education and the Arts in Tasmania, originated a project entitled "My Patch" for primary schools that conveys a sense of place in the world and shows how to reverse land degradation. She devised a resource booklet on trees and a calendar of agricultural festivals. The booklet, initially prepared under a 1982 "Year of the Tree" initiative for United Nations World Environment Day, led into a subsequent "Decade of the Tree" project. Her booklet included diagrams of the importance of trees, the parts of trees, activities to do on trees, such as smelling and touching them, explorations of a tree and its leaves, children's poetry about trees, and mathematical exercises concerning trees. Through these approaches, children could adopt a tree, identify with it, and, through the use of all their senses, learn to care about it and other trees. They then went on to relate their observations to other subjects, such as music. One exercise asked them to listen to the trunk of a smooth-barked tree on a windy day, to collect parts of a tree with which to make sounds, such as a gumleaf (eucalyptus) whistle, and to combine them with sound patterns friends made. Then they experimented with listening to wood from different musical instruments, such as a flute, violin, guitar, and the didgeridoo—an aboriginal instrument.[27]

The Women's Environmental Education Centre in Sydney maintains a library and resource center that includes a collection of materials on women and environmental issues; supports women's environmental actions, campaigns, and lobbying; organizes conferences and contributes speakers; and creates networks with other women and environment groups throughout the world. At the University of Sydney, the Environmental Education Project, coordinated by Sharon Beder, distributes material for use in primary and secondary schools as well as at Sydney University. At the University level, a number of courses have been initiated on the topic of women and the environment. Among them are a master's level "Seminar on Eco-Feminism" offered by Ariel Salleh at the University of New South Wales in 1984 and 1988; "Women and Environments," by Sandra Taylor, offered since 1989 through the Mawson Graduate Centre for Environmental Studies at the University of Adelaide; "Ecofeminism," by Freya Mathews at Murdoch University in 1990 and "Ecology and Feminism" at LaTrobe University beginning in 1992; courses by Denise Russell and Val Plumwood at Sydney University; and the incorporation of feminist issues into environmental education at Deakin University by Giovanna Di Chiro and Annette Greenall Gough, and at the Royal Melbourne Institute of Technology by Lesley Instone.[28]

REPRODUCTION OF LAW AND GOVERNANCE

A fourth area of reproduction is the maintenance of society through law and governance. Here women are active in a variety of political efforts that have transformed governing bodies in greener directions. In October 1989, the federal government initiated a taskforce on ecologically sustainable development. Nine committees were formed to report on possibilities for sustainability in agriculture, forestry, fisheries, mining, energy production, manufacturing, transport, energy use, and tourism.[29] A tenth report, dealing with "Women and Ecologically Sustainable Development," was prepared by Valerie Brown and Margaret Switzer for the Office of the Status of Women in the Department of the Prime Minister and Cabinet for use by women and by the other working groups. In their initial draft, Brown and Switzer observed that "the structural changes needed to make our environment a safe place for the Longfooted Potaroo are the same as those needed to make it a safe place for women. The women's debate coupled with the environment debate is the most fundamental social debate to date." (The Potoroos, or rat kangaroos, are a species native to Australia whose habitats are now protected in a few locations.)[30]

Brown and Switzer see women as at once victims, vicars, and visionaries. As victims, they are first-line sufferers from environmental degradation. As

vicars, or caretakers, they are custodians of personal environments and social
sustainability. As visionaries, they are initiators of many of the transformative visions of sustainable development. The social conditions underlying the
need for a women's agenda for change are identical to those that lead to global degradation of the environment. These include poverty and violence
toward women, issues of human fertility, and the invisibility of women's
unpaid work. The social conditions that would create security and equity for
women in political and economic development are the same as those needed
to secure sustainability of the world's natural resources.[31]

The task force recommended strategies for change in the areas of equity, security, and resource management. To achieve greater equity, they
advised the government to include the female industry sector and the household sector in national sustainability strategies; to reduce the effects of unsustainable development on women; to increase women's choices; and to give
women an equal voice in policy. To achieve greater security, measures should
be adopted to increase financial and health security for women and children;
to reduce environmental costs to the household created by toxic chemicals
and pollutants; and to monitor toxic chemicals in the home. Improvements in
resource management would include: developing sustainable resource management in the context of sustainable household management; developing
supportive policies of reentry for women and men absent from the workplace
for reasons of domestic responsibility; developing products that are energy
efficient and which could be repaired, reused, and recycled; developing "cra-
dle to grave" resource usage from industry to household; and finally, involving women in all stages of resource planning and management.

Throughout the world, Green Parties have challenged the ways in which
mainstream political parties reproduce governance. Australian women have
been leaders in recasting politics in new, green directions at all levels of government. All over the country women have been elected to local offices on
green party principles. At the state level, Green Party women have been especially active in Tasmania, where two out of five Green representatives to the
state government included Di Hollister and Christine Milne. At the federal
level of government in Canberra, Western Australia's Senator Jo Vallentine
declared herself a Green Independent in 1990. Vallentine was a Quaker for
whom nonviolence, the witnessing of human and natural atrocities, and
engaging in civil disobedience had been a way of life. The basis of the
Quaker belief-system is to effect a correspondence between a person's out-

ward visible life and her inward spiritual concerns, as illuminated by the light from within. Since the 1660s Quakers have refused to bear arms for any purpose whatsoever.[32]

Vallentine's initial actions on behalf of the environment and human lives centered on antinuclear protests. She was arrested in the United States in 1987 at the Mother's Day action at the Nevada atomic bomb test-site, an action dedicated to restoring Mother's Day to its original intention as a day of peace. She was arrested again at Pine Gap, near Alice Springs in Australia's central deserts, at a protest on behalf of aboriginal lands "desecrated by the presence of a huge United States spy base, which provided information crucial to the U. S. military in their nuclear weapons targeting programmes." Since her alliance with the Green Party in 1990, Senator Vallentine worked on behalf of the Green Party's central principles of (1) ecology, (2) grassroots democracy, (3) social justice, and (4) nonviolence.[33]

In the 1993 elections, Western Australia chose two Green Senators to replace Jo Vallentine, who stepped down. They were Senators Christabel Charmarette and Dee Margetts. The election resulted in the Green Party holding the balance of power in a Labor government. In their first major encounters with the ruling Labor Party over the passage of the budget and the Native Title Bill of 1993, the two "remained true to the underlying principles of social justice, environment, peace and disarmament or participatory democracy." Their actions in opposing the Labor-backed bill on aboriginal land titles, on the grounds that it did not go far enough in support of aboriginal peoples, threatened to bring down the government. In tense negotiations between the Labor Party, the Democrats, and the Greens, the bill was finally amended in ways that made it possible for the Greens to support it, averting a federal disaster. The two senators also refused to make cross-issue trades with the other parties just to save a wetland or create a national park. Instead they promoted environmental and social justice issues within the federal budget negotiations and put pressure on environment minister Ros Kelly to protect ecologically-sensitive areas. Among the issues they addressed were protecting old-growth forests, reducing woodchip licenses, protecting threatened areas such as the Ningaloo Reef in Western Australia, supporting a "right to know" bill that would require industries to inform communities of the chemicals they use and their risks, reinforcing Landcare programs that deal with tree planting, bush conservation, and sustainable agriculture, and promoting an Ecological Cities Program.[34]

Green women in Australia are part of "a powerful and singular branch of the feminist movement, growing within and alongside civil rights, justice, and race agendas," sums up John Vidal in Melbourne's venerable newspaper, *The Age*. "Environmentalism is being driven inexorably to a new agenda that at root owes much to feminism."[35]

CONSCIOUSNESS

In moving toward a sustainable society that resolves the contradictions between ecology and production and between production and reproduction, a new consciousness about humanity's relations with nonhuman nature is vital. An earthcare ethic can guide policymaking as well as day-to-day decisions concerning future development. An ecofeminist consciousness that contributes to that emerging ethic has been a key contribution of Australian women. Many academic and activist women, as well as those who combine the two, consider themselves to be ecofeminists or are engaged with issues concerning women and nature. They have developed a body of ideas that overlap, yet also diverge from each other in significant ways.

Environmental planner and Green activist Janis Birkeland confronts the issue of essentialism in the woman–nature connection, i.e., the idea that women have inherent unchanging biological characteristics that make them closer to nature than men. Instead, she argues it is patriarchal theories that are essentialist because mainstream approaches such as economics are founded on an essentialist concept of "rational man." She attributes the very concept of essence—an intrinsic characteristic which makes something what it is—to patriarchal thinking. The idea that women are closer to nature than men is a construct of culture and not a result of differences in genes, hormones, or essences. Both men and women can alter their behaviors, power structures, and value systems, taking on characteristics that a given culture associates with the opposite sex. Women are capable of adopting cultural characteristics, such as aggressiveness or rationality, traditionally associated with masculinity, and men can adopt characteristics traditionally associated with femininity, such as gentleness or emotionality. But ecofeminism calls for moving beyond power and domination by delinking power from masculinity and redesigning society on feminist principles. "Men," she says, "can subscribe to ecofeminism and, in fact, their cooperation is necesssary if we are to save the planet."[36]

Philosopher and forest activist Val Plumwood proposes a "critical ecological feminism" that transcends such entrenched problems as nature/culture dualism and forms a third wave of feminism through its connection to nature. She rejects dualisms and forms of domination associated with the "instrumentaliz-ing self," drawing instead on the "relational self." The "instrumentalizing self " is the self of the master colonizer that defines "the other" (woman, nature, and indigenous peoples) as an alien object to be dominated. The "relational self " is an ecological self, a self-in-relation to others who are both different from our-selves and with whom we coexist in mutual dependency. Ecofeminism con-tributes to an understanding of the ecological self through considerations of relations and differences that break down the dualisms of nature/culture and self/other to allow for care, friendship, and respect for nature.[37]

For Plumwood, caring relationships are one aspect of the ecological self. As humans, we can care for and have benevolent feelings for individuals who are different from ourselves, respect their differences, and enter into friend-ships with them. These "others" may be people of different races, sexes, or bodily abilities, or they may be plumwood trees, lyre birds, or wombats. We may be dependent on them for emotional fulfillment and they in turn on us, or we may empathize with them, enjoy mutual friendships, or take pleasure in promoting their own good for their own sake. But we must also recognize that this good may be our own conception, not theirs, and that these others, including the "earth other," are agents in themselves whose actions may limit our own.[38]

Plumwood argues that a relational account of the ecological self avoids the problem of total merging and identification with "the other" that is found in deep ecology. Deep ecology, a term introduced by Norwegian philosopher Arne Naess in 1973, holds that reform environmentalism through regulation and legislation is insufficient to resolve the ecological crisis; instead a trans-formation in the funadmental assumptions of Western metaphysics, psy-chology, and ethics is needed. In the self-realization approach of the deep ecologist, the self identifies as much as possible with the rain forest or the wilderness, which then becomes part of the self. But the rain forest may include coke bottles, plastic containers, and other human artifacts, along with bower birds, pitas, and goanas. In total merging, difference is denied, and self-identity is lost in altruism. The "deep-ecological self," says Plumwood, is too powerful, too oceanic, and too embracing to be viable, inasmuch as it denies both difference and individual identity. The human self does not have to merge with or identify with the cosmic self or assume the interests of the cosmos in order to care for nature and respect it.[39]

Plumwood's critical ecological feminism is an integrative project that draws on women's experiences in creating sustainable ways of living with nature. Because of women's historical positioning within the sphere of nature, women are in an especially powerful position to question and transcend dualism. Women's tasks, skills, and knowledge cannot just be dismissed as powerless; they have real value and significance for an ecological way of life.[40]

But critical ecological feminism does not assume that nature is necessarily a sphere of harmony and peace with which women can never be in conflict or manipulate to their own advantage. Nor does it raise feminism or woman-centered culture to the forefront as a way of moving beyond dualism. Rather, it redefines reproduction as involving powerful forms of creativity and knowledge that are positioned in alliance with nature rather than against it.[41]

In addition to differences from others, Plumwood's "ecological self" also recognizes continuities. Human identity is continuous with nature, not totally alien to it. Other animals, such as dolphins, wallabies, and crocodiles, along with humans of other races, share characteristics with us, such as needs for food, shelter, space, and freedom to move about, and they have abilities to feel pain and to suffer. Plants of the Western Australian jarrah forests and the spinifex grasses of the central deserts require light, air, and space as do humans, but have different needs for chemicals such as carbon dioxide and nitrogen in order to remain healthy. For Plumwood, therefore, the recognition of both difference and continuity between people and nature and between self and other helps to break down the logic of dualism at the root of the Western culture/nature split and to build a new critical ecofeminist philosophy based on relations and the ecological self.

Ecofeminist consciousness has been further developed in its political aspects by "green" theorist/activists Robyn Eckersley and Ariel Salleh. Eckersley's specific concern is to place women's struggles in the context of a wider political framework of social movements that nest within an ecological approach to emancipation. For Eckersley, ecofeminism is one of several varieties of ecocentrism—the idea of valuing "not just individual living organisms, but also ecological entities at different levels of aggregation, such as populations, species, ecosystems, and the ecosphere (or Gaia)."[42] Because ecofeminism assumes an ecocentric approach, it embodies a green, political value-system from which most new socio-ecological movements, such as ecomarxism, ecosocialism, and ecoanarchism, fall short. It therefore provides both values and visions for a new society that could result in greater ecological and social security for human and nonhuman life.

According to Eckersley, ecofeminism shares with intrinsic value theory and transpersonal ecology an ecocentric approach to the placing of humans within rather than above or outside of nature. Intrinsic value theory places value on all entities that are self-renewing (autopoietic), from individual organisms to the ecosphere itself. Transpersonal ecology views the cosmos as an expanded self that includes other organisms, species, and the ecosystem.[43] Although intrinsic value theory potentially treats women as self-renewing, valued beings and transpersonal ecology subsumes them under the larger cosmic self (an outside-in approach), ecofeminism differs from these theories by starting from women's unique physically and culturally-based experiences and working outward to a wider sense of self (an inside-out approach).[44]

While Eckersley points out the compatibility between ecofeminism and the transpersonal version of deep ecology, sociologist Ariel Salleh has been prominent in differentiating the two approaches on gendered terms. Salleh's now famous 1984 article "Deeper than Deep Ecology, the Eco-Feminist Connection," is a critique of Arne Naess's 1973 and Bill Devall's 1980 papers outlining the assumptions of the deep, long-range ecology movement. She argues that deep ecologists failed to show how the master–slave relationship, which characterizes human anthropocentrism and chauvinism toward nonhuman nature, is also replicated in the domination of women by men and in the treatment of both nature and women as commodities in class society. Salleh has continued to develop her critique of the masculinist assumptions that so far have framed deep ecology, while also holding to the importance and appropriateness of deep ecology as a new philosophy of nature.[45]

Salleh situates ecofeminism within a transformative politics that criticizes capitalist patriarchy and sees class, race, and gender as interlocking components of contemporary society that need to be transcended. Ecofeminism has three overlapping objectives that must be pursued through a zig-zag dialectical approach—a feminist objective of increasing women's political voice, an ecofeminist project of dismantling the patriarchal structures of men's historical relation to nature, and an ecological goal of incorporating women's ways of living with respect to nature into society.[46] In both the First and Third Worlds, women's labor provides the largely invisible social infrastructure that mediates between nature and men's economic production. Women grow and prepare food, build and tend homes, craft clothing, and reproduce the young who provide the next generation's labor force. For Salleh, the deep ecological method by which many middle-class men in the North reconnect to nature via meditation and backpacking contrasts sharply with the "hands-on involvement of the African subsistence farmer who tends her field with an astonishing knowledge of seeds, water habits, and insect catalysts—and whose land is the continuing staff of the children she has born out of her body." Women's work in reciprocity with nature provides a more appropriate model for ways of relating to nature than do some manifestations of deep ecology.[47]

Philosopher Patsy Hallen presents a comprehensive vision for a new worldview with ecofeminism, feminist science, and process philosophy as its core components. Eschewing essentialism (the view that women have different essential "natures" than men) for existentialism (the idea that existence precedes essence), Hallen argues that women can reclaim their historical past without being chained to it and can choose their historical future. Cognisant that women have been stereotyped as nurturers and caregivers, Hallen locates the roots of this stereotype in society, not in anatomy. Because of the way history has developed, women have had more experience than men with nurturing and caring. But this history and socialization places women in a strategically important position to develop a desperately needed ethic of earthcare.[48]

Like deep ecologists who have drawn on past thinkers who represent alternatives to reform environmentalism, Hallen brings together women who exemplify alternative scientific and philosophical traditions. Thus feminist science, as defined by Hillary Rose, unites hand, brain, and heart, emphasizing holism, harmony, and complexity as opposed to reductionism, domination, and linearity. Feminist biology, as proposed by Evelyn Fox Keller and practiced by Barbara McClintock, is based on a "feeling for nature" as a self-generating, complex, and resourceful process, not nature as a passive, simple, useful resource. The former set of assumptions also characteristize ecology, the scientific study of the earth's household, as pursued by Rachel Carson. Thus feminist science and ecology are not only philosophically compatible, they need each other. Moreover, they can be combined with an ethic of care, such as that proposed by Nel Noddings, that is grounded in receptivity, relatedness, and responsiveness, rather than the abstract principles of rights and justice. When these ideas and approaches are synthesized and applied to concrete situations, such as saving Australia's ancient forests, an ecofeminist ethic of earthcare results.[49]

Hallen sees ecofeminism as a broad, diverse, worldwide movement, dedicated to preventing "further deterioration of both women's condition and that of nonhuman nature." She summarizes the movement as having generated a number of unique ecofeminist approaches, bringing together women and men who offer a variety of ideas and strategies:[50]

•Liberal ecofeminists who seek reform from within existing political and economic structures;

• Radical ecofeminists who wish to dismantle those very structures through direct action;

• Cultural ecofeminists who focus on the cultural manifestations of the woman–nature connection, earth-based spirituality, goddess religions, and witchcraft;

• Social ecofeminists who build on the social ecology movement of the American anarchist philosopher Murray Bookchin in an attempt to restructure hierarchical society into egalitarian, decentralised, bioregional communities;

• Socialist ecofeminists who draw on neo-Marxist philosophies to focus on the relationship between production and reproduction and on women's work in the continued biological and social reproduction of life on Earth;

• Ecological ecofeminists who strive to show the respects in which ecofeminism and the science of ecology (specifically ecosystem ecology) share vital similarities;

• Deep-ecological ecofeminists who draw on the work of the Norwegian philosopher Arne Naess and strive to dismantle both anthropocentrism (human-centeredness) and androcentrism (male-centeredness);

• Critical or transformative ecofeminists who wish to transform the very categories of masculine and feminine and the divisive nature of dualistic rationality;

• Aboriginal or native ecofeminists who live close to nature, nurturing sacred lands and reconsecrating degraded spaces;

• Ecofeminists of the Third World who criticize maldevelopment in the First World and show us how women of color may be in a privileged position because their minds are not yet colonised and because they do not profit from the oppression of others.

Through the collective work of theorists such as Mathews, Birkeland,

Plumwood, Eckersley, Salleh, and Hallen, ecofeminism has emerged as a new consciousness about nature. When their own activism is combined with that of women engaged in the day-to-day struggles of resolving the contradictions between ecology and production and between production and reproduction, Australian women can indeed be seen as the vanguard third wave of the feminist revolution.

CONCLUSION

PARTNERSHIP

ETHICS

EARTHCARE FOR A
NEW MILLENNIUM

The women's tent at the 1992 Earth Summit in Rio de Janeiro bustled with activity. Stands of colorful scarves and saris from India, intricately decorated bowls and wooden utensils from the Pacific islands, and woven bags from Africa lined the tent's entryway. Tables of literature on population, women's rights, forest restoration, agriculture, and water purification surrounded the huge central amphitheatre, its rows of chairs occupied by hundreds of brightly dressed women from all over the world. A microcosm of the world's women, their collective problems, achievements, and energy, the tent was christened Planeta Fêmea (the female planet) by the Brazilian Women's Coalition. It had organized the women's portion of the Global Forum—the NGO (non-governmental organizations) conference running parallel to the Earth Summit. Tape-recorders, translation headsets, and microphones hummed with the sounds of human voices emmanating from the speakers' table in front. The speakers' words, processed into many languages and common understandings, were finally interpreted by those eagerly listening to the reading of the final women's documents arrived at after months of preparatory conferences and two hot, exciting weeks of negotiations in Rio.[1]

Planeta Fêmea, a remarkable event by one of the most diverse groups of women yet assembled on a global scale, put forward the political dimensions needed for a new partnership ethic of earthcare. The need for a new ethic had been building out of the experiences of women in Third World

FIG. 10.1 / EARTH SUMMIT MARCH. WOMEN JOIN A MARCH DURING THE EARTH
SUMMIT, JUNE 10, 1992, TO PROTEST THE DEPLORABLE LIVING CONDITIONS
SUFFERED BY MUCH OF THE BRAZILIAN POPULATION. (PHOTO BY NANDO
NEVED, IMAGENS DA TERRA, IMPACT VISUALS)

countries for over a decade through the recognition that women and nature
together bore the brunt of malconceived development programs. Women all
over the globe in both the North and the South began to insist that women's
issues and environmental issues be addressed in the same context. Allowed to
attend development conferences, but not involved in policy formation and
planning, women saw vital questions affecting their livelihoods, resources, and
security ignored and neglected. Realizing that women's concerns would not be
a part of the preparation for the Earth Summit unless they themselves seized
the initiative, they drew on their experiences, history, and political skills to
place their issues on the agenda. But while they succeeded in many of their
aspirations for inclusion in the process and many of their demands appear in
the resulting documents, concrete results remain as yet elusive and difficult to
evaluate. Hoped-for outcomes have yet to be realized. (Figure 10.1)

Planeta Fêmea was the culmination of more than a decade of advancement on the roles of women in environment and development. While women
had barely been acknowledged in development programs in the 1960s, their

contributions to agriculture in Third World households gained recognition as part of a Women in Development (WID) approach in the 1970s.[2] The United Nations Decade on Women, which concluded with a 1985 conference in Nairobi, brought women into development through access to education, resources, and grants that would help to eliminate poverty. As development agencies began to incorporate gender analysis into their programs in the late 1980s, women's concerns were added onto mainstream agency approaches in a shift to Gender and Development (GAD). An explicit environmental strand in development, Women, Environment, and Development (WED) gradually emerged from the United Nations Conference on the Human Environment in Stockholm in 1972 and within the subsequent United Nations Environmental Program (UNEP). After the completion of the 1987 United Nations' report, *Our Common Future*, chaired by Norwegian Prime Minister Gro Harlem Brundtland, and in preparation for the 1992 Earth Summit in Rio de Janeiro, the emphasis changed to sustainable development, or "development that meets the needs of the present without compromising the ability of future generations to meet their needs."[3]

In order to present the policy recommendations of women at the Earth Summit, two back-to-back conferences were held in Miami Florida in November 1991. The first, the Global Assembly of Women and the Environment—Partners in Life, presented environmental case studies of the ways in which women throughout the world were managing and conserving resources to achieve sustainability. The second, the World Women's Congress for a Healthy Planet, attended by 1500 women from 83 countries, presented case studies of the impacts of past development projects on women and the environment to an international tribunal of female judges. Through an outstanding exercise in cooperation and consensus, the conference formulated the Women's Action Agenda 21 (an agenda for the twenty-first century), to be brought to the Earth Summit.[4]

The Planeta Fêmea conference, organized in cooperation with the Women's Environment and Development Organization (WEDO) in New York City, co-chaired by former Congresswoman Bella Abzug, was attended by representatives from women's and environment organizations from all over the world, as well as a constant stream of well-known female heads of state and local governments. After examining and debating the themes of the Miami Women's Action Agenda 21, the women's tent adopted the "Global Women's Treaty for NGOs Seeking a Just and Healthy Planet," which was incorporated into the Global Forum's final NGO treaty.

At the official Earth Summit held simultaneouly in Rio Centro, the second document to emerge from the preparatory process was also adopted. "The Global Action for Women Towards Sustainable and Equitable Development," was included as Chapter 24 of UNCED's final document, *Agenda 21* (the 500 page agenda for the twenty-first century ratified at the Earth Summit). Moreover, women's interests were part of the Rio Declaration, the Earth Summit's 27 point proclamation replacing the intended Earth Charter that was to have enunciated far-reaching ethical principles on human–human and human–environment relations. Item 20 of the Rio Declaration stated that "women have a vital role in environmental management and development. Their full participation is therefore essential to achieve sustainable development."[5]

A prominent plank in the Miami Women's Action Agenda, to which a session was devoted at Planeta Fêmea, was the "Code of Environmental Ethics and Accountability." The code asserted that "the women's global environmental model is cooperative rather than competitive, values women's roles, work, and participation, and acknowledges the responsibility that accompanies power and is owed to future generations." Drawing on the work of women economists, such as Marilyn Waring's *If Women Counted*, it made a number of specific recommendations for economic and ethical accountability, such as including the full value of women's labor, the value of environmental resources and pollution, and the intrinsic value of biodiversity in national accounting systems and international trade.[6]

The women's "Code of Environmental Ethics and Accountability" exemplifies the first prong of what I have called a partnership ethic of earthcare; the second is the autonomy of nature itself. Partnership ethics differs from the three major forms of environmental ethics that currently dominate human–environment relations—egocentric, homocentric, and ecocentric. These three forms of environmental ethics can be exemplified by three major interests represented at the Earth Summit—GATT, the General Agreement on Tariffs and Trade; UNCED, the United Nations Commission on Environment and Development; and many environmental organizations attending the Global Forum. I shall first illustrate the assumptions of egocentric, homocentric, and ecocentric ethics and then show how a new transcendent ethic of earthcare emerges out of the women's "Code of Environmental Ethics and Accountability."[7]

The Uruguay round of GATT, which began in 1986 and by 1995 was concluded and had been ratified, assumes a free market model of world trade and an egocentric ethic. Based on the idea of trickle-down economic benefits, an egocentric ethic is the idea that what is good for the individual, or the corporation acting as an individual, is good for society as a whole. Nature comprises resources that can be turned into commodities for trade. It consists of free goods from an inexhaustible tap whose wastes go into an inexhaustible sink. Following the model of a factory, nature is conceptualized as a dead machine, isolated from its environment, whose parts are manipulated for assembly line production. Resource depletion (the tap) and environmental pollution (the sink) are not part of the profit–loss accounts, hence there is no accountibility to or for nature. Because the individual, or individual corporation, is free to profit, there are no ethical restraints on nature's "free" goods or on free trade. The result is the Hobbesian Good Society and an egocentric ethic.[8]

GATT's egocentric ethic, like that of NAFTA (the North American Free Trade Agreement), eliminates barriers to trade and with it environmental and consumer-safety measures, despite the possibility of environmental side-agreements. For example, in 1990, the United States, in response to a consumer boycott of tuna caught in drift nets that trapped and killed dolphins, enacted an embargo on Mexican tuna. Mexico protested and a GATT review panel ruled that no country can restrict imports on the basis of methods of production, essentially invalidating a U.S. law protecting dolphins (the Marine Mammal Protection Act).[9] GATT harmonizes environmental and consumer safety standards to the lowest common denominator worldwide. It increases corporate control and decreases local control. Communities and resources are forced to comply with the demands of the global market. This approach essentially removes control from local communities, homelands, and indigenous and tribal peoples over their own resources. In addition, tropical and temperate old-growth forests suffer along with marine mammals and other components of local ecosystems. GATT further externalizes environmental costs and penalizes sustainable technologies that attempt to internalize costs.

GATT's egocentric ethic promotes Trans-National Corporations (TNCs) and limits democracy in these industries. The successful completion of GATT's Uruguay Round is the dream of the self-made man, the darling of Reagan–Bush–Thatcher economics, and the ethic of capitalist patriarchy. The Women's NGO treaty, adopted by the Global Forum, contains an indictment of GATT as a major cause of environmental degradation.[10]

In contrast to GATT's egocentric ethic, the ethic of UNCED's sustainable development program is a homocentric ethic. It is a utilitarian ethic based on the precept of the greatest good for the greatest number of people. Developed by Jeremy Bentham and John Stuart Mill in the nineteenth century, utilitarian ethics became the conservation ethic of Theodore Roosevelt and Gifford Pinchot during the Progressive Era in the early twentieth century with the addition of the phrase "for the longest time." The idea of "the greatest good for the greatest number for the longest time," is a public-interest, social-interest ethic that considers conservation of natural resources to be consistent with the needs and interests of the majority over those of the individual. In Bentham and Mill's formulations it promotes the general good, the greatest happiness for the greatest number, and freedom from pain and suffering. In its purest form, it is the ethic of federal and state agencies, acting free of political forces and private lobbyists on behalf of the people for the common good. The utilitarian calculus of benefits and costs, rather than the bottom line of profits, guides the ethical choices made. In reality, however, homocentric ethics are always in conflict with the pressures of the egocentric ethic from the influence of private interests and lobbyists on government officials and the confluence of state/monopoly capitalist interests. Conflicts of interest therefore develop, one example of which is the ethics of GATT versus the ethics of UNCED.

For the homocentric ethic of UNCED, as for the egocentric ethic of GATT, nature is viewed primarily as a resource for humans and a source of commodities. But in contrast to GATT, the United Nations is dedicated to promoting the general good of all nations and all peoples in the world community. Its policies reflect the principle of the greatest good for the greatest number. Like the Progressive Era's conservation ethic, UNCED's sustainable development ethic adds the principle of the longest time. Sustainable development is development that fulfills the needs of the present generation without compromising the needs of future generations. This principle brings future generations into the accountability calculus. The Earth Summit's goal is to promote greater democracy for more people for a longer time by developing and conserving resources sustainably.[11]

Many (but not all) environmentalists attending the Earth Summit, subscribed to the assumptions of a third ethic—ecocentrism. Developed by ecologist Aldo Leopold, who formulated the land ethic in the 1940s, and elaborated as ecocentric (and biocentric) ethics by environmental philosophers over the past three decades, ecocentrism includes the entire biotic and abiotic world. Leopold's land ethic expanded the human community to include "soils, waters, plants, animals, or collectively the land." "A thing is right," Leopold said, "when it tends to preserve the integrity, beauty, and stability of

FIG. 10.2 / SAVE THE RAINFOREST ACTIVISTS.

Rainforest Action Network activists picket the Greater Los Angeles Auto Show while a giant banner is unfurled protesting Mitsubishi Corporation's international logging operations. One of the two climbers hanging the banner can be seen to the right and above the banner. (Photo by Robin Doyno, Impact Visuals)

the biotic community. It is wrong when it tends otherwise." Ecocentrism, as elaborated in the 1970s and 1980s, went a step further to assert that all things have intrinsic worth—value in and of themselves—not just instrumental or utilitarian value. Because biota have evolved over millennia, all organisms have a right to exist and should be preserved for future generations. Biodiversity is necessary not only for utilitarian and humanitarian reasons (for maintaining the present and future health of the entire biosphere, for enhancing the quality of life, and for aesthetic enjoyment), but for its own sake. Ecocentrism expands the good of the human community to embrace and include within it the good of the biotic community. From an ecocentric point of view, accountability must include the rights of all other organisms, such as those in a rainforest, to continue to exist.[12] (Figure 10.2)

Ethical dilemmas occur when real world situations produce conflicts among the three forms of ethics. Acting on the basis of GATT's egocentric ethic, with the goal of maximizing profits through free trade in natural resources, transnational corporations harvest rainforests for timbers and turn cutover areas into range lands for grazing cattle. Acting on the basis of eco-centric ethics, with the goal of saving rainforests and endangered species, environmentalists engineer debt-for-nature swaps that preserve and value whole ecosystems. Both ethics, however, can negatively affect communities of indigenous peoples by forcing them out of long-inhabited areas onto mar-ginal lands, where they increase their populations to obtain the labor to sur-vive, or migrate to cities where they end up jobless and homeless. In this example, the social-interest ethic of these communities to fulfill their basic needs conflicts with the egocentric ethic of transnational corporations and the ecocentric ethic of nature preservationists. From one point of view nature is victimized at the expense of people, from another people are victimized at the expense of nature.[13]

The three dominant forms of environmental ethics all have conceptual and practical shortcomings. Egocentric ethics are criticized for privileging the few at the expense of the many (narcissistic, cut-throat individualism), homocentric ethics for privileging majorities at the expense of minorities (tyranny of the majority, environmental racism), and ecocentric ethics for privileging the whole at the expense of the individual (holistic fascism). Egocentric and homocentric ethics are often lumped together as anthro-pocentrism (by deep ecologists, for example). But this approach masks the role of economics and particularly of capitalism, placing the onus on human hubris and domination rather than the capitalist appropriation of both nature and labor. Moreover, it fails to recognize the positive aspects of the social-jus-tice approach of homocentric ethics. On the other hand, the ecocentric approach of many environmentalists suggests the possibility of incorporat-ing the intrinsic value of nature into an emancipatory green politics.[14]

An alternative that transcends many of these problems is a partnership ethic. A partnership ethic sees the human community *and* the biotic commu-nity in a mutual relationship with each other. It states that "the greatest good for the human and the nonhuman community is to be found in their mutual, living interdependence."

A partnership ethic draws on the principles and advantages of both the homocentric social-interest ethic and the ecocentric environmental ethic, while rejecting the egocentric ethic associated with capitalist exploitation of people and nature. The term partnership avoids gendering nature as a moth-er or a goddess (sex-typing the planet), avoids endowing either males or females with a special relationship to nature or to each other (essentialism), and admits the anthropogenic, or human-generated (but not anthropocentric, or human-centered) nature of environmental ethics and metaphor. A partnership ethic of earthcare means that both women and men can enter into mutual relationships with each other and the planet independently of gender and does not hold women alone responsible for "cleaning up the mess" made by male-dominated science, technology and capitalism.

Just as egocentric ethics is grounded in the principle of self-interest, homocentric ethics in the concept of utility, and ecocentric ethics in intrinsic value, so partnership ethics is grounded in the concept of relation. A relation is a mode of connection. This connection may be between people or kin in the same family or community, between men and women, between people, other organisms, and inorganic entities, or between specific places and the rest of the earth. A relation is also a narrative; to relate is to narrate. A narrative connects people to a place, to its history, and to its multileveled meanings. It is a story that is recounted and told, in which connections are made, alliances and associations established. A partnership ethic of earthcare is an ethic of the connections between a human and a nonhuman community. The relationship is situational and contextual within the local community, but the community is also embedded in and connected to the wider earth, especially national and global economies.[15]

A partnership ethic has four precepts:

1. Equity between the human and nonhuman communities.

2. Moral consideration for humans and nonhuman nature.

3. Respect for cultural diversity and biodiversity.

4. Inclusion of women, minorities, and nonhuman nature in the code of ethical accountability.

A partnership ethic goes beyond egocentric and homocentric ethics in which the good of the human community wins out over the good of the biotic community (as in egocentric and homocentric ethics). It likewise transcends ecocentric ethics in which the good of the biotic community may take precedence over the good of the human community. In contrast to Leopold's extensionist ethic, in which the community is extended to encompass nonhuman nature, partnership ethics recognizes both continuities and differences between humans and nonhuman nature. It admits that humans are dependent on nonhuman nature and that nonhuman nature has preceded and will postdate human nature. But it also recognizes that humans now have the power, knowledge, and technology to destroy *life as we know it* today.

For millennia, Nature held the upper hand over humans. People were subordinate to nature and fatalistically accepted the hand that nature dealt. Since the seventeenth century, the balance of power has shifted and humans have gained the upper hand over Nature. We have an increasing ability to destroy nature through mechanistic science, technology, capitalism, and the Baconian hubris that the human race should have dominion over the entire universe. In the late twentieth century, however, the environmental crisis and developments in postmodern science and philosophy have called into question the efficacy of the mechanistic worldview, the idea of Enlightenment progress, and the ethics of unrestrained development as a means of dominating nature.

A partnership ethic calls for a new balance in which both humans and nonhuman nature are equal partners, neither having the upper hand, yet cooperating with each other. Both humans and nature are active agents. Both the needs of nature to continue to exist and the basic needs of human beings must be considered. As George Perkins Marsh put it in 1864, humanity should "become a co-worker with nature in the reconstruction of the damaged fabric," by restoring the waters, forests, and bogs "laid waste by human improvidence or malice." While thunderstorms, tornados, volcanos, and earthquakes represented nature's power over humanity to rearrange elementary matter, humans equally had the power "irreparably to derange the combinations of inorganic matter and of organic life, which through the night of aeons she had been proportioning and balancing...."[16] In the 1970s, Herbert Marcuse conceptualized nature an opposing partner, emphasizing the differences, as well as the continuities that people share with nature. Nature is "an ally," not mere inorganic matter,—a "life force in its own right," appearing as "subject–object." Nature as subject "may well be hostile to man, in which case the relation would be one of struggle; but the struggle may also subside and make room for peace, tranquility, fulfillment." A nonexploitative relation would be a "surrender, 'letting-be,' acceptance."[17]

A partnership ethic therefore has two components—a homocentric social-interest ethic of partnership among human groups and an ecocentric ethic of partnership with nonhuman nature. The first component, the idea of a partnership among human groups, is reflected in both the preamble to UNCED's *Agenda 21* of "a global partnership for sustainable development" and in the opening paragraph of the "Rio Declaration on Environment and Development" proclaiming that the conference met "with the goal of establishing a new and equitable global partnership through the creation of new levels of cooperation among states, key sectors of societies, and people." Article 7 of the Rio Declaration asserts that "States shall cooperate in a spirit of global partnership to conserve, protect, and restore the health of the Earth's Ecosystem." The concept of partnership is also called forth in the title of the Miami "Global Assembly of Women and the Environment—Partners in Life."[18] The document from the second Miami conference, the World Women's Congress for a Healthy Planet, exemplifies ways of actually putting the human side of the partnership into practice.

First, as they would apply to the sphere of production, the Women's Action Agenda 21 and its Code of Environmental Ethics and Accountability hold (among other things) that:

- Fulfillment of basic needs takes precedence over profit.

- Depletion and pollution are part of individual and corporate accounts and should be paid by the producer and polluter.

- Resources should be replenished, environments restored, and biodiversity maintained by all industries and businesses, especially transnational corporations.

- Air, water, and soil should be left clean and healthy.

- Corporations, institutions, organizations, states, and nations are accountable to the public.

- Environmental audits and impact assessments must be made for all proposals before funding.

Second, as they would apply to the sphere of reproduction, the Women's Action Agenda 21 and its "Code of Environmental Ethics and Accountability" hold (among other things) that:

- Voluntary birth control should be managed by women for women. Contraception should be safe and legal.

- Reproductive healthcare and family planning should be available to all women.

- Education, sex education, job education, and old age security should be available to all women.

- Men should participate in childcare.

The second component of the new partnership brings nature into an active relationship with humans and entails a new consciousness of nature as equal subject. Postmodern science reconstructs the relationship between humans and nature. While mechanistic science assumes that nature is divided into parts and that change comes from external forces (a billiard ball model), ecology emphasizes nature as continuous change and process. Chaos theory goes a step further, suggesting that the human ability to predict the outcome of those processes is limited. Disorderly order, the world represented by chaos theory, is the second component of the partnership ethic.[19]

While a certain domain of nature can be represented by linear, deterministic equations, and is therefore predictable (or can be subjected to probabilities, stochastic approximations, and complex systems analysis), a very large domain can be represented only through nonlinear equations that do not admit of solutions. The closed systems and determinism of classical physics described by Isaac Newton and Pierre Simon Laplace gives way to a postclassical physics of open complex systems and chaos theory. These theories suggest that there are limits to the knowable world. This is not the same as saying there is a non-knowable noumenal world behind the phenomena. It says there is a real, material, physical world, but a world that can never be totally known by means of mathematics. It is a world that is primarily chaotic and unpredictable and therefore cannot be totally controlled by science and technology. Science can no longer perform the god-trick—imposing the view of everything from nowhere. It cannot offer the totalizing viewpoint associated with modernism, the Enlightenment, and mechanistic science. The real world is both orderly and disorderly, predictable and unpredictable, controllable and uncontrollable, depending on context and situation.[20]

Chaos theory challenges two basic assumptions of ecology as it developed in the 1960s and 1970s and formed the basis of environmental management—the ideas of the balance of nature and the diversity–stability hypothesis. The historical concept of a balance of nature which humans could disrupt implied that people could repair damaged ecosystems with better practices. The idea that biodiversity led to ecosystem stability meant that species conservation and ecological restoration could improve ecosystem health. Yet chaos theory suggests that natural disturbances and mosaic patches that do not exhibit regular or predictable patterns are the norm rather than aberration. Moreover, the seemingly stable world that is the object of socially-constructed representations can be destabilized by human social practices (as when pesticides produce mutant insects or antibiotics produce resistant bacteria). Such theories undercut assumptions of stability at the root of Leopold's land ethic and of holism as a foundation for ecocentrism. They reinforce the idea that predictability, while still useful, is more limited than previously assumed and that nature, while a human construct and a representation, is also a real, material, autonomous agent. A postclassical, postmodern science is a science of limited knowledge, of the primacy of process over parts, and of imbedded contexts within complex, open ecological systems.[21]

This disorderly, ordered world of nonhuman nature must be acknowledged as a free autonomous actor, just as humans are free autonomous agents. But nature limits human freedom to totally dominate and control it, just as human power limits nature's and other humans' freedom. Science and technology can tell us that an event such as a hurricane, earthquake, flood, or fire is likely to happen in a certain locale, but not when it will happen. Because nature is fundamentally chaotic, it must be respected and related to as an active partner through a partnership ethic.

If we know that an earthquake in Los Angeles is likely in the next 75 years, a utilitarian, homocentric ethic would state that the government ought not to license the construction of a nuclear reactor on the faultline. But a partnership ethic would say that, we, the human community, ought to respect nature's autonomy as an actor by also limiting building and leaving open space. If we know there is a possibility of a 100 year flood on the Mississippi River, we respect human needs for navigation and power, but we also respect nature's autonomy by limiting our capacity to dam every tributary that feeds the river and build homes on every flood plain. We leave some rivers wild and free and leave some flood plains as wetlands, while using others to fulfill human needs. If we know that forest fires are likely in the Rockies, we do not build cities along forest edges. We limit the extent of development, leave open spaces, plant fire resistant vegetation, and use tile rather than shake roofs. If cutting tropical and temperate old-growth forests creates problems for both the global environment and local communities, but we cannot adequately predict the outcome or effects of those changes, we need to conduct partnership negotiations in which nonhuman nature and the people involved are equally represented.

Each of these difficult, time-consuming ethical and policy decisions will be negotiated by a human community in a particular place, but the outcome will depend on the history of people and nature in the area, the narratives they tell themselves about the land, vital human needs, past and present land-use patterns, the larger global context, and the ability or lack of it to predict nature's events. Each human community is in a changing, evolving relationship with a nonhuman community that is local, but also connected to global environmental and human patterns. Each ethical instance is historical, contextual, and situational, but located within a larger environmental and economic system.

Partnership ethics draws on feminist theory and on women's experiences of and historical connections to the environment, but it does not claim that women have a special knowledge of nature or a special ability to care for nature. Partnerships can be formed between women and women, men and men, women and men, people and nature, and North and South to solve specific problems and to work toward a socially-just, environmentally-sustainable world. Partnership ethics also draw on social and socialist ecology in making visible the connections between economic systems, people, and the environment in an effort to find new economic forms that fulfill basic needs, provide security, and enhance the quality of life without degrading the local or global environment. Finally, partnership ethics draws on work in the sciences that suggests possibilities for non-dominating relationships between humans and nonhuman nature.

As in all cases of applied ethics, the implementation of partnership ethics is not easy. Problems stem, for example, from the meaning of the term sustainable development and its relationship to power. Defined by the Brundtland Report as "development which meets the needs of the present without compromising the ability of future generations to meet their own needs" and as "meeting the basic needs of all and extending to all the opportunity to satisfy their aspirations for a better life," sustainable development can be used either to mean sustained economic growth or fulfillment of basic needs. Secondly, sustainable development cast as a partnership between North and South obscures existing, uneven power-relationships. The debt burden of Third World countries, imbalances between the G-7 and G-77 nations, the role of militarism, the export of military technology and toxic wastes, and the power of aid organizations such as the World Bank, the International Monetary Fund (IMF), and the economic power vested in TNCs and GATT are all implicated by their egocentric, self-interested ethical and power relationships.

Rather than sustainable development, which reinforces dominant approaches to development, women's environmental groups, and many other NGOs, have substituted the term "sustainable livelihood." Sustainable livelihood is a people-oriented approach that emphasizes the fulfillment of basic

needs—health, employment, and old-age security, the elimination of poverty, and women's control over their own bodies, methods of contraception,
and resources.[22]

A second potential problem for the implementation of partnership ethics
comes from relationships among women's groups themselves. Some women
of the South criticize the consumption-oriented lifestyles of many of those in
the North and of elites in the South. At the same time, they point out the burden on poor women of the South from Third World indebtedness to the
North; the effects on women's bodies of poor health and nutrition, involuntary sterilization, and "population control" programs; and the effects of environmental exposures to pesticides and toxics from cash crop production by
TNCs. From this perspective, the poor woman of the South is in a privileged
position to criticize maldevelopment and the many Northern environmental
groups who blame the environmental crisis on women's reproduction of
large numbers of children. Moreover, if a woman's body is her primary environment, the desperate need for food, water, and fuel just to stay alive would
seem to preclude the possibility of a partnership with nonhuman nature.
Women of the South focus instead on subsistence, healthcare, and security as
the primary needs. The approach of the South is not inconsistent with partnership ethics, however, and a reconciliation of North–South differences
might be achieved from other perspectives.[23]

From the perspective of socialist ecofeminism, for example, the key causes of the crisis are the twin impacts of production on ecology and of production on reproduction. Production oriented toward profit-maximization, sanctioned by the egocentric ethic, undercuts the conditions for its own perpetuation by destroying the environment from which it extracts "free" resources.
Production threatens biological reproduction by driving people onto marginal lands and into urban areas where they produce children as a labor asset to
survive, while also threatening social reproduction by creating homelessness,
poverty, crime, and political instability. Historically produced colonialism and
capitalism in First World/Third World relations results in the expansion of
profit-oriented market economies at the expense of basic-needs oriented
local/subsistence economies. An analysis of the role of colonial and capitalist
forms of production in the larger system of historically-generated power relations can illuminate common problems and suggest new strategies for change.

Thus to place the blame for the environmental crisis on the evolution of
domination and Western dualism (as do some social ecologists and social
ecofeminists) or on anthropocentrism (as do deep ecologists), or on the pri-

macy of power relations and enlightenment rationality (as do some postmodernists) is insufficient. These approaches tend to ignore or downplay the critical role played by capitalism (as well as state socialism). They can be helpful, however, when integrated into an economic analysis of the capitalist exploitation of people and nature. The emphasis placed by many environmental groups on "overpopulation" in the South and "overconsumption" in the North neglects the crucial role of production that underlies and unites both causes of degradation. Instead, reduction of production for profit and its reorientation toward fulfillment of basic needs and human security would go a long way towards creating sustainable livelihoods and stablizing populations.

A framework based on the dialectical, historical, structural, and systemic relations among the conceptual levels of ecology, production, reproduction, and consciousness can integrate these approaches into a comprehensive analysis and propose strategies for revolutionary transformation. Such strategies would analyze past and present power relations, identify the weak points in the system, and draw on the energy and vision of new social/ecology movements and NGOs to bring about a sustainable world.

If the goals of economic production were reoriented toward the reproduction of human and nonhuman life (rather than the reverse as is presently the case), many of the problems that promote exponential population growth, unlimited economic expansion, and environmental degradation would wither away. Such an ecological revolution could realize the goals of the Global Forum's Planeta Fêmea by implementing a partnership ethic of earthcare and a movement toward a sustainable world for the new millennium. Perhaps "the gaping void, chaos," Gaia, "the ancient earth-mother," and their offspring, "the world and the human race" could once again be reunited.[24]

NOTES

NOTES TO INTRODUCTION

1. Sherry Ortner, "Is Female to Male As Nature is to Culture?" in Michelle Rosaldo and Louise Lamphere, ed. *Woman, Culture, and Society* (Stanford, CA.: Stanford University Press, 1974), pp. 67–87.

NOTES TO CHAPTER 1

Revised from Carolyn Merchant, "Ecofeminism," in *Radical Ecology: The Search for a Livable World* (New York: Routledge, 1992), pp. 183–210.

1. Charlene Spretnak, *Lost Goddesses of Early Greece: A Collection of Pre-Hellenic Mythology* (Ann Arbor, MI.: Moon Books, 1978), pp. 30–31.

2. Spretnak wrote, "The seeds for this book were planted several years ago when I began reading of certain archaeological and anthropological discoveries. In the summer of 1975, I attended a weekend gathering on 'Women and Mythology' conducted by Hallie Inglehart. She showed slides of ancient goddess statues and artifacts from the Mediterranean area and the Near East...." Spretnak, *Lost Goddesses*, p. 23. In 1985, she wrote, "I remember exactly the moment when I first heard about the Gaia hypothesis. It was in 1978 that a friend told me about this scientific theory. I was quite delighted because at that time I was steeped in my research into the pre-Hellenic goddesses; the pre-Indo European religion of Europe," in Spretnak, "The Concept of Earth as Bountiful Goddess in Pre-Indo-European Cultures of Old Europe," *Conference Proceedings, National Audubon Society Expedition*

Institute, "Is the Earth a Living Organism?" held August 1985 (Sharon, CT.: Northeast Audubon Center, 1985), p. 62–61.

3. Spretnak drew on the following early works by women: Jane Ellen Harrison, *Prolegomena to the Study of Greek Religion* (Cambridge: Cambridge University Press, 1922; originally published 1903); *The Relgion of Ancient Greece* (London: Archibald Constable, 1905); *Myths of the Social Origins of Greek Religion* (Cambridge: Cambridge University Press, 1912); *Mythology* (New York: Harcourt, Brace & World/Harbinger Books, 1963; originally published 1924); Helen Diner, *Mothers and Amazons: The first Feminine History of Culture* (New York: Anchor Press/Doubleday, 1973; originally published 1929); M. Esther Harding, *Women's Mysteries, Ancient and Modern* (London: Rider, 1971; originally published 1955). Other feminists whose work in the 1970s focused on a reclaiming of ancient female earth deities included: Elizabeth Gould Davis, *The First Sex* (Baltimore: Penguin Books, 1972; originally published 1971); Adrienne Rich, *Of Woman Born* (New York: W.W. Norton, 1976); Merlin Stone, *When God Was a Woman* (New York: Harcourt, Brace, Jovanovich, 1976); Maria Gimbutas, *The Gods and Goddesses of Old Europe, 7000–3500 BC* (Berkeley, Ca.: University of California Press, 1974; second edition as *The Goddesses and Gods of Old Europe*, 1982).

4. Spretnak, *Lost Goddesses*, p. 33.

5. Charlene Spretnak, *The Spiritual Dimension of Green Politics* (Santa Fe, N.M.: Bear and Co., 1986), quotation on p. 63; Spretnak, "Our Roots and Our Flowering," in Irene Diamond and Gloria Orenstein, eds. *Reweaving the World: The Emergence of Ecofeminism* (San Francisco: Sierra Club Books, 1990), pp. 3–14, see p. 5; Spretnak, *States of Grace: The Recovery of Meaning in the Postmodern Age* (San Francisco: Harper and Row, 1991), pp. 112–13, 127–49.

6. James Lovelock, *Gaia: A New Look at Life on Earth* (New York: Oxford, 1979), quotation on p. 9; Lovelock, "Gaia as Seen Through the Atmosphere," *Atmospheric Environment*, 6 (1972): 579; Lovelock and Lynn Margulis, "Atmospheric Homeostasis by and for the Biosphere: The Gaia Hypothesis," *Tellus*, 26 (1973): 2; Lynn Margulis and Lovelock, "Biological Modulation of the Earth's Atmosphere," *Icarus*, 21 (1974): 471; Lovelock and S.R. Epton, "The Quest for Gaia," *New Scientist*, 6 (February 1975): 304; Lovelock, *The Ages of Gaia: A Biography of Our Living Earth* (New York: Bantam Books, 1988); Glennda Chui, "The Mother Earth Theory," *San Jose Mercury News*, March 8, 1988, 1C, 2C.

7. Music and poetry by Paul Winter and Kim Oler, "Missa Gaia: The Earth Mass" (Sausalito, CA.: Living Music Records, 1982); J. Donald Hughes, "Gaia: An Ancient View of Our Planet," *Environmental Review*, 6 no. 2 (1982); Norman Meyers, ed. *The Gaia Atlas of Planet Management* (New York: Doubleday Anchor, 1984); William Irwin Thompson, ed. *Gaia: A New Way of Knowing* (Great Barrington, MA.: Lindisfarne Press, 1987); Elisabet Sahtouris, *Gaia: The Human Journey from Chaos to Cosmos* (New York: Simon and Schuster Pocket Books, 1989); Michael Allaby, *A Guide to Gaia: A Survey of the New Science of Our Living Earth* (New York: Dutton, 1989); Joseph Lawrence, *Gaia: The Growth of an Idea* (New York: St. Martin's Press, 1990); Alan Miller, *Gaia Connections: An Introductin to Ecology, Ecoethics, and Economics* (Savage, MD.: Rowman & Littlefield, 1990).

8. Spretnak, "The Concept of Earth as Bountiful Goddess," p. 62–64, quote attributed to Elizabeth Dodson Gray; Val Plumwood, "Gaia and Greenhouse: How Helpful is the Use of Feminine Imagery for Nature?" in Ken Dyer and John Young, ed. *Changing Directions: The Proceedings of Ecopolitics IV* (Adelaide, Australia: Graduate Centre for Environmental Studies, University of Adelaide, 1990), pp. 622–28, quotation on p. 625.

9. Françoise d'Eaubonne, "Feminism or Death," in Elaine Marks and Isabelle de Courtivron, eds. *New French Feminisms: An Anthology* (Amherst: University of Massachusetts Press, 1980), pp. 64–67, but see especially p. 25; Françoise d'Eaubonne, *Le Féminisme ou la Mort* (Paris: Pierre Horay, 1974), pp. 213–52. For a translation see Françoise d'Eaubonne, "The Time for Ecofeminism," trans. Ruth Hottell, in Carolyn Merchant, ed. *Ecology* (Atlantic Highlands, N.J.: Humanities Press, 1994), pp. 174–97.

10. Ynestra King, "Toward an Ecological Feminism and a Feminist Ecology," in Joan Rothschild, ed., *Machina Ex Dea* (New York: Pergamon Press, 1983), pp. 118–29; Janet Biehl, "What is Social Ecofeminism?" *Green Perspectives*, 11 (October 1988).

11. Alison Jaggar, *Feminist Politics and Human Nature* (Totawa, N.J.: Roman and Allanheld, 1983); Karen Warren, "Feminism and Ecology: Making Connections," *Environmental Ethics*, vol. 9, no. 1 (1987): 3–10.

12. Karen Warren, "Toward an Ecofeminist Ethic," *Studies in the Humanities* (December 1988): 140–56, quotation on p. 151.

13. Karen Warren, "The Power and the Promise of Ecological Feminism," *Environmental Ethics*, 12, no. 2 (Summer 1990): 125–46.

14. Jaggar, *Feminist Politics and Human Nature*, pp. 27–47.

15. Simon de Beauvoir, *The Second Sex* [1949] (London: Penguin Books, 1972), pp. 95–96; Betty Friedan, *The Feminine Mystique* (New York: Dell, 1963), pp. 11–27, 326–63; Ynestra King, "Toward an Ecological Feminism and a Feminist Ecology," pp. 121–22; Rachel Carson, *Silent Spring* (Boston: Houghton and Mifflin, 1962), pp. 1–37.

16. Barbara Holzman, "Women's Role in Environmental Organizations," manuscript in possession of the author, Berkeley, CA.

17. Sherry Ortner, "Is Female to Male as Nature is to Culture," in Michelle Rosaldo and Louise Lamphere, eds., *Woman, Culture, and Society* (Stanford, CA.: Stanford University Press, 1974), pp. 67–86.

18. Stone, *When God Was a Woman;* Carolyn Merchant, *The Death of Nature: Women, Ecology, and the Scientific Revolution* (San Francisco: Harper and Row, 1980); Carolyn Merchant, "Earthcare: Women and the Environmental Movement," *Environment*, 23, no. 5 (June 1981): 6–13, 38–40 (see below, ch.7).

19. Starhawk, *The Spiral Dance: A Rebirth of the Ancient Religion of the Great Goddess* (San Francisco: Harper and Row, 1979); Carol Gilligan, *In a Different Voice: Psychological Theory and Women's Development* (Cambridge, MA.: Harvard University Press, 1982); Nel Noddings, *Caring: A Feminist Approach to Ethics and Moral Education* (Berkeley: University of California Press, 1984).

20. Ortner,"Is Female to Male as Nature is to Culture?" For a recent anthology of varieties of ecofeminism see Irene Diamond and Gloria Orenstein, eds. *Reweaving the World: The Emergence of Ecofeminism* (San Francisco: Sierra Club Books, 1990).

21. Dorothy Nelkin, "Nuclear Power as a Feminist Issue," *Environment*, vol. 23, no. 1 (1981): 14–20, 38–39.

22. Merchant, "Earthcare," quotation on p. 38.

23. Karen Stults, "Women Movers: Reflections on a Movement By Some of Its Leaders," *Everyone's Backyard*, vol. 7, no. 1 (Spring, 1989): 1; Ann Marie Capriotti–Hesketh, "Women and the Environmental Health Movement: Ecofeminism in Action," Department of Biomedical and Environmental Health Sciences, University of California, Berkeley, CA., unpublished manuscript in possession of the author.

24. Merchant, "Earthcare," p. 13.

25. Susan Prentice, "Taking Sides: What's Wrong with Ecofeminism?" *Women and Environments*, (Spring 1988): 9–10.

26. Janet Biehl, "What is Social Ecofeminism?" *Green Perspectives*, No. 11 (October 1988); 1–8, quotation on p. 7.

27. Janet Biehl, *Rethinking Ecofeminist Politics* (Boston: South End Press, 1991), pp. 1–7, 9–19.

28. Friedrich Engels, "Origin of the Family, Private Property, and the State," in *Selected Works* (New York: International Publishers, 1968), p. 455; Engels, *Dialectics of Nature*, ed. Clemens Dutt (New York: International Publishers, 1940), pp. 28–90. For another approach to a socialist ecofeminism, see Mary Mellor, *Breaking the Boundaries: Towards a Feminist Green Socialism* (London: Virago, 1992).

29. Abby Peterson, "The Gender-Sex Dimension in Swedish Politics," *Acta Sociologica*, 27, no. 1 (1984): 3–17, quotation on p. 6.

30. Carolyn Merchant, *Ecological Revolutions: Nature, Gender, and Science in New England* (Chapel Hill: University of North Carolina Press, 1989), p. 14.

31. Irene Diamond, *Fertile Ground* (Boston, MA.: Beacon, 1994), p. 56.

32. For examples see Merchant, "Earthcare," pp. 7–13, 38–40 and chapter 7, below.

33. Vandana Shiva, *Staying Alive: Women, Ecology, and Development* (London: Zed Books, 1988), p. 76. See also Maria Mies and Vandana Shiva, *Ecofeminism* (London: Zed Books, 1993).

34. Shiva, *Staying Alive*, pp. 55–77.

35. John Farrell, "Agroforestry Systems," in Miguel Altieri, *Agroecology: The Scientific Basis of Alternative Agriculture* (Berkeley: Division of Biological Control, University of California, Berkeley, 1983), pp. 77–83.

36. Wangari Maathai, *The Green Belt Movement: Sharing the Approach and the Experience* (Nairobi, Kenya: Environment Liaison Centre International, 1988), pp. 5–24, quotation on p. 5.

37. Maathai, *Green Belt Movement*, pp. 9–30. See also Lori Ann Thrupp, "Women, Wood, and Work in Kenya and Beyond," *UNASYLVA* (FAO, Journal of Forestry), (December 1984): 37–43.

38. Sithembiso Nyoni, "Women, Environment, and Development in Zimbabwe," in *Women, Environment, Development Seminar Report* (London: Women's Environmental Network, 1989), p. 25–27, quotation on p. 26.

39. Maloba, Robleto, Letelier, Castro, speaking at the conference on "The Fate and Hope of the Earth," Managua, Nicaragua, June 1989; Nyoni, "Women, Environment, and Development in Zimbabwe," pp. 23–24.

40. Chee Yoke Ling, "Women, Environment, Development: The Malaysian Experience," in Women's Environmental Network, *Women, Environment, Development Seminar Report* (London: Women's Environmental Network, 1989), pp. 23–24.

41. Jeanne Rhinelander, "Crusader in Krakow," *Worldwide News: World Women in Environment*, 8, no. 2 (March–April 1990): 1, 7; Interview with Soviet Environmentalist: Dr. Eugenia V. Afanasieva, *Worldwide News* (September–October 1989): 1, 5, quotations on p. 5.

42. "Women Meet in Moscow to Talk Environment," *Worldwide: News World Women in Environment* (November–December 1989), pp. 1–2.

43. Olga Uzhnurtsevaa speaking at the conference on "The Fate and Hope of the Earth," Managua, Nicaragua, June 1989.

NOTES TO CHAPTER 2

From: "Reinventing Eden: Western Culture as a Recovery Narrative," in William Cronon, ed. *Uncommon Ground: Toward Reinventing Nature* (New York: Norton, 1995)

1. Roland Nelson, Penobscot, as recorded by Frank Speck, "Penobscot Tales and Religious Beliefs," *Journal of American Folklore*, 48, no. 187 (January–March 1935): 1–107, on p. 75. This Corn Mother origin story is a variant on a number of eastern United States and Canadian transformative accounts, recorded from oral traditions, that attribute the origins of corn to a mythical Corn Mother who produces corn from her body, grows old, and then instructs her lover or son how to plant and tend corn. The killing of the corn mother in most of the origin stories may symbolize a transition from gathering/hunting to active corn cultivation. The snake lover may be an influence from the Christian tradition or a more universal symbol of the renewal of life (snakes shed their skins) and/or the male sexual organ. On Corn Mother origin stories, see John Witthoft, *Green Corn Ceremonialism in the Eastern Woodlands* (Ann Arbor: University of Michigan Press, 1949), pp. 77–85; Joe Nicholas, Malechite, Tobique Point, Canada, August 1910, as recorded by W.H. Mechling, *Malechite Tales*, (Ottawa: Government Printing Bureau, 1914), pp. 87–88; for the Passamaquoddy variant, see *Journal of American Folklore*, 3, (1890), p. 214; for Creek and Natchez variants, see J.R. Swanton, "Myths and Tales of the Southeastern Indians," *Bulletin of the Bureau of American Ethnology*, no. 88 (1929): 9–17; on Iroquois variants, see Jesse Cornplanter, *Legends of the Longhouse* (Philadelphia: J.B. Lippincott, 1938) and Arthur Parker, "Iroquois Use of Maize and Other Food Plants," *New York State Museum Bulletin* no. 144 (November 1, 1910): 36–9; Gudmund Hatt, "The Corn Mother in America and Indonesia" *Anthropos* 46 (1951): 853–914. Examples of corn mother origin stories from the Southwest include the Pueblo emergence from the dark interior of the earth into the light of the fourth world where Corn Mother plants Thought Woman's gift of corn. See Ramón Gutiérrez, *When Jesus Came the Corn Mothers Went Away* (Stanford, CA.: Stanford University Press), 1991. For a discussion of the relationship of the corn mother to mother earth, see Sam Gill, *Mother Earth: An American Story* (Chicago: University of Chicago Press, 1987), pp. 4, 125.

2. On Great Plains environmental histories as progressive and declensionist plots, see William Cronon, "A Place for Stories: Nature, History and Narrative," *Journal of American History*, 78 (March 1992): 1347–1376. The Indian and European origin stories can be interpreted from a variety of standpoints other than the declensionist and progressive narrative formats I have empha-

sized here (such as romance and satire). Additionally, the concepts of desert, wilderness, and garden are nuanced and elaborate motifs that change valences over time in ways I have not tried to
deal with here.

3. *Holy Bible,* King James version, Genesis, Book 1. On the comic and tragic visions of the human,
animal, vegetable, mineral, and unformed worlds see Northrup Frye, *Fables of Identity* (New
York: Harcourt Brace, 1963), pp. 19–20. In the comic state, or vision, the human world is a community, the animal world consists of domesticated flocks and birds of peace, the vegetable world
is a garden or park with trees, the mineral world is a city or temple with precious stones and star-
lit domes, and the unformed world is a river. In the tragic state or vision, the human world is an
anarchy of individuals, the animal world is filled with beasts and birds of prey (such as wolves,
vultures, and serpents), the vegetable world is a wilderness, desert, or sinister forest, the mineral
world is filled with rocks and ruins, and the unformed world is a sea or flood. The plot of the
tragedy moves from a better or comic state to a worse or tragic state; the comedy from an initial
tragic state to a comic outcome. On history as narrative, see Hayden White, *Metahistory: The
Historical Imagination in Nineteenth-Century Europe* (Baltimore, MD.: Johns Hopkins University
Press, 1973); White, *Tropics of Discourse: Essays in Cultural Criticism* (Baltimore, MD.: Johns
Hopkins University Press, 1978); White, *The Content of the Form: Narrative Discourse and
Historical Representation* (Baltimore, MD.: Johns Hopkins University Press, 1987).

4. Benjamin Franklin, "Remarks Concerning the Savages of North America," in Richard E.
Amacher, ed., *Franklin's Wit and Folly: The Bagatelles* (New Brunswick, N.J.: Rutgers
University Press, 1953), pp. 89–98. Franklin's story is probably satirical rather than literal.

5. The concept of a recovery from the original Fall appears in the early modern period. See the
Oxford English Dictionary, compact edition, vol. 2, p. 2447: The act of recovering oneself from a
mishap, mistake, fall, etc. See Bishop Edward Stillingfleet, *Origines Sacrae* (London, 1662), II, i,
sec 1.: "The conditions on which fallen man may expect a recovery." William Cowper,
Retirement (1781), 138: "To...search the themes, important above all Ourselves, and our recovery
from our fall." See also Richard Eden, *The Decades of the Newe Worlde or West India* (1555), 168:
"The recoverie of the kyngedome of Granata." The term "recovery" also embraced the idea of
regaining a "natural" position after falling and a return to health after sickness. It acquired a legal
meaning in the sense of gaining possession of property by a verdict or judgment of the court. In
common recovery, an estate was transferred from one party to another. John Cowell, *The
Interpreter* (1607), s.v. "recoverie": "A true recoverie is an actuall or reall recoverie of anything,
or the value thereof by Judgement." Another meaning was the restoration of a person or thing to
a healthy or normal condition, or a return to a higher or better state, including the reclamation of
land. Anonymous, *Captives bound in Chains...the misery of graceless Sinners, and the hope of their
recovery by Christ* (1674); Bishop Joseph Butler, *The Analogy of Religion Natural and Revealed*
(1736), II, 295: "Indeed neither Reason nor Analogy would lead us to think...that the
Interposition of Christ...would be of that Efficacy for Recovery of the World, which Scripture
teaches us it was." Joseph Gilbert, *The Christian Atonement* (1836), i, 24: "A modified system,
which shall include the provision of means for recovery from a lapsed state." James Martineau,
Essays, Reviews, and Address (1980-91), II, 310: "He is fitting to be among the prophets of recovery, who may prepare for us a more wholesome future." John Henry Newman, *Historical
Sketches* (1872-3) II, 1, iii, 121: "The special work of his reign was the recovery of the soil."

6. On the Genesis 1, or priestly version (Genesis P), composed in the fifth century B.C. versus the Genesis 2, or Yahwist version (Genesis J), composed in the ninth or tenth century B.C. and their relationships to the environmental movement, see J. Baird Callicott, "Genesis Revisisted: Muirian Musings on the Lynn White, Jr. Debate," *Environmental Review*, 14, nos. 1–2 (Spring/Summer 1990): 65–92. Callicott argues that Lynn White, Jr. mixed the two versions in his famous article "The Historical Roots of Our Ecologic Crisis," *Science* 155 (1967): 1203. On the historical traditions behind the Genesis stories, see Artur Weiser, *The Old Testament: Its Formation and Development*, trans., Dorthea M. Barton (New York: Association Press, 1961).

7. John Prest, *The Garden of Eden: The Botanic Garden and the Recreation of Paradise* (New Haven: Yale University Press, 1981), pp. 1–37; J.A. Phillips, *Eve: The History of an Idea* (San Francisco: Harper and Row, 1984), Francis Russell, *The World of Dürer* (New York, Time, 1967), pp. 83, 109.

8. "Paradise" derives from the old Persian word for "enclosure" and in Greek and Latin takes on the meaning of garden. Its meanings include heaven, a state of bliss, an enclosed garden or park, and the Garden of Eden. "Parousia" derives from the Latin *parere* meaning to produce or bring forth. The Parousia is the idea of the End of the World, expressed as the hope set forth in the New Testament that "he shall come again to judge both the quick and the dead." See A.L. Moore, *The Parousia in the New Testament* (Leiden: E.J. Brill, 1966). I thank Anthony Chennells for bringing this concept to my attention. Capitalism and Protestantism were initially mutually reinforcing in their common hope of a future golden age. But as capitalism became more materialistic and worldly it began to undercut the Church's parousia hope. Communism retained the idea of a future golden age in its concern for community and future direction (pp. 2–3). The parousia hope was a driving force behind the Church's missionary work in its early development and in the New World (p. 5). The age of glory was a gift of God; an acknowledgement of the future inbreaking of God (JHWH) into history (pp. 16, 17). "The scene of the future consumation is a radically transformed earth. The coming of this Kingdom was conceptualized as a sudden catastrophic moment, or as preceded by the Messianic kingdom, during which it was anticipated that progressive work would take place" (p. 20). "Concerning the central figure in the awaited End-drama there is considerable variation. In some visions the figure of Messiah is entirely absent. In such cases 'the kingdom was always represented as under the immediate sovereignty of God'" (p. 21). "The divine intervention in history was the manifestation of the Kingdom of God...[T]his would involve a total transformation of the present situation, hence the picture of world renewal enhanced sometimes by the idea of an entirely supernatural realm" (pp. 25–26). "The fourth Eclogue of Virgil presents the hope of a 'golden age' but in fundamental contrast to apocalyptic expectation; although it is on a cosmic scale, it is the hope of revolution from within rather than of intervention from without" (p. 28).

9. Max Oelschlaeger, *The Idea of Wilderness: From Prehistory to the Age of Ecology* (New Haven, CT.: Yale University Press, 1991), pp. 49–60.

10. Francis Bacon, "Novum Organum," in James Spedding, Robert Leslie Ellis, and Douglas Devon Heath, eds. *Works*, 14 vols. (London: Longmans Green, 1870), vol. 4, pp. 247–48, 114–15. See also Bacon's statement, "I mean (according to the practice in civil causes) in this great plea or suit granted by the divine favor and providence (whereby the human race seeks to recover its right over nature) to examine nature herself and the arts upon interrogatories." Bacon, "Preparative Towards a Natural and Experimental History," *Works*, vol. 4, p. 263. William Leiss, *The*

Domination of Nature (New York: George Braziller, 1972), pp. 48–52; Merchant, *The Death of Nature: Women, Ecology, and the Scientific Revolution*, pp. 185–86. Charles Whitney, *Francis Bacon and Modernity* (New Haven, CT.: Yale University Press, 1986), p. 25.

11. Marshall Sahlins, *Culture and Practical Reason* (Chicago: University of Chicago Press, 1976), p. 53: "The development from a Hobbesian state of nature is the origin myth of Western capitalism."

12. On the definition of natural resources, see John Yeats, *Natural History of Commerce* (London, 1870), p. 2. Thomas Hobbes, "Leviathan" (1651), in *English Works*, 11 vols (reprint edition, Aslen, W. Germany: Scientia, 1966), vol. 3, pp. 145, 158. John Locke, *Two Treatises of Government* (1690), ed. Peter Laslett (Cambridge: Cambridge University Press, 1960), Second Treatise, Chap 5, secs., 28, 32, 35, 37, 46, 48.

13. The Fall from Eden may be interpreted (as can the Corn Mother origin story, see note 1) as representing a transition from gathering/hunting to agriculture. In the Garden of Eden, Adam and Eve pick the fruits of the trees without having to labor in the earth (Genesis 1: 29–30; Genesis 2: 9). After the Fall they had to till the ground "in the sweat of thy face" and eat "the herb of the field." (Genesis 3: 18, 19, 23). In Genesis 4, Abel, "keeper of sheep," is the pastoralist, while Cain, "tiller of the ground" is the farmer. Although God accepted Abel's lamb as a first fruit, he did not accept Cain's offering. Cain's killing of Abel may represent the ascendancy of farming over pastoralism. Agriculture requires more intensive labor than either pastoralism or gathering. See Oelschlaeger, *The Idea of Wildnerness;* Callicott, "Genesis Revisited," p. 81.

14. Victor Rotenberg, "The Lapsarian Moment," mss. Hesiod, "Works and Days," in *Theogony and Works and Days*, trans. M.L. West (Oxford, N.Y.: Oxford University Press, 1988), p. 40.

15. Publius Ovid, *Metamorphoses* (written A.D. 7), trans. Rolfe Humphries (Bloomington: Indiana University Press, 1955), Bk. 1, p. 6, lines 100–11.

16. On the meanings of nature and nation and the following interpretation of Virgil, see Kenneth Olwig, *Nature's Ideological Landscape* (London: George Allen and Unwin, 1984), pp. 3–9. In the *Eclogues*, Virgil characterized the pastoral landscape as the grazing of tame animals on grassy hillsides. Human labor domesticated animals, transformed the forest into meadows, and dammed springs to form pools for watering livestock. But the shepherd was relatively passive, watching flocks while reclining in the shade of a remnant forest tree.

17. Olwig, *Nature's Ideological Landscape*, p. 6. Agriculture is initiated by Jove who "endowed that cursed thing the snake with venom and the wolf with thirst for blood." "Toil...taught men the use and method of the plough." Agricultural instruments were hammered out by the use of fire, becoming "weapons hardy rustics need ere they can plow or sow the crop to come." Virgil, *Georgics*, I, 151–52, as quoted in Olwig, *Nature's Ideological Landscape*, p. 6.

18. Olwig, *Nature's Ideological Landscape*, pp. 3–9; Virgil, *Georgics*, II (1946), 106–07; *Eclogues*, IV, 4–34. Virgil's temporal and spatial stages prefigure Frederick Jackson Turner's frontier stages and Johann Heinrich von Thünen's rings, discussed by William Cronon in the conversion of hinterland resources (first nature) into commodities (second nature) in Chicago. See William Cronon, *Nature's Metropolis: Chicago and the Great West* (New York: Norton, 1991), pp. 46–54.

19. Lucretius, *Of the Nature of Things*, trans. William Ellery Leonard (New York: E.P. Dutton, 1950), Book V, lines 922–1008. Lucretius's image of "the state of nature was strikingly similar to

that of Thomas Hobbes in *Leviathan*. Lucretius wrote that in the early days "men led a life after the roving habit of wild beasts." They chased and ate wild animals and were in turn hunted and devoured by them. In the state of nature, they "huddled in groves, and mountaincaves, and woods" without any regard for "the general good" and did not "know to use in common any customs, any laws." Just as Hobbes characterized life before civil law as "nasty, brutish, and short," so Lucretius wrote that "the clans of savage beasts" would make "sleep-time horrible for those poor wretches." Men were "snatched upon and gulped by fangs," while those who escaped "with bone and body bitten, shrieked," as the "writhing pangs took them from life." In a time before agricultural plenty, starvation was rampant as "lack of food gave o'er men's fainting limbs to dissolution." Procreation, for Lucretius, was likewise beastlike and brutal. Men took women "with impetuous fury and insatiate lust" or bribed them with berries and fruit. When finally women moved "into one dwelling place" with men "the human race began to soften," as they saw "an offspring born from out themselves." Neighbors intervened on behalf of women and children and urged compassion for the weak.

20. Lucretius, *Of the Nature of Things*, Book V, lines 1135–1185: "So next some wiser heads instructed men to found the magisterial office, and did frame codes that they might consent to follow laws."... "For humankind, o'er wearied with a life fostered by force...of its own free will yielded to laws and strictest codes." Because "each hand made ready in its wrath to take a vengeance fiercer than by man's fair laws," people voluntarily submitted to "fear of punishment."

21. Lucretius, *Of the Nature of Things*, Book VI, lines 1136–1284. "For now no longer men did mightily esteem the old Divine, the worship of the gods: the woe at hand did overmaster."

22. Lucretius, *Of the Nature of Things*, Book V, lines 811–870.

23. On Edenic imagery in American history see, R.W.B. Lewis, *The American Adam: Innocence, Tragedy, and Tradition in the Nineteenth Century* (Chicago: University of Chicago Press, 1955); David Noble, *The Eternal Adam and the New World Garden: The Central Myth in the American Novel since 1830* (New York: George Braziller, 1968); David Watt, *The Fall into Eden: Landscape and Imagination in California* (New York: Cambridge University Press, 1986); Cecelia Tichi, *New World, New Earth: Environmental Reform in American Literature from the Puritans through Whitman* (New Haven, CT.: Yale University Press, 1979).

24. Vladimir Propp, "Morphology of the Folktale," *International Journal of American Linguistics*, 24, no. 4 (October 1958), pp. 46–48. Roland Barthes, "The Struggle with the Angel," *Image, Music, Text*, trans. Stephen Heath (New York: Noonday Press, 1977), pp. 139–41.

25. Quoted in Peter N. Carroll, *Puritanism and the Wilderness, 1629–1700* (New York: Columbia University Press, 1969), pp. 13–14.

26. William Bradford, *History of Plymouth Plantation, 1620-1647*, Edited by Worthington C. Ford, 2 vols. (Boston: Published for the Massachusetts Historical Society by Houghton Mifflin Co., 1912).

27. Charles Morton, *Compendium Physicae*, from the 1697 manuscript copy, (Boston, MA.: Colonial Society of Massachusetts Publications, 1940), vol. 33, pp. xi, xxix, xxiii, xxxi; Nathaniel Ames, *An Astronomical Diary or Almanac*, (Boston: J. Draper, 1758), endpapers.

28. Robert Beverley, *The History and Present State of Virginia* (London: R. Parker, 1705), pp. 246–48.

29. Matthew Baigell, *Thomas Cole* (New York: Watson Guptill, 1981), plates 15, 16. On Cole's use of Eden as metaphor see Henry Adams, "The American Land Inspired Cole's Prescient Visions," *Smithsonian*, 25, no. 2 (May 1994): 99–107.

30. Baigell, *Thomas Cole*, plates 10, 15.

31. Ralph Waldo Emerson, "The Young American," *The Dial*, 4 (April 1844): 484–507, quotation on pp. 489, 491.

32. Leo Marx, *The Machine in the Garden: Technology and the Pastoral Ideal in America* (New York: Oxford University Press, 1964).

33. John Winthrop, "Winthrop's Conclusions for the Plantation in New England," in *Old South Leaflets* no. 50 (1629) (Boston: Directors of the Old South Work, 1897), no. 50, pp. 4–5; John Quincy Adams, *Congressional Globe*, 29, no. 1 (1846): 339–42. Thomas Hart Benton, *ibid*, pp. 917–8

34. Reverend Dwinell, quoted in John Todd, *The Sunset Land, or the Great Pacific Slope* (Boston: Lee and Shepard, 1870), p. 252; Henry Nash Smith, *Virgin Land: the American West as Symbol and Myth* (Cambridge, MA.: Harvard University Press, 1950); L. Marx, *The Machine in the Garden*.

35. Frederick Jackson Turner, "The Significance of the Frontier in American History," American Historical Association, Annual Report for the Year 1893. (Washington, D.C., 1894), 199–227.

36. Francis Paul Prucha, *The Indians in American Society* (Berkeley: University of California Press, 1985), quotations on pp. 7, 10.

37. Prucha, *Indians in American Society*, quotation on p. 12.

38. Prucha, *Indians in American Society*, pp. 14–20; Lloyd Burton, *American Indian Water Rights and the Limits of the Law* (Lawrence, KA.: University of Kansas Press, 1991), pp. 6–34; Carolyn Merchant, *Ecological Revolutions: Nature, Gender, and Science in New England* (Chapel Hill: University of North Carolina Press, 1989), chapters 2 and 3; William Cronon, *Changes in the Land: Indians, Colonists, and the Ecology of New England* (New York: Hill and Wang, 1983); Richard White, *The Roots of Dependency: Subsistence, Environment, and Social Change Among the Choctaws, Pawnees, and Navajos* (Lincoln, NB.: University of Nebraska press, 1983); "Wilderness Act," 1964.

39. Chief Luther Standing Bear, *Land of the Spotted Eagle* (Boston: Houghton Mifflin, 1933), p. xix. On the ethnocentricity of wilderness values, see J. Baird Callicott, "The Wilderness Idea Revisited: The Sustainable Development Alternative," *The Environmental Professional*, 13 (1991): 236–45.

40. Neal Salisbury, "Red Puritans: The 'Praying Indians' of Massachusetts Bay and John Eliot," *William and Mary Quarterly*, 3rd ser. 31, no. 1 (1974): 27–54; William Simmons, "Conversion From Indian to Puritan," *New England Quarterly*, 52, no. 2 (1979): 197–218.

41. Franklin, "Remarks Concerning the Savages of North America," p. 91.

42. On images and metaphors of nature as female in American history, see Annette Kolodny, *The Lay of the Land: Metaphor as Experience and History in American Life and Letters* (Chapel Hill: University of North Carolina Press, 1975); *idem, The Land before Her: Fantasy and Experience of the American Frontier, 1630–1860* (Chapel Hill: University of North Carolina Press, 1984); Vera

Norwood and Janice Monk, eds., *The Desert Is No Lady: Southwetern Landscapes in Women's Writing and Art* (New Haven: Yale University Press, 1987), Vera Norwood, *Made from This Earth: American Women and Nature* (Chapel Hill: University of North Carolina Press, 1993); Sam Gill, *Mother Earth* (Chicago: University of Chicago Press, 1987).

43. Thomas Morton, *New English Canaan*, in Peter Force, ed. *Tracts and Other Papers...* (Washington, D.C., 1838), vol. 2, p. 10.

44. Henry Colman, "Address Before the Hampshire, Franklin and Hampden Agricultural Society Delivered in Greenfield, Oct. 23, 1833," (Greenfield, MA.: Phelps and Ingersoll, 1833), pp. 5–6, 15, 27.

45. Frank Norris, *The Octopus, A Story of California* (New York: Penguin Books, 1986; originally published 1901), p. 127. I thank David Igler for bringing these passages to my attention.

46. Norris, *Octopus*, p. 127.

47. Norris, *Octopus*, pp. 130–31.

48. *Scribner's Monthly*, 21, no. 1 (November 1880), p. 61. On the association of women with civilization and culture in nineteenth century America, see Christopher Lasch, *The New Radicalism in America, 1889–1963* (New York: W.W. Norton, 1965), p. 65; Nancy Woloch, *Women and the American Experience* (New York: Knopf, 1984), chap. 6; Merchant, *Ecological Revolutions*, chap. 7.

49. J. Hector St. John de Crévecoeur, "What is an American?" *Letters from an American Farmer* (New York: E.P. Dutton, 1957; originally published 1782), pp. 39–43.

50. Richard F. Burton, *The City of the Saints and across the Rocky Mountains to California*, (1861) (New York: Knopf, 1963), p. 72.

51. See also Roderick Nash, *Wilderness and the American Mind*, 3rd ed. (New Haven, CT.: Yale University Press, 1982); Richard Slotkin, *Regeneration through Violence: The Mythology of the Frontier* (Middletown, CT.: Wesleyan University Press, 1973); idem, *Gunfighter Nation: The Myth of the Frontier in Twentieth–Century America* (New York: Atheneum, 1992).

52. On the Greek and Renaissance distinction between *Natura naturans* and *Natura naturata* see Eustace M.W. Tillyard, *The Elizabethan World Picture* (New York: Random House Vintage, 1959), p. 42: "This giving a soul to nature—nature, that is, in the sense of *natura naturans*, the creative force, not of *natura naturata*, the natural creation—was a mildy unorthodox addition to the spiritual or intellectual beings... Hooker, orthodox as usual, is explicit on this matter. [Nature] cannot be allowed a will of her own... She is not even an agent... [but] is the direct and involuntary tool of God himself." See also Whitney, *Bacon and Modernity*, p. 123: [T]he extreme dehumanization of [nature by] the Baconian scientist... is linked not simply to a complementary dehumanization of the feminine object of study, but to a somewhat anachronistic return to a more robust feminine image of nature as *natura naturans*." Spinoza also used the two terms but with rather different meanings than implied here. See Baruch Spinoza, *Spinoza Selections*, ed. John Wild (New York: Charles Scribner's Sons, 1930), pp. 80–2; Harry A. Wolfson, *The Philosophy of Spinoza*, 2 vols. (New York: Meridian, 1958), I, 253–5.

53. John Gast, *American Progress*, painting, 1872, reproduced as a chromolithograph. Reproduced in Jules David Prown, et al, *Discovered Lands, Invented Pasts* (New Haven, CT.: Yale University

Press, 1992), p. 97. On landscape paintings as narrative moments, see William Cronon, "Telling Tales on Canvas: Landscapes of Frontier Change," *Discovered Lands, Invented Pasts*, pp. 37–87.

54. For representations and interpretations of the four paintings discussed below, see William H. Truettner, ed. *The West as America: Reinterpreting Images of the Frontier, 1820–1920* (Washington: National Museum of Art, 1991), pp. 135, 120, 136, 137.

55. Frank Norris, *The Pit, A Story of Chicago*, (1903) (New York: Grove Press, 1956).

56. William Cronon, *Nature's Metropolis; Chicago and the Great West* (New York: W.W. Norton, 1991). Cronon quotes the passage below from *The Pit* on the page preceding his "Prologue."

57. Norris, *The Pit*, p. 62.

58. Norris, *The Pit*, p. 60–3.

59. On Marx's concept of the endowment of money with organic, living properties and its application among the Indians of the Cauca valley in Colombia, see Michael Taussig, "The Genesis of Capitalism amongst a South American Peasantry: Devil's Labor and the Baptism of Money," *Comparative Studies in Society and History*, 19 (April 1977): 130–53.

60. Norris, *The Pit*, p. 374.

61. Nash, *Wilderness and the American Mind*.

62. Carol P. MacCormack, "Nature, Culture, and Gender," in Carol MacCormack and Marilyn Strathern, eds. *Nature, Culture, and Gender* (Cambridge: Cambridge University Press, 1980), pp. 6–7; Sherry Ortner, "Is Female to Male as Nature Is to Culture?" in Michelle Rosaldo and Louise Lamphere, eds. *Woman, Culture, and Society* (Stanford, CA.: Stanford University Press, 1974), pp. 67–87.

63. Philip Elmer-Dewitt, "Fried Gene Tomatoes," *Time* (May 30, 1994): 54–55; Richard Keller Simon, "The Formal Garden in the Age of Consumer Culture: A Reading of the Twentieth-Century Shopping Mall," in Wayne Franklin and Michael Steiner, ed. *Mapping American Culture* (Iowa City, IA.: University of Iowa Press, 1992), pp. 231–50.

64. Max Horkheimer and Theodor Adorno, *Dialectic of Enlightenment* (1944) (New York: Continuum, 1993), quotations on pp. 3, 7, 9.

65. Maria Gimbutas, *The Goddesses and Gods of Old Europe, 6500–3500 B.C.* (Berkeley, CA.: University of California Press, 1982); Merlin Stone, *When God Was a Woman* (New York: Harcourt Brace Jovanovich, 1976); Riane Eisler, *The Chalice and the Blade* (San Francisco: Harper and Row, 1988); Elinor Gadon, *The Once and Future Goddess* (San Francisco: Harper and Row, 1989); Monica Sjöö and Barbara Mor, *The Great Cosmic Mother: Rediscovering the Religion of the Earth* (San Francisco: Harper and Row, 1987); Pamela Berger, *The Goddess Obscured: The Transformation of the Grain Protectress from Goddess to Saint* (Boston: Beacon Press, 1985). On cultural ecofeminism see some of the essays in *Reweaving the World: The Emergence of Ecofeminism*, Irene Diamond and Gloria Orenstein, eds., (San Francisco: Sierra Club Books, 1990).

66. Londa Schiebinger, *The Mind Has No Sex? Women in the Origins of Modern Science* (Cambridge, MA.: Harvard University Press, 1989); Evelyn Fox Keller, *Reflections on Gender and Science* (New Haven, CT.: Yale University Press, 1985).

67. Examples include Oelschlaeger, *The Idea of Wilderness;* Donald Worster, *The Wealth of Nature* (New York: Oxford University Press, 1993); Barry Commoner, *The Closing Circle: Nature, Man, and Technology* (New York: Knopf, 1971).

68. Bill McKibben, *The End of Nature* (New York: Random House, 1989). For a critique see Tom Athanasiou, "US Politics and Global Warming," (Westfield, New Jersey: Open Magazine Pamphlet Series, 1991).

69. Carolyn Merchant, *Radical Ecology: The Search for a Livable World* (New York: Routledge, 1992).

70. Alan Hastings, Carole L. Hin, Stephen Ellner, Peter Turchin, and H. Charles J. Godfray, "Chaos in Ecology: Is Mother Nature a Strange Attractor?" *American Review of Ecological Systems,* 24, no. 1 (1993): 1–33; N. Katherine Hayles, "Gender Encoding in Fluid Mechanics: Masculine Channels and Feminine Flows," *Differences: A Journal of Feminist Cultural Studies,* 4, no. 2 (1992): 16–44; Hayles, *Chaos Bound: Orderly Disorder in Contemporary Literature and Science* (Ithaca: Cornell University Press, 1990); Hayles, ed. *Chaos and Order: Complex Dynamics in Literature and Science* (Chicago: University of Chicago Press, 1991); Daniel Botkin, *Discordant Harmonies: A New Ecology for the Twenty-First Century* (New York: Oxford University Press, 1990); James Gleick, *Chaos: The Making of a New Science* (New York: Viking, 1987): Edward Lorenz, *The Essence of Chaos* (Seattle, WA: University of Washington Press, 1993).

NOTES TO CHAPTER 3

Portions of this chapter appeared previously in Carolyn Merchant, "Isis Consciousness Raised," *Isis* 73 (1982): 398–409.

1. George Sarton, *A History of Science,* 2 vols. (Cambridge, MA.: Harvard University Press, 1959), vol. 1, pp. 125, 152. Sarton cites Herodotus, IV, 186 and quotes Plutarch, "Isis and Osiris," (I-2) in *Moralia* (Loeb Classical Library), vol. 5, inscription on 354c. Herodotus, *The History of Herodotus* (New York: Tudor, 1928), writes: "Even at Cyrene, the women think it wrong to eat the flesh of the cow, honoring in this Isis, the Egyptian goddess, whom they worship both with fasts and festivals." (p. 260). Herodotus also writes: "... the females [i.e., cows] they are not allowed to sacrifice, since they are sacred to Isis. The statue of this goddess has the form of a woman, but with horns like a cow, resembling thus the Greek representations of Io; and the Egyptians, one and all, venerate cows much more highly than any other animal.... The Egyptians do not all worship the same gods, excepting Isis and Osiris, the latter of whom they say is the Grecian Bacchus." (p. 95) Also, "The Egyptians tell the following story: 'Latona, one of the eight gods of the first order, who dwelt in the city of Buto, where now she has her oracle, received Apollo as a sacred charge from Isis, and saved him by hiding him in what is now called the floating island. Typhon meanwhile was searching everywhere in hopes of finding the child of Osiris.' According to the Egyptians, Apollo and Diana are the children of Bacchus and Isis; while Latona is their nurse and their preserver. They call Apollo, in their language Horus; Ceres they call Isis; Diana Bubastis" (p. 137).

2. Painting of *Isis Conducts Queen Nefretere to her Tomb,* as reproduced by Nina de Garis Davies in *Ancient Egyptian Paintings, Selected, Copied, and Described,* 3 vols. (Chicago: University of Chicago Press, 1936), vol. 2, Plate XCI. Description by Davies quoted from vol. 3, p. 177.

3. George Sarton, *The Study of the History of Science* (New York: Dover, 1936), pp. 41–42.

4. George Sarton, *The Studyof the History of Science*, p. 5. On historiograpy in the history of science, see Tore Frängsmyr, "Science or History: George Sarton and the Positivist Tradition in the History of Science," *Lychnos* (1973–74): 104–44.

5. Sarton, *Introduction to the History of Science*, (Baltimore, 1927), p. 6. See Frängsmyr, p. 115.

6. Sarton, *Introduction to the History of Science*, p. 19.

7. Sarton, *A History of Science*, vol. 1, p. xii.

8. Aristotle, *De Generatione Animalium*, trans. Arthur Platt (Oxford, Eng.: Clarendon Press, 1910), Bk. 1, Ch. 19, lines, 279b13.

9. See Georg Simmel (1859–1918), *Philosophische Kultur*, as quoted in Karen Horney, "The Flight from Womanhood," in *Women and Analysis*, ed. Jean Strouse (New York: Grossman, 1974), p. 172. See also Evelyn Fox Keller, "Gender and Science," *Psychoanalysis and Contemporary Thought*, 1 (1978): 409–433, on p. 409.

10. Vincent di Norcia, "From Critical Theory to Critical Ecology," *Telos*, no. 22 (1974/75): 85-95, on pp. 88–89; Max Horkheimer and Theodor Adorno, *Dialectic of Enlightment*, Max Horkheimer, *The Eclipse of Reason* (New York: Oxford University Press, 1947); Jürgen Habermas *Toward a Rational Society* (London: Heineman, 1971), pp. 81–122; William Leiss, *The Domination of Nature* (New York: George Braziller, 1972); Theodor Adorno, et al. *The Positivist Dispute in German Sociology*, trans. Glyn Adey and David Frisby (New York: Harper and Row, 1976). For a feminist extension of the Frankfurt school's critique of objectivity, see Marcia Westkott, "Feminist Criticism of the Social Sciences," *Harvard Educational Review*, 49 (November 1979); 422–30. See also Dorothy Smith, "Women's Perspective as a Radical Critique of Sociology," *Sociological Inquiry*, 44 (1974): 7–13. On Bacon, Harvey, Hobbes, Glanvill, and Boyle, see Carolyn Merchant, *The Death of Nature* (San Francisco: HarperCollins, 1980).

11. Londa Schiebinger, "Feminine Icons: The Face of Early Modern Science," *Critical Inquiry* 14, no. 4 (Summer 1988): 661–91, see pp. 663, 688. See also Schiebinger, *The Mind Has no Sex? Women in the Origins of Modern Science* (Cambridge, MA.: Harvard University Press, 1989), pp. 119–59.

12. Ruth Bleier, *Science and Gender: A Critique of Biology and Its Theories on Women* (New York: Pergamon, 1984), pp. 193-200. For other feminist critiques of science see Sandra Harding, *The Science Question in Feminism* (Ithaca: Cornell University Press, 1986); Nancy Tuana, ed., *Feminism & Science* (Bloomington: Indiana University Press, 1989); Keller, *Reflections on Gender and Science;* Brian Easlea, *Science and Sexual Oppression: Patriarchy's Confrontation with Woman and Nature* (London: Weidenfeld and Nicholson, 1981); Merchant, "*The Death of Nature: Women and Ecology in the Scientific Revolution*," Chapter 4, below.

13. John A. Schuster, "(New) Master Narrative(s), Yes: 'Scientific Revolution,' No Thanks," paper presented to the annual meeting of the History of Science Society, Seattle, October 26, 1990; Robert Westman, *ibid.*, comment.

14. For feminist reappraisals of the Scientific Revolution see Merchant, *The Death of Nature;* Schiebinger, *The Mind Has No Sex?*, Keller, *Reflections on Gender and Science;* Brian Easlea, *Witch-hunting, Magic, and the New Philosophy* (Sussex: Harvester, 1980).

15. Elizabeth Ann R. Bird, "The Social Construction of Nature: Theoretical Approaches to the History of Environmental Problems," *Environmental Review*, 11, no. 4 (Winter 1987): 255-64. Bird argues that the concept of representation implies an independently-existing, evolving nature behind the representation that is accessible and knowable by science. Yet human social practice, not just "Natural" evolution changes nature. Applications of pesticides and antibiotics, for example, create the conditions through which nature resists human technologies and mutates to new life forms. On perspective versus participatory ways of knowing see Thomas Merriam, "The Disenchantment of Science," *The Ecologist*, 7, no. 1 (1977): 23-28; Morris Berman, *The Reenchantment of the World* (Ithaca: Cornell University Press, 1981). On the distancing process created by perspective art and satellite images, see Yaakov Garb, "The Use and Misuse of the Whole Earth Image," *Whole Earth Review* no. 45 (March 1985): 18–25.

16. Stephen Shapin and Simon Schaffer, *Leviathan and the Airpump* (Princeton, N.J.: Princeton University Press, 1985).

17. I thank Yaakov Garb for his analysis of the painting by Joseph Wright of Derby.

18. On the philosophy of metaphor see George Lakoff and Mark Johnson, *Metaphors We Live By* (Chicago: University of Chicago Press, 1980); Robin Lakoff *Language and Woman's Place* (New York: Harper and Row, 1975); Garb, personal communication.

19. On contextualism see Robert F. Berkhofer, Jr., "A New Context for a New American Studies?" *American Quarterly*, 41, no. 4 (December 1989): 588–613; AHR Forum: "The Old History and the New," *The American Historical Review*, 94, no. 3 (June 1989): 581–698.

20. Evelyn Fox Keller and Christine R. Grontkowski, "The Mind's Eye," in Sandra Harding and Merrill B. Hintikka, eds. *Discovering Reality* (Dordrecht, Holland: D. Reidel, 1983), pp. 207–24; Martin Jay, *Downcast Eyes: The Denigration of Vision in Twentieth–Century French Thought* (Berkeley: University of California Press, 1993), pp. 526–42. On participatory consciousness see Morris Berman, *The Reenchantment of the World* (Ithaca, N.Y.: Cornell University Press, 1981).

21. Alain de Lille, *The Complaint of Nature*, trans. Douglas Moffat (New York: Henry Holt, 1908), pp. 15, 33, 41. For the original see Alanus de Insulis, *De Planctu Naturae*, in Thomas Wright, ed. *The Anglo-Latin Satirical Poets and Epigrammatists of the Twelfth Century* (London: Longman & Trubner, 1892), vol. 2, pp. 429–522, esp. pp. 441, 467. On the proper role of nature as teacher in revealing her truths to mankind, see p. 457 (Alain, *Complaint*, p. 31). For a commentary, see George Economou, *The Goddess Natura in Medieval Literature* (Cambridge, MA.: Harvard University Press, 1972), esp. pp. 72–80; Merchant, *The Death of Nature*, pp. 10–20, 31–33.

22. See the French painting *St. Genevieve with Her Flock*, (16th Cent.) depicting the virgin with her flock of sheep within a protective stone circle on a hillside of trees and blooming flowers, reproduced in John Mitchell, *The Earth Spirit* (New York: Avon, 1975). Geoffrey Chaucer, "The Merchant's Tale," *Works*, ed. F.N. Robinson (Boston, Ma.: Houghton Mifflin, 1957), lines 2044–2046; 2143–2146. On garden symbolism, see Stanley Stewart, *The Enclosed Garden: The Tradition and Image in Seventeenth-Century Poetry* (Madison, WI.: University of Wisconsin Press, 1966).

23. Francis Bacon, "De Dignitate et Augmentis Scientarum," *Works*, ed. James Spedding, Robert Ellis, and Douglas Heath, 14 vols. (London: Longmans Green 1857–1874), vol. 4, pp. 343, 287; Bacon, "The Refutation of Philosophies," in Benjamin Farrington, ed. and trans. *The Philosophy*

of Francis Bacon (Liverpool: Liverpool University Press, 1964), p. 130; Bacon "De Dignitate et Augmentis Scientarum," *Works,* vol. 4, pp. 294, 296.

24. Joseph Glanvill, *Plus Ultra* (Gainesville, Fl.: Scholar's Facsimile reprints, 1958; originally published, 1668), pp. 87, 10, 56; Glanvill, *The Vanity of Dogmatizing* (New York: Columbia University Press, 1931; originally published, 1661), pp. 247, 118.

25. For the illustration of "Nature Revealing Herself to Science," see Merchant, *Death of Nature,* p. 191. For the illustration of *Le Dejeuner sur l'Herbe,* see George Mauner, *Manet: Peintre–philosophe* (University Park, Pa.: Pennsylvania State University Press, 1975), pp. 11–17, 34.

26. Inaugural editorial, *Le Radium,* 1 (January 1904): 2, quotation translated by Spencer Weart (I thank Dr. Weart for this and the following three quotations); Sir William Crookes, "Modern Views on Matter," *Scientific American Supplement,* 56 (July 1903): 23014; Hans Reichenbach, *Atom and Cosmos: The World of Modern Physics,* trans. and revised by Edward S. Allen (New York: MacMillan, 1933), p. 222; editor's note in *Harper's,* 149 (July 1924): 251, as quoted in Daniel Kevles, *The Physicists* (New York: Knopf, 1978), p. 174.

27. Sarton, *Study of the History of Science,* pp. 41–2.

28. Sarton, *A History of Science,* vol. 1, quotation on p. 18; Sarton, *The Study of the History of Mathematics* (New York: Dover, 1936), pp. 8–9, quotation on p. 9.

29. Davies in *Ancient Egyptian Paintings,* vol. 3, writes: "Her [Isis'] yellow complexion, contrasting markedly with the rosy flesh-tint of the queen, is traditional; the appearance of deities did not change with the times like that of mortals." (p. 177). She also notes, "Hair is very often modelled [with] the blobs being arranged... so as to create the appearance of short curls; these break up the surface pleasantly when the entire wig is painted black or grey." (vol. 3, p. xlii.) On Isis as the prototype of the black madonna, see Danita Redd, "Black Madonnas of Europe: Diffusion of the African Isis," in Ivan Van Sertima, ed. *African Presence in Early Europe* (1985; New Brunswick, N.J.: Transaction Publishers, Rutgers—The State University, 1993), pp. 106–33, illustration of Isis with Horus on p. 109. See also Monica Sjöö and Barbara Mor, "The Original Black Mother," in Sjöö and Mor, *The Great Cosmic Mother: Rediscovering the Religion of the Earth* (San Francisco: Harper and Row, 1987), pp. 21–32, illustration of Isis with Horus, on p. 158. On Isis as exemplar of fertility and matriarchy in black Africa, see Cheikh Anta Diop, *The Cultural Unity of Black Africa* (1959; Chicago: World Press, 1990), pp. 58–62. Frances C. Welsing, *The Isis Papers* (Chicago, 1991).

30. David Kubrin, "How Sir Isaac Newton Helped Restore Law and Order to the West," *Liberation* 16, no. 10 (March 1972): 32–41, quotation on p. 38. See also Londa Schiebinger, *Nature's Body: Gender in the Making of Modern Science* (Boston: Beacon Press, 1993), chapter 6. Schiebinger points out that Constantin-François Volney in 1787 cited Herodotus on the blackness of Egyptians in his defense of the Egyptian roots of Greek science. See Volney, *Voyage en Syrie et Egypte* (1787; Paris: Mouton & Co., 1959), pp. 62–64.

31. Winthrop Jordan, *White Over Black: American Attitudes Toward the Negro, 1550–1812* (Chapel Hill, N.C.: University of North Carolina Press, 1968); Ronald Takaki, *Iron Cages* (New York: Alfred Knopf, 1979).

32. Athenasius Kircher, *Oedipus Aegypticus* (1652); W. Wynn Wescott, *The Isiac Tablet, or the Bembine Table of Isis* (Los Angeles: The Philosophical Research Society, 1976 [1887]).

33. Schiebinger, *Nature's Body,* chap. 6. Schiebinger points out that the Egyptian roots of modern sci- ence had been celebrated in the 16th and 17th centuries by such commentators as Ambroise Paré (1575) who stated that "Ethiopians, Egyptians, Africans, Jews, Phoenicians, Persians, Assyrians, and Indians have invented many curious sciences, revealed the mysteries and secrets of Nature, ordered mathematics, observed the motions of the heavens, and introduced the worship of the gods." (Paré quoted in Chapter 6, headnote). Galileo noted that the ancients had mapped the heavens and Newton was fascinated by the sacred cubit of the Egyptians as the underlying unit of the great pyramid of Cheops. See also Kubrin, "How Sir Isaac Newton Helped Restore Law and Order to the West," p. 38: "Most historians of science today, it is true, trace the roots of ancient science back to the thinkers in pre-Socratic Ionia, in sixth century B.C. Greece. Yet, cer- tainly during the scientific revolution, this was not the opinion of the scientists themselves. Rather, many of them agreed that their knowledge and discipline was more properly traced back to Egypt. To take merely one example, Isaac Newton wrote in his *Chronology of Ancient Kingdoms Amended* that it was after 655 B.C., when Psamminticus became king of all Egypt, that the Greek Ionians had 'access into Egypt; and thence came the Ionian Philosophy, Astronomy, and Geometry.'" [Newton, *Chronology of Ancient Kingdoms* (London, 1727, p. 37]. On racism in English science, see Nancy Leys Stepan, *The Idea of Race in Science: Great Britain, 1800-1960* (North Haven, CT.: Archon Books, 1982).

34. Martin Bernal, *Black Athena* (New Brunswick, N.J.: Rutgers University Press), p. 2. For other reappraisals of science from a racial perspective see Londa Schiebinger, "The Anatomy of Difference: Race and Sex in Eighteenth Century Science," *Eighteenth Century Studies* 23 (1990); 387–406; Anne Fausto-Sterling, "The Dissection of Race and Gender in the Nineteenth Century," paper presented to the annual meeting of the History of Science Society, Seattle, October 26, 1990.

35. Sandra Harding, ed. *The "Racial" Economy of Science: Toward a Democratic Future* (Bloomington: University of Indiana Press, 1993).

36. See Linda Nicholson, ed. *Feminism/Postmodernism* (New York: Routledge, 1990); Irene Diamond and Lee Quinby, ed. *Feminism & Foucault: Reflections on Resistance* (Boston: Northeastern University Press, 1988); Robert Young, ed. *Untying the Text: A Post-Structuralist Reader* (Boston: Routledge & Kegan Paul, 1981); Mark Poster, *Critical Theory and Poststructuralism: In Search of a Context* (Ithaca, N.Y.: Cornell University Press, 1989); William Leiss, *The Domination of Nature* (New York: George Braziller, 1972); Jürgen Habermas, *The Philosophical Discourse of Modernity* (Cambridge, MA.: MIT Press, 1990); Michel Foucault, *Power/Knowledge* (New York: Pantheon, 1980).

37. Martin Heidegger, "The Age of the World Picture," in *The Question Concerning Technology* (New York: Harper and Row, 1977), pp. 127–36; Heidegger, *Der Satz vom Grund,* quoted in Hubert Dreyfus, *What Computers Can't Do* (New York: Harper and Row, 1972), p. 242, n. 16.

38. Donna Haraway, *Primate Visions: Gender, Race, and Nature in the History of Modern Science* (New York: Routledge, 1989), pp. 1–15, quotation on p. 3. See also Haraway, "Situated Knowledges: The Science Question in Feminism and the Privilege of Partial Perspective," *Feminist Studies,* 14, no. 3 (Fall 1988): 575–99.

39. Jan Golinski, "The Theory of Practice and the Practice of Theory: Sociological Approaches in the History of Science," *Isis,* 81, no. 308 (September 1990): 492–505, quotation on p. 503.

NOTES TO CHAPTER 4

From: Michael Zimmerman, et al, eds. *Environmental Philosophy: From Animal Rights to Radical Ecology* (Englewood Cliffs, N.J.: Prentice Hall, 1992), pp. 268–83. [Excerpted by Karen Warren from *The Death of Nature: Women, Ecology, and the Scientific Revolution* (San Francisco: Harper and Row, 1980)]

1. On the tensions between technology and the pastoral ideal in American culture, see Leo Marx, *The Machine in the Garden* (New York: Oxford University Press, 1964). On the domination of nature as female, see Annette Kolodny, *The Lay of the Land* (Chapel Hill: University of North Carolina Press, 1975); Rosemary Radford Ruether, "Women, Ecology, and the Domination of Nature," *The Ecumenist* 14 (1975): 1–5; William Leiss, *The Domination of Nature* (New York: Braziller, 1972). On the roots of the ecological crisis, see Donald Hughes, *Ecology in Ancient Civilizations* (Albuquerque: University of New Mexico Press, 1976); Lynn White, Jr., *Medieval Technology and Social Change* (New York: Oxford University Press, 1966); and L. White, Jr., "Historical Roots of Our Ecologic Crisis," in White, Jr. *Machina ex Deo* (Cambridge, MA.: M.I.T. Press, 1968), pp. 75–94; Reijer Hooykaas, *Religion and the Rise of Modern Science* (Grand Rapids, MI: Eerdmans, 1972); Christopher Derrick, *The Delicate Creation: Towards a Theology of the Environment* (Old Greenwich, CN.: Devin-Adair, 1972). On traditional rituals in the mining of ores and in metallurgy, see Mircea Eliade, *The Forge and the Crucible*, trans. Stephan Corrin (New York: Harper & Row, 1962), pp. 42, 53–70, 74, 79–96. On the divergence between attitudes and practices toward the environment, see Yi-Fu Tuan, "Our Treatment of the Environment in Ideal and Actuality," *American Scientist* (May-June 1970): 246–49.

2. On capitalism in early modern Europe see Immanuel Wallerstein, *The Modern World System* (New York: Academic Press, 1975). On forests and the development of mining see John U. Nef, *The Rise of the British Coal Industry* (North Haven, CT.: Archon, 1966), vol. 1, pp. 156–64. On the energy base of premodern society see Lewis Mumford, *Technics and Civilization* (New York: Harcourt Brace Jovanovich, 1934), ch. 3–4.

3. Treatments of Francis Bacon's contributions to science inlcude Paolo Rossi, *Francis Bacon: From Magic to Science* (London: Routledge & Kegan Paul, 1968); Lisa Jardine, *Francis Bacon: Discovery and the Art of Discourse* (Cambridge, Eng.: Cambridge University Press, 1974); Benjamin Farrington, *Francis Bacon, Philosopher of Industrial Science* (New York: Schumann, 1949); Margery Purver, *The Royal Society: Concept and Creation* (London: Routledge & Kegan Paul, 1967).

4. Bacon, "The Great Instauration" (written 1620), *Works*, vol. 4, p. 20; "The Masculine Birth of Time," ed. and trans. Benjamin Farrington, in *The Philosophy of Francis Bacon* (Liverpool, Eng.: Liverpool University Press, 1964), p. 62; "De Dignitate," *Works*, vol. 4, pp. 287, 294.

5. Quoted in Moody E. Prior, "Bacon's Man of Science," in Leonard M. Marsak, ed. *The Rise of Modern Science in Relation to Society* (London: Collier-Macmillan, 1964), p. 45.

6. Rossi, p. 21; Leiss, p. 56; Bacon, *Works*, vol. 4, p. 294; Henry Cornelius Agrippa, *De Occulta Philosophia Libri Tres* (Antwerp, 1531): "No one has such powers but he who has cohabited with the elements, vanquished nature, mounted higher than the heavens, elevating himself above the angels to the archetype itself, with whom he then becomes cooperator and can do all things," as quoted in Frances A. Yates, *Giordano Bruno and the Hermetic Tradition* (New York: Vintage Books, 1964), p. 136.

7. Bacon, "Novum Organum," Part 2, in *Works*, vol. 4, p. 247; "Valerius Terminus," *Works*, vol. 3, pp. 217, 219; "The Masculine Birth of Time," trans. Farrington, p. 62.

8. Bacon, "The Masculine Birth of Time," and "The Refutation of Philosophies," trans. Farrington, pp. 62, 129, 130.

9. Bacon, "De Augmentis," *Works*, vol. 4, p. 294; see also Bacon, "Aphorisms," *Works*, vol. 4.

10. "De Augmentis," *Works*, vol. 4, pp. 320, 325; Plato, "The Timaeus," in *The Dialogues of Plato*, trans. B. Jowett (New York: Random House, 1937), vol. 2, p. 17; Bacon, "Parasceve," *Works*, vol. 4, p. 257.

11. Bacon, "De Augmentis," *Works*, vol. 4, pp. 343, 287, 343, 393.

12. Bacon, "Novum Organum," *Works*, vol. 4, p. 246; "The Great Instauration," *Works*, vol. 4, p. 29; "Novum Organum," Part 2, *Works*, vol. 4, p. 247.

13. Bacon, "Thoughts and Conclusions on the Interpretation of Nature or A Science of Productive Works," trans. Farrington, *The Philosophy of Francis Bacon*, pp. 96, 93, 99.

14. Bacon, "De Augmentis," *Works*, vol. 4, pp. 294; "Parasceve," *Works*, vol. 4, pp. 257; "Plan of the Work," vol. 4, pp. 32; "Novum Organum," *Works*, vol. 4, pp. 114, 115.

15. René Descartes, "Discourse on Method," Part 4, in E.S. Haldane and G.R.T. Ross, eds. *Philosophical Works of Descartes* (New York: Dover, 1955), vol. 1, p. 119.

16. Joseph Glanvill, *Plus Ultra* (Gainesville, FL.: Scholar's Facsimile Reprints, 1958; first published 1668), quotations on pp. 9, 87, 13, 56, 104, 10.

17. J.C. Smuts, *Holism and Evolution* (New York: Macmillan, 1926), pp. 86, 87. On holism in the biological sciences, see Arthur Koestler, "Beyond Holism and Reductionism: The Concept of the Holon," in *Beyond Reductionism: New Perspectives in the Life Sciences*, ed. A. Koestler and J.R. Smythies (Boston: Beacon Press, 1969).

18. On ecological cycles, see Barry Commoner, *The Closing Circle: Nature, Man, and Technology* (New York; Bantam Books, 1971), Chap. 2.

19. Samuel P. Hays, *Conservation and the Gospel of Efficiency: The Progressive Conservation Movement*, 1890–1920 (Cambridge, MA.: Harvard University Press, 1959), pp. 142–43.

20. Murray Bookchin, "Ecology and Revolutionary Thought," in *Post-Scarcity Anarchism* (San Francisco: Ramparts Press, 1971), pp. 57–82, and M. Bookchin, "Toward an Ecological Solution" (Berkeley, CA.: Ecology Center Reprint, n.d.). See also Victor Ferkiss, *Technological Man* (New York: New American Library, 1969), Chap. 9, pp. 205–11; Theodore Roszak, *Where the Wasteland Ends* (Garden City, N.Y.: Doubleday, 1973), pp. 367–61; Paul Goodman and Percival Goodman, *Communitas*, 2nd ed., rev. (New York: Vintage, 1960); Paul Goodman, *People or Personnel* (New York: Random House, 1965); E.F. Schumacher, *Small Is Beautiful: Economics as if People Mattered* (New York: Harper and Row, 1973); Ernest Callenbach, *Ecotopia* (Berkeley, CA.: Banyan Tree Books, 1976).

NOTES TO CHAPTER 5

Excerpted from: *Ecological Revolutions: Nature, Gender, and Science in New England*. (Chapel Hill, NC.: University of North Carolina Press, 1989).

1. For a more detailed analysis of the environmental history of New England, see Merchant, *Ecological Revolutions: Nature, Gender, and Science in New England*.

2. On the relationships between cosmology, mythology, ethics, and rituals, see Clifford Geertz, "Ethos, Worldview, and the Analysis of Sacred Symbols," in *The Interpretation of Cultures* (New York: Basic Books, 1973), p. 127. On the history of corn cultivation by the Indians of southern New England, see M.K. Bennett, "Food Economy of the New England Indians, 1605–75," *Journal of Political Economy*, 63, no. 5 (October 1955): 369–97; Eva L. Butler, "Algonkian Culture and the Use of Maize in Southern New England," *Bulletin of the Archeological Society of Connecticut* (December 1948): 1–39.

3. Roger Williams, *A Key into the Language of America: Or, An Help to the Language of the Natives in That Part of America, Called New England* (Providence, R.I.: Publications of the Narragansett Club, 1899; originally published, London, 1643), quotation on p. 23.

4. On the crow story, see Williams, *Key*, pp. 24–25, 114. On the Corn Mother story, see Frank Speck, "Penobscot Tales and Religious Beliefs," *Journal of American Folklore*, 48, no. 187 (January–March 1935): 1–107, see p. 75; Speck, *Penobscot Man: The Life History of a Forest Tribe in Maine* (Philadelphia, PA.: University of Pennsylvania Press, 1940), pp. 194–95; W.H. Mechling, *Malecite Tales* (Ottawa: Canada Department of Mines, Government Printing Office, 1914). On the relationship between the two origin stories, see John Witthoft, *Green Corn Ceremonialism in the Eastern Woodlands* (Ann Arbor, MI.: University of Michigan Press, 1949), pp. 81, 77–79.

5. Bennett, "Food Economy of the New England Indians," p. 392; William S. Fowler, "Agricultural Tools and Techniques of the Northeast," *Massachusetts Archeological Society Bulletin*, 15, no. 3 (1954): 41–51.

6. Van Wassenaer, "Historical Verhael," quoted in J. Franklin Jameson, ed. *Narratives of New Netherland 1609–1664*, (New York: Charles Scribner's Sons, 1909), pp. 61–96, see pp. 72, 69; Lynn Ceci, "Watchers of the Pleiades: Ethnoastronomy Among Native Cultivators in Northeastern North America," *Ethnohistory*, 25, no. 4 (Fall 1978): 301–17.

7. Letter of Isaack de Rasieres to Samuel Blommaert, (1628?), in Jameson, ed. *Narratives of New Netherland*, pp. 97–115, quotation on p. 107; Geertz, *Agricultural Involution*, pp. 24–25.

8. Howard Russell, *Indian New England Before the Mayflower* (Hanover, N.H.: University Press of New England, 1980), pp. 165–70.

9. William Wood, *New England's Prospect* (London: Thomas Coates, 1634), quotation on p. 100; John Winthrop, Jr. "Indian Corne," in Fulmer Mood, "John Winthrop, Jr. on Indian Corn," *New England Quarterly*, 10, no. 1 (March 1937): 121–33, see p. 127; Lawrence Kaplan, "Archeology and Domestication in American Phaseolus (Beans)," *Economic Botany*, 19, no. 4 (October–December 1965): 358–68, see p. 359. On the use of maize and beans with other foods, see Daniel Gookin, "Historical Collections of the Indians in New England," (1674) in *Collections of the Massachusetts Historical Society*, 10 vols., (Boston: Massachusetts Historical Society, 1792), 1st ser., 1: 144–229, p. 150.

10. Williams, *Key*, quotation on p. 124; Gookin, "Historical Collections," pp. 190–91; Bennett, "Food Economy of the New England Indians," pp. 391–94.

11. Wood, *New England's Prospect*, quotation on p. 100.

12. On changes in perceptions of wilderness from satanic to sublime among elites, see Roderick Nash, *Wilderness and the American Mind* (New Haven, CT.: Yale University Press, 1967), pp. 44–66; Perry Miller, "From Edwards to Emerson," in Miller, *Errand into the Wilderness* (New York: Harper and Row, 1956), pp. 184–203; Michael Rogin, "Nature as Politics and Nature as Romance in America," *Political Theory*, 5 (February 1977): 5–30.

13. Isaac Greenwood, *A Philosophical Discourse Concerning the Mutability and Changes of the Material World, Read to the Students of Harvard College, April 7, 1931, Upon the News of the Death of Thomas Hollis of London*, (Boston: S. Gerrish, 1931), pp. 8, 11.

14. Edward Taylor, "The Description of the Great Bones Dug up at Claverack on the Banks of Hundson River, A.D. 1705," in Donald Stanford, "The Giant Bones of Claverick, New York, 1705," *New York History* 40, no. 1 (January 1959): 46–61, quotation on p. 57; Leventhal, *In the Shadow of the Enlightenment: Occultism and Renaissance Science in Eighteenth Century America*, (New York: New York University Press, 1976), p. 226. On beliefs about a golden tree growing in the center of the earth, see Frank Dawson Adams, *Birth and Development of the Geological Sciences* (New York: Dover, 1938), pp. 286–89.

15. Leventhal, *Shadow of the Enlightenment*, pp. 226–29; Samuel Willard, *A Compleat Body of Divinity* (Boston: B. Green & S. Kneeland, 1726), p. 117; Benjamin Martin, *The Philosophical Grammar*, 2nd. ed. (London: J. Noon, 1738), p. 257; Charles Morton, *Charles Morton's Compendium Physicae* (from manuscript copy of 1697), Colonial Society of Massachusetts Publications, vol. 33 (Boston, MA.: Colonial Society of Massachusetts, 1940), p. 117.

16. Nathaniel Ames, *Astronomical Diary or Almanac*, (Boston: J. Draper, 1744), see also 1760 (March and April) and the August entries for 1746, 1754, and 1760.

17. Ames, *Astronomical Diary or Almanac*, 1754, May, September; 1761, December; quotation from 1750, August.

18. Ames, *Astronomical Diary, or Almanac*, 1753, June, July; John Tully, *An Almanack*, (Boston, 1688), July; Anonymous, *Almanack*, (Boston, 1709), August; Marion B. Stowell, *Early American Almanacs: The Colonial Weekday Bible* (New York: Burt Franklin, 1977), p. 59.

19. Ames, *Astronomical Diary, or Almanac*, 1758.

20. Leventhal, *Shadow of the Enlightenment*, pp. 223–31.

21. John Stilgoe, *Common Landscape of America* (New Haven, CT.: Yale University Press, 1982), pp. 159–66; Laurel Ulrich, *Good Wives: Image and Reality in the Lives of Women in Northern New England, 1650–1750* (New York: Alfred A. Knopf, 1982), pp. 51–54, 65–67.

22. Anonymous, *North American Calendar, or the Columbian Almanac for... 1835*, (Wilmington, DE.: P.B. Porter, 1835), January. On women in patriarchal society in colonial America, see Mary Beth Norton, "Evolution of White Women's Experience in Early America," *American Historical Review*, 89, no. 3 (June 1983): 593–619. Scholars have used the idea of the separation of male and female social roles—that is, the doctrine of separate spheres—both as evidence of the structures that subordinated women to men and as a means by which women established support networks and therefore gained autonomy. For a review of this scholarship, see Linda Kerber, "Women's History," *Journal of American History*, 75, no. 1 (June 1988): 9–39.

23. On women's accounts and trade with other women, see Ulrich, *Good Wives*, pp. 26–27, 45.

24. Sarah McMahon, "A Comfortable Subsistence: A History of Diet in New England, 1630–1850" Ph.D. dissertation, Brandeis University, 1982, pp. 50–61.

25. On Dunghill fowl, see Amelia Simmons, *First American Cookbook*, p. 7. On food preservation, see McMahon, "A Comfortable Subsistence: History of Diet," pp. 104–18.

26. McMahon, "A Comfortable Subsistence: History of Diet," pp. 99–104; Alice Morse Earle, *Home Life in Colonial Days* (Stockbridge, MA.: Berkshire Traveler's Press, 1974; originally published 1898), pp. 149–50.

27. Sarah Anna Emery, *Reminiscences of a Nonagenarian* (Newburyport, MA.: W.H. Huse, 1879), quotation on p. 7.

28. *New England Farmer*, 2, no. 16 (November 15, 1823): 124–25; *ibid* 4, no. 44 (May 26, 1826): 350–51; *ibid* 6, no. 47 (June 13, 1826): 370.

29. *New England Farmer*, 2, no. 9 (September 27, 1823): 67; *ibid* 2, no. 38 (April 17, 1824): 297; *ibid* 3, no. 9 (September 25, 1824): 67.

30. Nancy Cott, *The Bonds of Womanhood: Woman's Sphere in New England, 1780–1835* (New Haven: Yale University Press, 1977); Amy Dru Stanley, "Home Life and the Morality of the Market," paper for the Commonwealth Fund Conference, London, February, 1994.

31. Anonymous, "Successful Application of Labor and Skill," *New England Farmer*, 1, no. 16 (July 21, 1949): 244; A Butter Dealer, "Directions for Making and Preserving Butter," *New England Farmer*, 3, no. 9 (April 26, 1851): 145–46; [J.W. Proctor], "Dairy Management," *New England Farmer*, 2, nos. 1–3 (January 5, 19, February 2, 1850): 20–23, 36–37, 51–52.

32. Percy Wells Bidwell and John I. Falconer, *History of Agriculture in the Northern United States, 1620–1860*, (New York: Peter Smith, 1941; originally published, 1925), p. 242; Arthur Cole, "Agricultural Crazes: A Neglected Chapter in American Economic History," *American Economic Review*, 16, no. 4 (December 1926), pp. 634–65; Alan W. Dodge, "Poultry: A Profitable Part of Farm Production," *New England Farmer*, 1, no. 1 (December 9, 1848): 4–5; W. Bacon, "Poultry," *New England Farmer*, 2, no. 5 (March 2, 1850): 76; Howard B. Coffin, "Size of Fowls," *New England Farmer*, 2, no. 5 (March 2, 1850): 78.

33. Rolla Milton Tryon, *Household Manufacturers in the United States, 1640–1860*, (New York: Augustus M. Kelley, 1966), pp. 202–16.

34. Thomas Dublin, *Women at Work: The Transformation of Work and Community in Lowell, Massachusetts, 1826–1860* (New York: Columbia University Press, 1979), pp. 15–17; Tryon, *Household Manufactures*, pp. 242–53, 268, 271–76, 291–39.

35. On the background to domesticity in nineteenth-century America, see Barbara Welter, "Cult of True Womanhood," *American Quarterly*, 18 (Summer 1966): 151–74; Nancy F. Cott, *The Bonds of Womanhood: Woman's Sphere in New England* (New Haven: Yale University Press, 1977); Barbara Epstein, *Politics of Domesticity: Women, Evangelism, and Temperance in Nineteenth-Century America* (Middletown, CT.: Wesleyan University Press, 1981); Linda Kerber and Janet Dehart-Matthews, ed. *Women's America: Refocusing the Past* (New York: Oxford University Press, 1982).

36. Reverend H.M. Eaton, "Address Delivered Before the Kennebec County Agricultural Society," in E. Holmes ed. *Transactions of the Agricultural Societies in the State of Maine for 1853* (Augusta, Maine: William T. Johnson, 1854), pp. 60, 63–64, quotations on pp. 66–67; Perham, "An Address Delivered Before the Oxford Country Agricultural Society," in E. Holmes ed. *Transactions of the*

Agricultural Societies in the State of Maine for 1853 (Augusta, Maine: William T. Johnson, 1854), pp. 186–87, 189, quotation on p. 186.

37. M.T. True, M.D., "An Address Delivered Before the Cumberland County Agricultural Society in Portland...October 19, 1853," in E. Holmes ed. *Transactions of the Agricultural Societies in the State of Maine for 1853*, pp. 29–31.

38. Margaret Rossiter, *Women Scientists in America: Struggles and Strategies to 1940* (Baltimore: Johns Hopkins University Press, 1982), p. 3; Elizabeth Kenney, *The Botanizers: Amateur Scientists in Nineteenth Century America* (Chapel Hill, N.C.: University of North Carolina Press, 1992); Carolyn Merchant, "Women of the Progressive Conservation Movement, 1900–1916" *Environmental Review*, 11, no. 4 (Winter 1987): 265–74, see chapter 6, below.

39. Hannah Gale, *Diary* (1837–38) American Antiquarian Society Women's History Sources, vol. 1, collection 7631, NUCMC no. 62–3096, pp. 9–10, 12–14, 17.

40. Caroline Barrett White, *Diary* (Worcester, MA.: American Antiquarian Society, 1849–1915), October 17, 1849, November 13, 1849, March 14, 1850, September 1, 9, 1850.

NOTES TO CHAPTER 6

From *Environmental Review*, 8, no. 1 (Spring 1984): 57–85.

1. Gifford Pinchot, *The Fight for Conservation* (New York: Doubleday and Page, 1910), pp. 101, 105–106.

2. Samuel Hays, *Conservation and the Gospel of Efficiency: The Progressive Conservation Movement, 1890–1920* (New York: Atheneum, 1975; originally published 1959), pp. 142–44; Robert Welker, *Birds and Men* (Cambridge: Harvard University Press, 1955) pp. 184–99; Stephen Fox, *John Muir and His Legacy: The American Conservation Movement* (Boston: Little Brown and Company 1981), pp. 341–45, 173–78.

3. Karen Blair, *The Clubwoman as Feminist: True Womanhood Redefined, 1868–1914* (New York: Holmes & Meier, 1980); Aileen S. Kraditor *The Ideas of the Woman Suffrage Movement, 1890–1920* (New York: Columbia University Press, 1965); Hans Huth, *Nature and the American* (Lincoln, NA.: University of Nebraska Press, 1957) ch, 7, 9; Liz Keeney, "Women and Popular Botany: A Study in Nineteenth-Century American Social Values," paper given at the Berkshire Conference on Women's History, Vassar College, 1981; Fox, p. 341; Peter Schmitt, *Back to Nature: The Arcadian Myth in Urban America* (New York: Oxford University Press, 1969); Suellen M. Hoy, "Municipal Housekeeping: The Role of Women in Improving Urban Sanitation Practices, 1880–1917," in Martin V. Melosi, ed. *Pollution and Reform in American Cities, 1870–1930* (Austin; University of Texas Press, 1980), pp. 173–98.

4. Mary S. Gibson, ed. *A Record of Twenty-five Years of the California Federation of Women's Clubs 1900–1925* (n.p.: The California Federation of Women's Clubs, 1927), pp. 6, 7.

5. Gibson, *Twenty-Five Years*, pp. 10–11.

6. *Club Life, Official Organ of the California Federation of Women's Clubs*, 4, no. 6 (February, 1906), p. 1.

7. Gibson, ed. *Twenty-five Years*, p. 174; *Club Life*, 1, no. 11 (March, 1903, p. 7; H.E. Rensch, E.G. Rensch, and Mildred Brooke, *Historic Spots in California*, sponsored by the State Conference of

the National Society of the Daughters of the American Revolution (Stanford; Stanford University Press, 1933), pp. 51, 499; R. Coke Wood, *Big Tree Bulletin: Historical and Botanical Facts about the North and South Grove of the Calaveras Big Trees* (Murphys, Ca., 1960).

8. Gibson, ed. *Twenty-five Years,* p. 175.

9. Gibson, ed. *Twenty-five Years,* pp. 176–77; *Club Life,* 2, no. 8 (December, 1903), p. 2; *Club Life,* 2, no. 10 (February, 1904), p. 5; *Club Life,* 3, no. 2 (June, 1904), p. 4; *Club Life,* 3, no. 8 (February, 1905), p. 4.

10. The General Federation of Women's Clubs, *Tenth Biennial Convention Official Report* (Newark, New Jersey, 1910), p. 127; "Calaveras Big Trees Saved," Gibson, ed. *Twenty-five Years,* p. 177; Calaveras Grove Association, "South Grove, Calaveras Big Trees" (Stockton, Ca., n.d.).

11. Gibson, ed. *Twenty-five Years,* pp. 13–18.

12. *Club Life,* 1, no. 10 (February, 1903), p. 1; *Club Life,* no. 11 (March, 1903), p. 7; *Club Life,* 2, no. 10 (February, 1904), p. 6; Gibson, ed. *Twenty-five Years,* pp. 17–18.

13. *Club Life,* 1, no. 9 (January, 1903), pp. 1–2; Gibson ed. *Twenty-five Years,* p. 178; Paul Casamajor, ed. *Forestry Education at the University of California* (Berkeley, California Alumni Foresters, 1965), pp. 11–12.

14. Mrs. L.P. Williams, Chairman Forestry Committee, "Address," General Federation of Women's Clubs; American Forestry Association, *Proceedings of the American Forest Congress* (Washington, D.C., 1905), pp. 428–35.

15. *Proceedings of the American Forest Congress,* p. 432.

16. *Proceedings of the American Forest Congress,* p. 434.

17. Mrs. Welch, General Federation of Women's Clubs, "Address," *Proceedings of the Second National Conservation Congress at Saint Paul, September 5–8, 1910* (Washington: National Conservation Congress, 1911), p. 161; Mrs. F.W. Gerard, Chairman, "Report of the Forestry Committee," in the General Federation of Women's Clubs, (cited as G.F.W.C.) *Tenth Biennial Convention* (Newark, New Jersey, 1910), pp. 127–31; Lydia Phillips Williams, "Announcement of the Forestry Committee," *Federation Bulletin: Official Organ of the Massachusetts State Federation of Women's Clubs,* 2, no. 6 (March, 1905), p. 192; *Federation Bulletin,* 5, no. 2 (November, 1907), pp. 58–59, quotation on p. 58.

18. Mrs. Mary Gage Peterson, General Federation of Women's Clubs, "Address," in *Proceedings of the First National Conservation Congress Held at Seattle, Washington, August 26–28, 1909* (n.p., 1909), pp. 136–40.

19. Mrs. Overton Ellis, "The G.F.W.C.s in Conservation Work," *First National Conservation Congress,* pp. 149–58. Welch, *Second National Conservation Congress,* p. 161; Gerard, G.F.W.C. *Tenth Biennial,* p. 130; Mary L. Wood, *The History of the General Federation of Women's Clubs* (New York: G.F.W.C., 1912), pp. 149, 170–71, 195, 208–209, 217, 221, 231, 245, 253, 257, 263, 282, 296.

20. *Federation Bulletin,* 2, no. 5 (February, 1905), pp. 144–45; *Federation Bulletin,* 2, no. 3 (1904), pp. 99–100.

21. Gerard, *Tenth Biennial,* pp. 128–29, 140.

22. Jennie June Croly, *The History of the Woman's Club Movement in America* (New York: Henry G. Allen & Co., 1898), p. 105. The frontispiece of Croly's book bears the following inscription: "This book has been a labor of love, and it is lovingly dedicated to the Twentieth-Century Woman by one who has seen and shared in the struggles, hopes and aspirations of the woman of the nineteenth century, J.G. Croly." On Mira Lloyd Dock see also, *Federation Bulletin*, 2, no. 3 (1904), p. 99; G.F.W.C. *Eleventh Biennial Convention, June 25 to July 5, 1912, San Francisco, Ca.* (n.p. 1912), p. 266.

23. Mira Lloyd Dock, "Practical Conservation in Pennsylvania," in G.F.W.C., *Eleventh Biennial*, pp. 266–72.

24. "Women as Workers," *Conservation*, 15 (1909), p. 156.

25. Mrs. J.D. Wilkinson, Chairman Waterways Committee, "Report of the G.F.W.C.," *Second National Conservation Congress*, pp. 412–13. Wilkinson, "Report of Waterways Committee," in G.F.W.C., *Tenth Biennial Convention*, 1910, pp. 140–3.

26. Wilkinson, "Report on Waterways Committee," pp. 140–43.

27. Joseph Ransdell, "Our National Waterways," G.F.W.C., *Tenth Biennial*, pp. 144–50, quotations on p. 150.

28. Wood, *History of the G.F.W.C.*, p. 282.

29. Mrs. Emmons Crocker, "Other National Wastes," in G.F.W.C., *Tenth Biennial Convention*, 1910, pp. 151–59; Crocker, "Report of the Conservation Department," in G.F.W.C., *Eleventh Biennial Convention*, 1912, pp. 242–7.

30. Crocker, "Address," in *Proceedings, Fourth National Conservation Congress* (Indianapolis, 1912), pp. 257–62, quotation on p. 258.

31. Crocker, *Fourth Conservation Congress*, pp. 259, 260, 261.

32. Lydia Adams-Williams, "Forestry at the Biennial," *Forestry and Irrigation*, Official Organ of the American Forestry Association, 14, (1908), pp. 435–37; "Fighting for her Trees," *Forestry and Irrigation*, 14 (1908), p. 230. See also pp. 17, 127, 231.

33. Lydia Adams-Williams, "Conservation—Woman's Work," *Forestry and Irrigation*, 14 (June, 1908), pp. 350–51, quotation on p. 350. See also Adams-Williams, "Waste of Natural Resources and Need for Conservation," *Forestry and Irrigation*, 14 (1908), pp. 266–269, on the expenditures and projects of the U.S. Reclamation Service, the Inland Waterways Commission, rate of consumption of coal and wood, and the need for scientific management.

34. Lydia Adams-Williams, "A Million Women for Conservation," *Conservation*, Official Organ of the American Forestry Association, 15 (1909), pp. 346–47; Adams-Williams, "Upholding the Government," *Forestry and Irrigation*, 14 (May, 1908), p. 270.

35. *Fourth Conservation Congress*, p. 241; *Proceedings of a Conference of Governors in the White House, Washington, D.C., May 13–15, 1908* (Washington, 1909), p. xxvii. Gerard, "Report of the Forestry Committee," G.F.W.C. *Tenth Biennial*, p. 127.

36. *Fourth Conservation Congress*, pp. 240–41, 248; Wood, *History of the G.F.W.C.*, pp. 244–45.

37. Mrs. Hoyle Tomkies, "Address," *Second Conservation Congress*, p. 163–66.

38. Margaret Russell Knudsen, Women's National Rivers and Harbors Congress, "The Conservation of the Nation's Natural Resources," *First Conservation Congress*, pp. 206–11.

39. Knudsen, *First Conservation Congress*, p. 207.

40. "The Women's National Rivers and Harbors Congress," *Conservation*, 14 (1908), pp. 568–69.

41. Frances Shuttleworth, Women's National Rivers and Harbors Congress, "Interest of Women in Conservation," Letter to Editor, *Conservation*, 14 (1908), pp. 568–69.

42. Lydia Adams-Williams, "The Women's National Rivers and Harbors Congress," *Conservation*, 15 (1909), pp. 98–101.

43. Margaret Gibbs, *The D.A.R.* (New York: Holdt Reinhart and Winston, 1969), pp. 79–80. Mrs. Carl Vrooman, D.A.R., "Address," in *Proceedings of the Third National Conservation Congress at Kansas City, Missouri September 25, 26, and 27, 1911* (Kansas City, Missouri 1912), pp. 117–19, quotation on p. 117.

44. Gibbs, pp. 78, 82; *American Monthly*, April 19, 1909; *Third Conservation Congress*, p. 117.

45. *Third Conservation Congress*, p. 117, J. Horace McFarland, "How the Power Companies Beautify Niagara," *Ladies Home Journal*, 23, (October, 1906); *Ladies Home Journal*, 22 (Sept. 1905) and 23 (Jan. 1905).

46. Mrs. Jay Cooke, "Address," *Second Conservation Congress*, p. 167; Vrooman, *Third Conservation Congress*, p. 118.

47. Mrs. Matthew T. Scott, "Address," *Third Conservation Congress*, p. 127; Gibbs, D.A.R., p. 79.

48. Welker, *Birds and Men*, pp. 196–99, figures 35, 38, 40 of illustrations from *Godey's Ladies Book*, 1883 and the *Delineator*, 1898.

49. Welker, pp. 200–204; "History of the Audubon Movement," *Bird Lore*, 7, no. 1 (January-February, 1905), pp. 45–57; Paul Brooks, "Birds and Women," *Audubon*, 82, no. 5 (September, 1980): 88–97; Robin W. Doughty, "Concern for Fashionable Feathers," *Forest History*, 16, no. 2 (July, 1972), pp. 4–11.

50. Florence Merriam Bailey, "How to Conduct Field Classes," *Bird-Lore*, 2, no. 1, (February, 1900), p. 83.

51. "History of the Audubon Movement," op. cit. *Bird-Lore*, 1905, p. 47.

52. Welker, pp. 207, 189; "The Connecticut Society," *Bird-Lore*, 1, no. 1 (February, 1899), pp. 30–31.

53. *Bird-Lore*, 1, no. 1 (February, 1899), pp. 28–29; Welker, 187–92; Brooks, "Birds and Women;" Deborah Strom, ed. *Birdwatching with American Women* (NY.: Norton, 1986).

54. *Bird-Lore*, 1, no. 1 (April 1899), p. 66; *Bird Lore*, 1, no. 3, (June 1899), p. 103; *Bird-Lore* 1, no. 6 (December, 1899), p. 204.

55. *Bird-Lore*, 1, no. 6 (December 1899), p. 206.

56. *Bird-Lore*, 2, no. 1 (February, 1990), p. 32; *Bird-Lore*, 7, no. 1 (January-February, 1905), pp. 58, 296.

57. *Bire-Lore*, 14, no. 6 (December, 1905), p. 308; T. Gilbert Pearson, "The White Egrets," *Bird-Lore*, 14, no. 1 (Jan.-Feb., 1912), p. 62.

58. "The Wearing of Bird Plumage," *Club Life*, 2, no. 1 (May, 1903), p. 5.

59. William L. Finley, National Association of Audubon Societies, "Conservation of Wild Birds," *First Conservation Congress*, p. 112; Miss Gillette, *First Conservation Congress*, p. 211–212.

60. Mrs. F.W. Gerard, "Report of the Forestry Committee," G.F.W.C., *Tenth Biennial*, p. 129.

61. Crocker, *Fourth Conservation Congress*, pp. 260–61.

62. *Bird-Lore*, 15, no. 6 (November-December, 1913), p. 399.

63. *Bird-Lore*, 17, no. 6 (November-December, 1915), pp. 441, 495, 497; *Bird-Lore*, 14, no. 1 (January-February, 1912), p. 62.

64. Mrs. Matthew T. Scott, *Second Conservation Congress*, p. 271, 275; *Fourth Conservation Congress*, p. 252.

65. Mrs. Overton Ellis, "The General Federation of Women's Clubs in Conservation Work," *First Conservation Congress*, p. 150.

66. Mrs. Philip N. Moore, *Tenth Biennial*, pp. 29–30.

67. Mrs. Carl Vrooman, *Third Conservation Congress*, p. 119.

68. Mrs. Orville T. Bright, National Congress of Mothers, *Fourth Conservation Congress*, pp. 196–200, quotations on pp. 196, 200, 196.

69. Margaret Russell Knudsen, *First Conservation Congress*, p. 208.

70. Mrs. John Walker, *Fourth Conservation Congress*, p. 255.

71. Mrs. Overton Ellis, *First Conservation Congress*, p. 155.

72. Mrs. Welch, *Second Conservation Congress*, pp. 161, 162–63.

73. Mrs. Matthew T. Scott, *Fourth Conservation Congress*, p. 254.

74. Aileen Kraditor, *The Ideas of the Woman Suffrage Movement, 1890-1920* (New York: Columbia University Press, 1965), pp. 4–6.

75. Kate N. Gordan, "Equal Suffrage," *Tenth Biennial*, pp. 233–39, quotations on pp. 238–39.

76. Alice Chittendon, "Anti-Suffrage," G.F.W.C., *Tenth Biennial*, pp. 243–53, quotations on pp. 253, 243, 252. For more on antisuffragism, see Kraditor, pp. 114–42.

77. Chittendon, *Tenth Biennial*, pp. 251–52, 253.

78. *Report of the Forestry Committee of the First National Conservation Congress*, (Washington, D.C. 1913), especially pp. 385–89.

79. *American Forestry*, 19 (November, 1913), banquet photograph on p. 970.

80. "The Forestry Committee," *American Forestry*, p. 834.

81. On women in the forestry profession in recent years see Sally K. Fairfax and Lois White, "Women in Forestry," *Proceedings of the Eighth World Forestry Congress*, Jakarta, Indonesia, October 16–18, 1978.

82. Hays, Conservation and the Gospel of Efficiency, p. 193.

83. U.S. Congress, House Committee on Public Lands, Hearings on HJ Res 223, "San Francisco and the Hetch Hetchy Reservoir," 60th Congress, 2nd, session (January 9, 12, 20, 21, 1909).

84. "San Francisco and the Hetch-Hetchy Reservoir," p. 177.

85. "San Francisco and the Hetch Hetchy Reservoir," pp. 201, 216, 221.

86. "San Francisco and the Hetch-Hetchy Reservoir, "pp. 241, 332, 153.

87. U.S. Congress, Senate, Committee on Public Lands, Hearing on Jt. Res. S.R. 123, 60th Congress, 2nd session (February 10, 1909), pp. 30–32, quotation on p. 32.

88. Roderick Nash, *Wilderness and the American Mind* (New Haven: Yale University Press, 1973), pp. 168–69; Fox, *Muir*, p. 142.

89. John Muir, "Brief Statement of the Hetch Hetchy Question," G.F.W.C., *Federation Courier*, 1, no. 2 (December, 1909); p. 2. Muir, "Brief Statement," *The Federation Bulletin for the Woman of Today*, 7, no. 4 (Boston, January, 1910), pp. 110–111. Gerard, "Report of the Forestry Committee," G.F.W.C., *Tenth Biennial*, p. 130; Nash, *Wilderness*, p. 169.

90. Marsden Manson to G.W. Woodruff, April 6, 1910, Manson correspondence, Bancroft Library, University of California, Berkeley; Manson "Names and Addresses of people objecting to use of Hetch Hetchy;" ms., n.d.

91. Caroline K. Sherman to Marsden Manson, October 15, 1909, Manson correspondence, Bancroft Library, U.C., Berkeley.

92. Nash, *Wilderness*, pp. 170–71.

93. National Committee for the Preservation of the Yosemite National Park, "The Hetch Hetchy Grab," Bulletin no. 1 (1913); *idem*, "Comments of the United States Press on the Invasion of the Yosemite National Park," Bulletin no. 2 (1913). "Comments of the United States Press on the Invasion of the Yosemite National Park," Bulletin no. 2 (1913). Hays, *Conservation and the Gospel of Efficiency*, p. 194, letter from Kent to Pinchot, October 8, 1913, Gifford Pinchot manuscripts, #1823, Library of Congress.

94. Ruth E. Prager, "Remembering the High Trips," Sierra Club Oral History Project, "Sierra Club Women," Bancroft Library, University of California Berkeley, Vol. I, p. 6 & 8; Fox, *John Muir*, p. 343 and note, p. 422.

95. Hayes, *Conservation and the Gospel of Efficiency*, pp. 185–98; Fox, *John Muir*, pp. 344–345; "List of Members," *Bird-Lore*, 7 (November-December, 1905), pp. 345–48; "List of Members," *Bird-Lore*, 17 (November-December, 1915), pp. 541–48.

NOTES TO CHAPTER 7

Revised from: *Environment* 22 (June 1981): 7–13, 38–40.

1. Robert Clark, *Ellen Swallow: The Woman Who Founded Ecology*, (Chicago: Follet, 1973): "One Hundred Years of Women at MIT," *Technology Review*, (June 1973): 42, 52; Ellen H. *(Swallow)* Richards *Air, Water, and Food* (New York: John Wiley, 1890); Caroline L. Hunt, *Life of Ellen H. Richards* (Boston, 1912).

2. Rachel Carson, *Silent Spring* (Boston: Houghton-Mifflin, 1962), pp. 8, 15–37, quotations on p. 277.

3. Betty Friedan, *The Feminine Mystique* (New York: Dell, 1963) pp. 11–27, 326–63; Phyllis McGinley, *Sixpence in Her Shoe* (New York: Macmillan 1960).

4. Mary Daly, *Gyn/Ecology: The Metaethics of Radical Feminism* (Boston: Beacon, 1978); Sherry Ortner, "Is Female to Male as Nature is to Culture?" in M. Rosaldo and L. Lamphere, eds.,

Woman, Culture, and Society Stanford, CA.: Stanford University Press, 1974) pp. 67–87; Susan Griffin, *Woman and Nature*, (New York: Harper & Row, 1978). Dolores LaChapelle, *Earth Wisdom* (Los Angeles: Guild of Tutors Press, 1978); Adrienne Rich, *Of Woman Born* (New York, 1977); Merlin Stone, *When God was a Woman* (New York: Harcourt Brace Jovanovich, 1976).

5. Griffin, *Woman and Nature*, p. 227.

6. Rosemary Radford Reuther, *New Woman, New Earth* (New York: Seabury Press, 1975); Barbara Ward Jackson and René Dubos, *Only One Earth* (New York: Norton, 1972); René Dubos, *The Wooing of Earth* (New York: Charles Scribner's Sons, 1980); René Dubois, "A Theology of the Earth," in Ian Barbour. ed. *Western Man and Environmental Ethics,* (Reading, MA.: Addison-Wesley, 1973) pp. 43–54.

7. David Barash, "Sexual Selection in Birdland," *Psychology Today* (March 1978), pp. 82–86. On the Department of Energy and solar power see Sierra Club, San Francisco. *The Yodeler,* (January 1981), p. 41. I am grateful to John Sinton and Michael Reardon for the Mount St. Helen's quotation from a television interview with Michael Beeson, Portland State University, May 1980.

8. Dorothy Dinnerstein, *The Mermaid and the Minotaur,* (New York: Harper and Row, 1976); Evelyn Fox Keller, "Gender and Science." *Psychoanalysis and Contemporary Thought 1* (1978): 409–33; Nancy Chodorow, "Family Structure and Feminine Personality," in Rosaldo and Lamphere, eds. *Woman, Culture, and Society*, pp. 43–66.

9. Shulamith Firestone, "Feminism and Ecology," in *The Dialectic of Sex* (New York: Bantam, 1971). pp. 192–202.

10. Eleanor Leacock, "Women in Egalitarian Societies," in Renaté Bridenthal and Claudia Koonz, eds. *Becoming Visible: Women in European History* (Boston: Houghton Mifflin, 1977), pp. 11–35; Patricia Draper, "!Kung Women," in Rayna R. Reiter, ed. *Toward an Anthropology of Women* (New York: Monthly Review Press, 1975); Mina Caulfield, *Universal Sex Oppression? A Critique from Marxist Anthropology,* manuscript. See also Mona Etienne and Eleanor Leacock, *Women and Colonization* (New York: Praeger, 1980).

11. Carolyn Merchant, *The Death of Nature: Women, Ecology, and the Scientific Revolution* (San Francisco: HarperCollins, 1980), ch. 6, 7.

12. Karl Marx, *Capital* (New York: International Publishers, 1967), vol. 3, p. 745.

13. Comptroller General of the United States, *Indoor Air Pollution: An Emerging Health Problem*, U.S. General Accounting Office, Gaithersburg, Maryland, September 24, 1980; Thomas H. Maugh, II, "New Study Links Chlorination and Cancer," *Science* 211 (February 1981): p. 694.

14. Barbara Riley, "Chemical Exposures in Institutions," *Common Knowledge* 2 (1980): 56–57; Robert E. Gosselin, et al. *Clincal Toxicology of Commercial Products* (Baltimore: Williams and Wilkins, 1976), p. 271; Center for Science in the Public Interest, *The Household Pollutants Guide* (New York: Garden City, 1978).

15. See, for example, Anita Johnson, "Unnecessary Chemicals," *Environment* (March 1978), p. 6.

16. Michael Jacobson, *How Sodium Nitrite Can Affect Your Health: Don't Bring Home the Bacon*, Center for Science in the Public Interest, 1980; Michael Klein et al. "Earthenware Containers as a Source of Fatal Lead Poisoning," *New England Journal of Medicine* 283 (September 24, 1970): 669–72; Comptroller General, *Indoor Air Pollution*, p. 7.

17. *Women and Life on Earth. Ecofeminism in the '80's,* pamphlet series, Amherst, MA. 1980.

18. Dorothy Nelkin, "Nuclear Power as a Feminist Issue," *Environment* (January/February 1981), pp. 14–20, 38–39.

19. Carl Irving, "Conservative Nominated to Head EPA," *San Francisco Chronicle,* 22 February 1981, p. 1; Frank Greve, "Reagan's Choice to Head EPA May Symbolize a Weakening of That Agency," *San Francisco Sunday Examiner and Chronicle,* 29 March, 1981, sec. A, p. 12; Larry Eichel, "Environmentalists' Fearsome Foursome: Allies from Colorado," *San Francisco Sunday Examiner and Chronicle,* 5 April, 1981, sec. A, p. 14.

20. Nelkin, *Nuclear Power as a Feminist Issue;* H. Patricia Hynes, *The Recurring Silent Spring* (New York: Pergamon Press, 1989), pp. 181–2.

21. *Unity Statement of the Women's Pentagon Action,* New York, 1980.

22. B.J. Phillips, "The Case of Karen Silkwood, *Ms. Magazine* (February 1975), p. 59–66; Michael E.C. Gery, "Silkwood on Stage," *New Roots* (December/January 1981), pp. 15–17.

23. Helen Caldicott, *Nuclear Madness* [1978], rev. ed. (New York: W.W. Norton, 1994).

24. Sierra Club, San Francisco, "A Conversation with Dr. Helen M. Caldicott," *The Yodeler* (January 1981), p. 4; Caldicott, *If You Love This Planet* (NY.: Norton, 1992).

25. Sierra Club, "A Conversation with Dr. Helen M. Caldicott," p. 7.

26. Sierra Club, "A Conversation with Dr. Helen M. Caldicott," p. 6.

27. Sierra Club, "A Conversation with Dr. Helen M. Caldicott".

28. Catherine Georgia Carlotti, *W.A.R.S.: Women Against Racism and Sexism,* Conference on "Women and Life on Earth," pamphlet series, Amherst, Mass., P.O. Box 580, 1980.

29. Petra Kelly, "Women Aware! The Interrelationship Between Feminism and Ecology," *Women's International Network News* 6 (Summer 1980): 44; Kelly, *Thinking Green* (Berkeley: Parallax, 1994).

30. *Akwesasne Notes* (Winter, 1978), p. 15; Ibid. Summer 1979, p. 23; Ibid. Early Spring, 1980, p. 22; William K. Tabb, "1980 Black Hills Survival Gathering," *In These Times* (August 13–26, 1980).

31. *Akwesasne Notes,* Summer, 1980, p. 23.

32. Lois Gibbs, *Love Canal,* Conference on "Women and Life On Earth," pamphlet series, Amherst, MA.: P.O. Box 580, 1980.

33. Constance Holden, "Love Canal Residents Under Stress," *Science* 208 (June, 1980): 1242–44.

34. Gibbs, *Love Canal.*

35. Holden, "Love Canal Residents Under Stress," p. 1244.

36. Beverly Paigen, "Public Health Issues: Benedictin, Love Canal," *Science* 211 (January 2, 1981): 7–8; R. Jeffrey Smith, "Love Canal Reviewed," *Science* (October 31, 1980); 513.

37. Sierra Club, San Francisco, "Hazardous Waste in the Bay Area," *The Yodeler* (November, 1980), p. 3.

38. Anne Bancroft, "How the PCB Outcry Began," *San Francisco Chronicle,* 14 August 1980, p. 19.

39. See David Kriebel, "The Dioxins," *Environment* (January/February 1981), p. 12.

40. Mark Kirkmeier, "2,4-D Spraying Starts in Oregon," *San Francisco Chronicle*, 27 September, 1979.

41. Kirkmeier, "2,4-D Spraying Starts in Oregon."

42. Kirkmeier, "2,4-D Spraying Starts in Oregon."

43. Carl Irving, "Children Poisoned: Modesto Pesticide Case Coming to Trial," *San Francisco Sunday Examiner and Chronicle*, 25 November, 1979, sec. A, p. 13.

44. Laura Merlo, "The Poisoning of Berkeley," *Grassroots* (June 25–July 15, 1980). pp. 6–7.

45. Judy Smith, *Something Old, Something New, Something Borrowed, Something Due: Women and Appropriate Technology*, National Center for Appropriate Technology, Butte, Mont., 1978; Conference Proceedings, *Women and Technology: Deciding What's Appropriate*, Missoula, Montana, 1979; Bev Eaton, "Women Changing Technology," *New Roots* (December/January 1981), pp. 23–26.

46. Lois Gibbs, personal communication; Robbin Lee Zeff, Marsha Love, and Karen Stults, *Empowering Ourselves: Women and Toxics Organizing* (Arlington, VA.: Citizen's Clearing House for Hazardous Wastes, n.d.), p. 25.

47. Hawley Truax, "Minorities at Risk," *Environmental Action* (January/February 1990): 20–21; Robert W. Collin and William Harris, Sr., "Race and Waste in Two Virginia Communities," in Robert D. Bullard, ed. *Confronting Environmental Racism: Voices from the Grassroots* (Boston: South End Press, 1993), pp. 98–100.

48. Charles Lee, "Toxic Wastes and Race in the United States: A National Report on the Racial and Socio-Economic Characteristics of Communities with Hazardous Waste Sites" (New York: United Church of Christ Commission for Racial Justice, 1987).

49. Robert D. Bullard, "Anatomy of Environmental Racism and the Environmental Justice Movement," in Bullard, ed. *Confronting Environmental Racism*, pp. 15–39.

50. Sue Greer, quoted in Andrew Szasz, *Ecopopulism: Toxic Waste and the Movement for Environmental Justice* (Minneapolis, MN.: University of Minnesota Press, 1994), pp. 70–71, 192.

51. Kay Kiker, quoted in Szasz, *Ecopopulism*, p. 155.

52. Cora Tucker, quoted in Celene Krauss, "Blue Collar Women and Toxic Waste Protests," in Richard Hofrichter, ed. *Toxic Struggles: The Theory and Practice of Environmental Justice* (Philadelphia, PA.: New Society Publishers, 1993), p. 112.

53. Dick Russell, "Environmental Racism: Minority Communities and Their Battle Against Toxics," *Amicus*, 11, no. 2 (Spring 1989): 4–5; Cynthia Hamilton, "Women, Home, and Community: The Struggle in an Urban Environment," *Race, Poverty, and Environment Newsletter*, 1, no. 1 (April 1990): 3, 10–13; Robert D. Bullard, "Anatomy of Environmental Racism," in Hofrichter, ed. *Toxic Struggles*, p. 31.

54. Esperanza Maya, "Environmental Justice and Racism," presentation at Land, Air, and Water (LAW), Public Interest Law Conference, University of Oregon, Eugene, Oregon, March 1994; Magdalena Avila, "David Vs. Goliath," *Crossroads/forward motion* (April 1992): 13–15.

55. Charon Asetoyer, presentation to "Women as Social Conscience" conference, Eleventh Annual Women's Research Conference, University of South Dakota, April 16, 1994.

NOTES TO CHAPTER 8

Revised from: Carolyn Merchant and Abby Peterson (Department of Sociology, University of Gothenburg) *Women's Studies International Forum*, London, England, 9, no. 5–6 (1986): 465–79.

1. Elin Wägner, *Väckarklocka* (Stockholm: Bonniers, reprinted Proprius, 1990. 1941), p. 238; On Wägner, see Abby Peterson, "Elin Wägner and Radical Environmentalism in Sweden: The Good Earthworm," *Environmental History Review*, 18, no. 3 (Fall 1994): 61–74. On women and the American environmental movement see this volume, chapters 6, 7.

2. Wägner *Ibid*. pp. 249, 236; Elisabeth Tamm and Elin Wägner, *Fred med jorden* (Stockholm: Bonniers, 1940); Rachel Carson, *Silent Spring* (Boston: Houghton-Mifflin, 1962) pp. 8, 15–37.

3. Wägner, *Väckarklocka*, pp. 237, 250; Johann Jacob Bachofen, *Das Mutterrecht* (Basel, 1897; first printed 1861); Robert Briffault, *The Mothers* (London, 1927) 3 vols.: Wägner *Tusen år i Småland*, (Stockholm, 1939).

4. Interview with Flory Gate, Östra Grevie, June 1, 1984; Ulla Isaksson and Erik Jhalmar Linder, *Elin Wägner: Dotter av Moderjord, 1922-1949* (Stockholm, Bonniers 1980) pp 240, 272.

5. Tamm and Wägner, *Fred med jorden, op. cit.;* Flory Gate, "Fred med Jorden: En Bakgrundsskiss," *Fogelstad–Förbundet, 1925–75*, (Katrineholm, 1976) pp. 67–72.

6. Interview with Flory Gate, Östra Grevie, June 1–2, 1984.

7. Interview with Sara Lidman, Missenträsk, May 19, 1984.

8. Sara Lidman, *Varje löv är ett öga*, (Stockholm: Bonniers, 1980) pp. 76, 80, 83, 94; Karin Berglund, "Sara Lidman bland de döende träden: Skam över dem som förstör vår skog," *Dagens Nyheter*, April 22, 1984.

9. Interview with Elisabet Hermodsson, Uppsala, April 3, 1984; Elisabeth Möback, "Traditionella vetenskapen—ett hot mot naturen! intervju med Elisabet Hermodsson," *Djurfront* 9 (February 1982): pp. 3–5; Asa Freij, "Porträtt av Elisabet Hermodsson: Vår civilisation tog själen från naturen," *Alternativet* (March 16, 1984): pp. 6–7; Hermodsson, *DagensNyheter*, 6 Dec. (1994), p. B3.

10. Hermodsson, *Gör dig synlig (Make Yourself Visible)* (Stockholm: Rabén & Sjögren 1980) pp. 93–101, quotation on p. 93, see also note, p. 112. Poem trans. Birgitta Ivarson in K.W. Berg and G. Amansson, eds. *Mothers, Saviours, Peacemakers: Swedish Women Writers in the Twentieth Century* (Uppsala: University of Uppsala, 1983), pp. 171–97.

11. Eva Moberg, "Förnyelsens källor," *Alternativet*, no. 9 (March 9, 1984): 18; *idem, Vad tar vi oss för?* (Stockholm: Timo Förlag, 1983), pp. 41–57, 112–140; *Dagens Nyheter*, 2 Nov., 8 Dec. (1994).

12. Barbro Andréen, et al. *Häxkraft* (Gothenburg, 1983); Lisbet Ahnoff, "Myter kring häxen i frölunda," *Göteborgs-Tidningen*, 10 October, 1983.

13. Susan Griffin, *Woman and Nature* (New York: Harper and Row, 1978); Mary Daly, *Gyn/Ecology* (Boston: Beacon, 1978); Carol Christ, "Why Women Need the Goddess: Phenomenological, Psychological, and Political Reflections," in Charlene Spretnak, ed. *The Politics of Women's Spirituality* (Garden City, N.Y.: Anchor, 1982).

14. Wägner, *Väckarklocka*, p. 248.

15. Those arguing for the political praxis of Wägner's *Väckarklocka* were: Maria Bergom-Larsson, "Kvinnor värnar livet, männen förstör det," *Dagens Nyheter,* 16 June 1979, p. 4 and "*Väckarklockans* tid inte förbi, än härskar manssamhället," *Dagens Nyheter,* 6 July 1979, p. 4; Maj Wechselmann, "Elin Wägner hade rätt," *Dagens Nyheter,* 10 July 1979, p. 4; Ebba Witt-Brattström, "På med skyddshjälmen och ner i gruvan, systrer!" *Dagens Nyheter,* 24 July 1979, p. 4; Elisabet Hermodsson, "Demokratiska matriarkat," *Dagens Nyheter,* 31 July 1979, p. 4. Those arguing against the political praxis of Wägner's book were: Barbro Backberger, "Elin Wägner i dag politisk omöjlig," *Dagens Nyheter,* 28 June 1979, p. 4; Anita Sandberg, "Vi har inget att vinna på att bli känslor experter," *Dagens Nyheter,* 21 July 1979, p. 4.

16. The Swedish Institute, "The Economic Situation in Swedish Households," Stockholm, 1981; Boel Berner, "New Technology and Women's Education in Sweden," *World Yearbook of Education 1984: Women and Education* (New York: Nichols, 1983–84) p. 228; Louise Waldén, "Kvinnokultur-skruvstävstång?" *Vi mänskor,* no. 1 (1981): 20.

17. Eva-Lena Neiman, *Veckans Eco,* no. 14 (1982): 7.

18. For an extensive discussions of the politics of reproduction see Abby Peterson, "The Gender-Sex Dimension in Swedish Politics," *Acta Sociologica,* 27, no. 1 (1984): 3–17. For data on women in the workplace, see Ingmarie Froman, "Sweden for Women," Swedish Institute, Stockholm, November 1994, pp. 1–2.

19. Kurt Törnqvist, "Opinion 82," *Psykologisk Försvar,* Beredskapsnämnden, Stockholm, no. 116 (1982).

20. Kenneth Berglund, "Besvär och hälsoeffekter av luftföroreningar i Sundsvall och Timrå," Statens Miljömedicinska Laboratorium, Stockholm, rapport no. 14, 1983; *Miljötidningen,* no. 8 (1980): 12–15.

21. Abby Peterson, "Kvinnofrågor, kvinnomedvetande och klass," *Zenit,* no. 2 (1981). On American women, see Dorothy Nelkin, "Nuclear Power as a Feminist Issue," *Environment,* 23, no. 1 (January-February, 1981): 14–20, 38–39.

22. *Alternativet* (February 4, 1983): 3–8; "Stop and Reconsider," *Connexions: An International Women's Quarterly,* no. 6 (Fall, 1982): 20–21, quotation on p. 21. On women's protest of a proposed uranium mine in Pleutojokk, see *Miljötidningen,* no. 8 (1980): 36.

23. Abby Peterson, "The New Women's Movement—Where Have All the Women Gone," paper presented at the Nordic Conference on Women and Politics, Gothenburg, Sweden, May, 1984; Ulla Torpe, "Kvinnokamp för Fred mot Krig," *Vi mänskor,* no. 2, (1978): pp. 21–28, quotation on p. 24.

24. Interview with Marit Paulson, April 16, 1984; *Miljötidningen,* no. 6 (1977): 6–11; On women's protest of herbicide use in Darlarna see *Vi mänskor,* no. 2 (1978): 26.

25. *Veckans Eco,* no. 10–11 (1982): 16–19; *Miljötidningen,* no. 2 (1977).

26. Editors, *Vi mänskor,* no. 5/6 (1980).

27. *Vi mänskor,* no. 5 (1980): 33.

28. *Miljötidningen,* no. 8 (1980).

29. *Miljötidningen*, no. 2 (1979).

30. Berner, "New Technology and Women's Education," *op. cit.*, p. 229.

31. Interview with Christina Mörtberg, Institution för Arbetsvetenskap, Luleå University, May 4, 1984; *International Business Week*, (April 23, 1984), pp. 75, 78.

32. *Veckans Eko*, no. 14 (1982): pp. 13–15.

33. Interviews with Ingrid Stjernquist and Sif Johansson, Östra Grevie, June 1, 1984.

34. *Miljötidningen*, no. 7 (1978): 16–18.

35. Interview with Erika Daléus, Friends of the Earth (Jordens Vänner), Linköping, April 4, 1984; interview with Birgitta Wrenfelt, Stockholm, May 14, 1984.

36. *Ny livsstil*, no. 3 (1983); *Ibid*, no. 4 (1983); *Ibid*, no. 1 (1984).

37. Interview with Stina Deurell, May 24, 1984.

38. Ella Ödmann, Elivor Bucht, and Maria Nordström, *Vildmarken och välfärden: Om naturskyddslagstiftningens tillkomst* (Stockholm, 1982); Eva-Lena Neiman-Tiren, Stockholm, personal communication, May 21, 1984; interview with Gunilla Olsson, Östra Grevie, June 1, 1984.

39. The Swedish Institute, "The Swedish Political Parties," Stockholm, February 1983; Frank Viviano, "Swedish Women Saying No to European Union," *San Francisco Chronicle*, 14 September 1994; "Swedes Reject Rightists, Turn Again to Socialists," *San Francisco Chronicle*, 19 September 1994; Ingmarie Froman, "Sweden for Women," p. 1.

40. Centerparty program, in "The Swedish Political Parties," *ibid.*, quotation on p. 2.

41. Birgitta Hambraeus, lecture, Stockholm, May 15, 1984.

42. Centerpartiet motion 1973: 1467; 1983/4: 651, Birgitta Hambraeus; personal communication, May 16, 1984.

43. "Swedes Reject Rightists." *op. cit.*; Ingmarie Froman, "Sweden for Women," p. 3.

44. "Miljöpartiet-politisk programm," Lund, 1981.

45. Interview with Margareta Gisselberg, Umeå, April 19, 1984.

46. "Swedish Women Saying No to EU," *op. cit.*

47. Ortner, "Is Female to Male as Nature is to Culture?" in Michelle Rosaldo and Louise Lamphere, eds. Woman, Culture, and Society (Stanford, CA.: Stanford University Press, 1974), pp. 67–87; Ynestra King, "Toward an Ecological Feminism and a Feminist Ecology," in Joan Rothschild, ed., *Machina Ex Dea* (New York: Pergamon, 1983), pp. 118–29; Judith Stacey, "The New Conservative Feminism," *Feminist Studies*, 9, no. 3 (fall, 1983): 559–83; Michele Barrett and Mary McIntosh, *The Anti-Social Family* (London: Verso Editions, 1982), pp. 20, 33.

48. Tamm and Wägner, *Fred med jorden*.

NOTES TO CHAPTER 9

1. Virginia Westbury, "The Nature of Women," *Elle* (May 1991): 40–6; Westbury, "God the Mother," *Elle*, (June 1991): 28–33; Westbury, "Mother Nature's Sisters," *Canberra Times*,

Midweek Magazine, 15 May 1991, p. 21. The first wave of the women's movement is generally considered to be the late nineteenth- and twentieth-century campaigns for women's rights, equality, and suffrage. The second wave is the women's liberation movement beginning in the 1960s. On the second wave of the women's movement in Australia, see Marian Sawer and Marian Simms, "The Women's Movement: Then and Now," in Sawer and Simms, *A Woman's Place: Women and Politics in Australia* (Sydney: George Allen and Unwin, 1984), pp. 171–96.

2. Freya Mathews, "Relating to Nature," *The Trumpeter,* 11, no. 4 (Fall 1994): 159–66.

3. Freya Mathews, *The Ecological Self* (London: Routledge, 1991), chapter 4, "Value in Nature and Meaning in Life," esp. pp. 117–18.

4. Mathews, *Ecological Self,* pp. 121–26.

5. Mathews, *Ecological Self,* p.133.

6. For an account of the structure of ecological revolutions, see Merchant, *Ecological Revolutions* (Chapel Hill: University of North Carolina Press, 1980).

7. On the global ecological crisis and its potential resolution through environmental movements, see Carolyn Merchant, *Radical Ecology: The Search for a Livable World* (New York: Routledge, 1992).

8. Peter Daniels and Lex Brown, *Environmental Attitudes of the Queensland Population in 1990,* Institute of Applied Environmental Research, Griffith University, Brisbane, Queensland, September 1990.

9. Valerie A. Brown and Margaret A. Switzer, *Engendering the Debate: Women and Ecologically Sustainable Development,* Report prepared for the Ecologically Sustainable Development Working Groups by the Office of the Status of Women, Department of the Prime Minister and Cabinet (Canberra, ACT: Centre for Resource and Environmental Studies, Australian National University, 1991), pp. 5, 11.

10. Brown and Switzer, *Engendering the Debate,* p. 2, Table 1, p. 5. Susan Ryan interview, Australian National Television, May 1991. Beginning in the 1970s, as more women were elected to parliament, laws benefitting women were passed. Examples include, the Sex Discrimination Act of 1984, the Equal Opportunities Act of 1986, and the adoption of the National Agenda for Women in 1988.

11. Brown and Switzer, *Engendering the Debate,* p. 4. In 1991, 34.5 percent of the work force was female, but women received on the average 17 percent lower wages than men for the same job and were largely concentrated in sex-stereotyped work. Female industry sectors (where women's representation was greater than the average for all industries) comprised unpaid household workers (with 65% females), community services (66 % females), recreation (55% females), finance (48% females), and wholesale and retail (45% females). The female industry sector as a whole contributed 46% to the Gross Domestic Product. The male industry sector comprised electricity (90% males), mining, (89% males), construction (86% males), transport (81% males), manufacturing (72% males), communications (71% males), agriculture etc. (70% males), public administration (60% males). Brown and Switzer, *Engendering the Debate,* Table 2, p. 10.

12. Brown and Switzer, *Engendering the Debate,* pp. 3–4.

13. Christine Sharp, "What is Green Development? Towards a Strategy for Creative Economic Development," (Balingup, WA: Small Tree Farm, 1988), quotations on pp. 3–5.

14. Sharp, "What is Green Development!" pp. 3–5, 6, 9, 12, 16.

15. CREST, "Workshops on 'Women in Landcare,'" Centre for Rural Environmental Studies and Technology, Wongon Hills, WA.

16. Mare Carter, "Nganyinytja: Teaching the Circle of Life," *ITA* (June 1991); 72–77, interview with Nganyinytja as interpreted by Diana James. For more information on women in aboriginal production see Diane Bell, *Daughters of the Dreaming* (Sydney, NSW: McPhee Gribble/George Allen & Unwin, 1983); Fay Gale, ed. *Women's Role in Aboriginal Society* (Canberra, ACT: Australian Institute of Aboriginal Studies, 1970) and Gale, "Seeing Women in the Landscape: Alternative Views of the World Around Us," in Jacqueline Goodnow and Carole Pateman, eds. *Women, Social Science, and Public Policy* (Sydney, NSW: Allen & Unwin, 1985). According to Jennifer Isaacs, "Sex roles are well defined in traditional Aboriginal communities. Women generally gather food; men hunt it. While men hunt large land and sea animals and catch fish, women collect vegetables, shellfish, small animals and eggs. Women, of course, as bearers and rearers of children, must carry out all their food-gathering activities with children present. However, they gather food extremely successfully and can provide up to 80 percent of the food in the community... I would suggest, therefore that the greatest repository of centuries of botanical knowledge and experience lies with Aboriginal women, rather than men...On all the bush tucker trips taken for this book the women were indisputably the experts." [Jennifer Isaacs, *Bush Food: Aboriginal Food and Herbal Medicine* (Willoughby, NSW: Ure Smith Press, 1987), p. 16].

17. Kate Short, "The Australian Toxics Network: Why Women Do It," *Ecopolitics V*, ed. Ronnie Harding (Sydney, NSW: Centre for Liberal and General Studies, University of New South Wales, 1992), pp. 506–58. *The A to Z of Chemicals in the Home*, 2nd. ed. (Sydney: Total Environment Centre, 1990); Robyn Smith, et al, *Chemical Risks and the Unborn* (Sydney: Total Environment Centre, 1991).

18. Short, "The Australian Toxics Network," Gender and the Environment conference session, *Ecopolitics V*, Sydney, University of New South Wales, April 5, 1991; Short, telephone interview, November 1991; Short, "Editorial," *Australian Toxic Network News* (June 1991): p. 1; "Act of Necessity: A Matter of Life and Money," Executive Producer Ron Saunders; Director Ian Munro; Producer, Pamela Williams, 90 minutes (Linfield, NSW: Film Australia, 1991).

19. Short, "The Australian Toxics Network," *Ecopolitics V*, conference session, April 1991; Short, telephone interview, November 1991.

20. Brown and Switzer, *Engendering the Debate*, pp. 7, 10, 11.

21. Brown and Switzer, p. 11; Janet Mackenzie, "HOPE for the Future," *Conserve: Women's Conservation and Environment Network* (June 1990); Interview with Mary Dykes, Department of Conservation and Environment, State of Victoria, Melbourne, Victoria, May 15, 1991.

22. Mina Sirianni, "Worldwide Home Environmentalists Network (WHEN)," *Conserve*, (June 1990): p. 13; Mina Sirianni, "Letter from the President," *The Home Environmentalist: The Newsletter of Worldwide Home Environmentalists Network Australia*, 1, no. 2 (Autumn, 1991); Interview with Mary Dykes, May 15, 1991.

23. *Network: Quarterly Newsletter of the Rural Women's Network* (Winter 1990); Interview with Mary Dykes, May 15, 1991.

24. Elisabeth Kirkby, "Women and the Environment," in Ronnie Harding, ed. *Ecopolitics V: Proceedings* (Sydney, NSW.: Centre for Liberal and General Studies, University of New South Wales, 1992), pp. 515–23.

25. Lesley Instone, "Green-House-Work," *Ecopolitics V,* ed. Ronnie Harding (Sidney, NSW: Centre for Liberal and General Studies, University of New South Wales, 1992), pp. 524–30.

26. Brown and Switzer, *Engendering the Debate,* quotation on p. 9.

27. Nel Smit, *Trees: A Book of Resource Ideas for the Teacher* (Tasmania: A.B. Caudell Government Printer, 1984). The booklet asked such questions as: What signs of birds and mammals, such as nesting, pecking, scratching, or chewing can you find? Can you see anything under the bark? Are the leaves the same? Smit encouraged children to smell the leaves and to think about words to describe the lines they saw in them. Further questions dealt with measurements and numerical comparisons: How wide is the trunk at the base of the tree? Compare the height of the tree to other trees in the area. Hug it. Try a bark rubbing. Other activities related the tree to its geophysical environment: What is growing under the tree? Examine the soil. Is it wet, dry, sandy, or like clay?

28. Sandra G. Taylor, "Teaching Environmental Feminism: The Potential for Integrating Women's Studies and Environmental Studies," *Proceedings of Gender, Science, and Technology,* 6 (1991): 656–63; Giovanna Di Chiro, "Environmental Education and the Question of Gender: A Feminist Critique," in Ian Robottom, ed. *Environmental Education: Practice and Possibility* (Geelong, Vic.: Deakin University Press, 1987), pp. 23–47; Giovanna Di Chiro, "Applying a Feminist Critique to Environmental Education," *Australian Journal of Environmental Education,* 3, no. 1 (1987). Annette Greenall Gough, "Universalized Discourses: In Whose Interests is Teacher Education?" Paper presented at the 1993 Annual Conference of the Australian Association for Research in Education, Fremantle, 21–25 November 1993, pp. 7–9. Another community education/action project is "Nursing the Environment," dedicated to reducing waste and pollution in hospitals and promoting environmental health in communities. See "Nursing the Environment," Papers from the first annual conference (Melbourne: Nursing the Environment A.N.F., 1991) and Helen Lucas, compiler, "Women and the Environment: A Victorian Environmental Action-Research Project," (Melbourne: National Women's Consultative Council, 1990).

29. Scott Henry, "Task Force, a Model for the World,'" *The Australian,* 18 March 1991.

30. Valerie A. Brown and Margaret A. Switzer, *Women and Sustainable Development: A Common Purpose?* Draft No. 1 of Issues Paper for Office of Status of Women, Centre for Resource and Environmental Studies, Australian National University, January 2, 1991, quotation on p. 1.

31. Valerie A. Brown and Margaret A. Switzer, "Victims, Vicars, and Visionaries: A Critique of Women's Roles in Ecologically Sustainable Development," in Ronnie Harding, ed. *Ecopolitics V: Proceedings* (Sydney, NSW.: Centre for Liberal and General Studies, University of South Wales, 1992), pp. 531–39; Brown and Switzer, *Engendering the Debate: Women and Ecologically Sustainable Development* (Canberra, Australia: Office of the Status of Women, Department of the Prime Minister and Cabinet, 1991).

32. Jo Vallentine and Peter D. Jones, *Quakers in Politics: Pragmatism or Principle?* (Aderley, QLD: Quaker Booksellers and Publishers, 1990).

33. Vallentine, *Quakers in Politics,* quotation on p. 24; Senator Jo Vallentine, "Rationale for Civil Disobedience," December 1988, pp. 18–20.

34. "Doing Politics Differently," *Newsletter of the Greens (WA) Senate and State Offices,* Issue 4 (January 1994). Geoffrey Barker, "How Green Can You Get," *The Age,* Melbourne, Saturday, 21 August 1993, p. 13; Geoffrey Barker, "Budget Still Not Right, Say Greens," *The Age,* Melbourne, Wednesday, 1 September 1993, p. 1. On feminism and green politics, see Ariel Salleh, "A Green Party: Can the Boys Do Without One?" in Drew Hutton, ed. *Green Politics in Australia* (Sydney: Angus and Robertson, 1987), p. 88.

35. John Vidal, "Green Women Take over the World," *The Age,* Melbourne, Wednesday, 1 September 1993, p. 18.

36. Janis Birkeland, "Ecofeminism and Ecopolitics," in Ronnie Harding, ed. *Ecopolitics V Proceedings,* (Sydney, NSW: Centre for Liberal and General Studies, University of New South Wales), pp. 546–54, quotation on p. 547. "We should work to disassociate masculinity from images of heroism, conquest, and death-defying so familiar in militaristic fantasies; from images of competitiveness, individualism, and aggression glorified in sport; from images of objectivity, linearity and reductionism exalted by science; and from images of hierarchy, progress and control entrenched in the technocracy." (p. 553) Birkeland has been active in the Tasmanian Greens and has worked to develop ecologically challenging environments for children.

37. Plumwood, *Feminism and the Mastery of Nature* (London: Routledge, 1993), pp. 39, 142–62. See also Plumwood, "Women, Humanity, and Nature," *Radical Philosophy,* 48 (1988): 16–24; Plumwood, "Nature, Self, and Gender: Feminism, Environmental Philosophy, and the Critique of Rationalism," *Hypatia,* 6, no. 1 (1991): 3–27.

38. Plumwood, *Feminism and the Mastery of Nature,* pp. 154, 160, 214–15.

39. Plumwood, *Feminism and the Mastery of Nature,* pp. 160, 173–82, 214–15. "Naess (1990: 187) says identification is a process in which 'the supposed interests of another being are spontaneously reacted to *as our own interests*' ....Naess's formulation glosses over our different placement with respect to these interests.... What we assume may be our conception of the others' good, not theirs.'" Plumwood, *Feminism and the Mastery of Nature,* pp. 214–15, citing Arne Naess, "Man Apart and Deep Ecology: A Reply to Reed," *Environmental Ethics,* 12: 183–92. See Arne Naess, "The Shallow and the Deep, Long-range Ecology Movement. A Summary," *Inquiry,* 16 (1973): 95–100.

40. Plumwood, *Feminism and the Mastery of Nature,* pp. 21, 35–40, 65. "To the extent that women's lives have been lived in ways which are less directly oppositional to nature than those of men... an ecological feminist position could and should privilege some of the experience and practices of women... as a source of change without being committed to any form of naturalism" (p. 35).

41. Plumwood, *Feminism and the Mastery of Nature,* pp. 21, 31, 35, 39, 199.

42. Robyn Eckersley, *Environmentalism and Poltical Theory: Toward an Ecocentric Approach* (Albany, N.Y.: State University of New York Press, 1992), quotation on p. 47. For Eckersley, ecofeminism derives from the way women experience the world in gender-specific ways. Two connections are especially significant—women's unique body-based experiences (ovulation, menstruation, childbearing, and suckling) and female experiences of oppression (whether stemming from biological differences or cultural practices). Yet for Eckersley, ecofeminism is not just a reversal that sets up

women's experiences as superior to those of men. It is important because of its emancipatory philosophy of including women and the rest of nature in the concept of the expanded self. (Eckersley has been active in the Tasmanian and Melbourne Green movements.)

43. See Warwick Fox, *Towards a Transpersonal Ecology: Developing New Foundations for Environmentalism* (Boston, MA.: Shambala, 1990).

44. Eckersley's efforts to connect ecofeminism to the expanded self may be vulnerable to Plumwood's argument that the expanded self is too powerful and too inclusive to adequately reflect differences, especially those deriving from women's unique physical or socially-constructed experiences.

45. Ariel Kay Salleh, "Deeper than Deep Ecology: The Eco-Feminist Connection," *Environmental Ethics*, 6, no. 4 (Winter 1984): 339–45; Ariel Salleh, "The Ecofeminism/Deep Ecology Debate," 14, no. 3 (Fall 1992): 195–216, see esp. 198–99; Ariel Salleh, "Class, Race, and Gender Discourse in the Ecofeminism/Deep Ecology Debate," *Environmental Ethics*, 15, no. 3 (Fall 1993): 225–44; Ariel Salleh, "Eco-Socialism/Ecofeminism," *Capitalism, Nature, Socialism*, 2, no. 1 (1991): 129–34. Arne Naess, "The Shallow and the Deep, Long Range Ecology Movement;" Bill Devall, "The Deep Ecology Movement," *Natural Resources Journal*, 20 (1980): 299–322. Salleh has been active in the Movement Against Uranium Mining, the Franklin Dam Blockade, the Australian Greens, the Society for Social Responsibility in Engineering, the Women in Science Enquiry Network, and was a convener of the Women's Environmental Education Centre in Sydney. She has written on women's activism in the development of the Australian Green movement. See Salleh, "A Green Party: Can the boys Do Without One?" pp. 67–90.

46. [Ariel] Kay Salleh, "Contribution to the Critique of Political Epistemology," *Thesis Eleven*, No. 8 (January 1984): 23–43; Salleh, "The Ecofeminism-Deep Debate," pp. 197–98, 203, 208, 211; "...thought is shaped in the context of a class, race, and gender stratified division of labor. Under capitalist patriarchy, all people, white or colored, men or women, are proscribed from knowing the full range of their own and each other's capacities." (Salleh, "The Ecofeminism-Deep Ecology Debate," p. 208). See also Salleh, "From Centre to Margin," *Hypatia*, 6 (1991): 206–14.

47. Salleh, "Class, Race, and Gender Discourse," p. 226, quotation on p. 229. See also Salleh, "Working with Nature: Reciprocity or Control," in J. Ronald Engel and Joan Gibb Engel, eds. *Ethics of Environment and Development* (Tucson, AZ.: University of Arizona Press, 1990), reprinted in Michael Zimmerman, et al, eds. *Environmental Philosophy: From Animals Rights to Radical Ecology* (Englewood Cliffs, N.J.: Prentice Hall, 1993) pp. 310–19.

48. Patsy Hallen, "Making Peace with Nature," *The Trumpeter*, 4, no. 3 (Summer 1987): 3–14; Hallen, "Making Peace with the Environment, or Why Ecology Needs Feminism," *Canadian Women's Studies*, 9, no. 1 (Spring 1988): 9–18. On the underlying principles of process philosophy see, Hallen, "How the Hegelian Notion of Relation Answers the Question, 'What's Wrong with Plastic Trees,'" *The Trumpeter*, 8, no. 1 (Winter 1991): 20–25.

49. Hallen, "Making Peace with the Environment." See also Patsy Hallen, "Careful of Science: A Feminist Critique of Science," *The Trumpeter*, 6, no. 1 (Winter 1989): 3–8, and Hallen, "Genetic Engineering: 'Miracle of Deliverance,' or 'Destroyer of Worlds'?" in Roslynn Haynes, ed., *High Tech: High Cost?: Technology, Society, and the Environment* (Chippendale, N.S.W.: Pan Macmillan Publishers Australia, 1991), pp. 36–47; Hilary Rose, "Hand, Brain, and Heart: A Feminist Epistemology for the Natural Sciences," *Signs: Journal of Women in Culture and Society* 9, no. 1

(1983); Evelyn Fox Keller, *A Feeling for the Organism: The Life and Work of Barbara McClintock* (New York: W.H. Freeman, 1983), pp. 99–102; Evelyn Fox Keller, *Reflections on Gender and Science* (New Haven, CT.: Yale University Press, 1985), pp. 162–64; Rachel Carson, *Silent Spring* (Boston, MA.: Houghton Mifflin, 1962); Nel Noddings, *Caring: A Feminine Approach to Ethics and Moral Education* (Berkeley, CA.: University of California Press, 1984).

50. Patsy Hallen, "Reawakening the Erotic: Why the Conservation Movement Needs Ecofeminism," *Habitat Australia: The Magazine of the Australian Conservation Foundation*, 22, no. 1 (February 1994): 18–21, paraphrased from p. 18.

NOTES TO CONCLUSION

This chapter is a revision of a paper presented at the Global Forum (The Nongovernmental Organizations' Earth Summit in Rio de Janeiro) at the Women's *Planeta Fêmea* conference, in the session on the "Code of Ethics and Accountability."

1. Rosiska Darcy de Oliveira and Thais Corral, *Planeta Fêmea: A Publication of the Brazilian Women's Coalition* (Rio de Janiero, IDAC, 1993); Rosiska Darcy de Oliveira and Thais Corral, eds. *Terra Femina* (Rio de Janeiro: Companhia Brasileira de Artes Gríficas, 1992).

2. Rosi Braidotti, Ewa Charkiewics, Sabine Häusler, and Saskia Wieringa, *Women, the Environment, and Sustainable Development* (London: Zed Books, 1994), pp. 78–80; Ester Boserup, *Women's Role in Economic Development* (New York: St. Martin's Press, 1970).

3. Braidotti, et al, *Women, the Environment, and Sustainable Development*, pp. 86–87; Sue Ellen M. Charlton, *Women in Third World Development* (London: Westview Press, 1984); Irene Dankelman and Joan Davidson, *Women and Environment in the Third World: Alliance for the Future* (London: Earthscan, 1988); Sally Sontheimer, ed., *Women and the Environment: A Reader, Crisis and Development in the Third World* (New York: Monthly Review Press, 1988); Vandana Shiva, *Staying Alive: Women, Environment, and Development* (London: Zed Books, 1989); Waafas Ofosu-Amaah, ed. *Asia-Pacific Regional Assembly: "Women and Environment: Partners in Life,"* (Washington, D.C.: WorldWIDE Network, 1991); Janet Henshall Momsen, *Women and Development in the Third World* (London: Routledge, 1991); Annabel Rodda, *Women and the Environment* (London: Zed Books, 1993); The World Commission on Environment and Development, *Our Common Future* (Oxford, Eng.: Oxford University Press, 1987), pp. ix–xv, 7–9, quotation on p. 8; Lisa Bunin, personal communication.

4. Braidotti, et al, *Women, the Environment, and Sustainable Development*, pp. 90–92; Women's International Policy Action Committee (IPAC), *Official Report, World Women's Congress for a Healthy Planet*, Miami Florida, 8–12 November, 1991 (New York: Women's Environment and Development Organization (WEDO), 1992).

5. "NGO's Meeting in Rio Adopt a Global Women's Treaty for a Just and Healthy Planet," and "Agenda 21 Defines the Role of Women in Sustainable Development," *Global Assembly of Women and the Environment—Partners in Life*, Washington, D.C.: WorldWIDE, Issue 4 (July 1992): 5–9; Michael Grubb, Matthias Koch, Abby Munson, Francis Sullivan, and Koy Thomson, *The Earth Summit Agreements: A Guide and Assessment* (London: Earthscan, 1993), p. 137; Braidotti, et al, *Women, the Environment and Sustainable Developoment*, p. 127.

6. Marilyn Waring, *If Women Counted: A New Feminist Economics* (London: Macmillan, 1988); IPAC, *Official Report, World Women's Congress for a Healthy Planet,* p. 17.

7. On egocentric, homocentric, and ecocentric ethics see "Environmental Ethics and Political Conflict," in Merchant, *Radical Ecology* (NY.: Routledge, 1992), pp. 63–82.

8. Environmental News Network, "GATT, the Environment, and the Third World: An Overview," (Berkeley, CA.: The Tides Foundation, 1992); "GATT vs. UNCED: Can Free Trade and Sustainable Development Coexist?" (San Francisco, CA.: Rainforest Action Network, 1992); World Wide Fund for Nature, "The GATT Report on Trade and Environment: A Critique" (Gland, Switzerland: WWF International, 1992); Third World Network, *Earth Summit Briefings,* (Penong, Malaysia, 1992); Marcia Stepanek, "GATT Group Turns up the Heat," *San Francisco Examiner,* 7 August 1994, B-1, 9; Kristin Dawkins, *NAFTA, GATT and the World Trade Organization: The Emerging World Order,* (Westfield, N.J.: Open Pamphlet Series, 1994).

9. Heinz Greijn, "GATT, Environment, and Development," *Earth Island Journal,* 7 (June 1992): 11–12.

10. The Global Women's Treaty contained the following paragraph: "We recognize the failure of governments to either address the true causes of the planetary crisis or reach agreement on urgent action to save our planet. We believe that the chief causes lie in militarism, debt and struc-tural adjustment and trade policies being promoted by multinational corporations and interna-tional financial and trade institutions such as the International Monetary Fund, the World Bank, and the General Agreement on Tariffs and Trade (GATT). The policies of these institutions are causing the degradation of human and natural environments, leading to the growing impoverish-ment of the majority of the world's people, perpetuating the inequity of the existing world order, and contributing to the continuing and intensified pressure on natural resources. We con-demn these policies and call for the immediate adoption of alternative policies based on principles of justice, equity, and sustainability." "NGO's Meeting in Rio Adopt a Global Women's Treaty," *Global Assembly of Women and the Environment,* No. 4 (July 1992), p. 8.

11. The Preamble to UNCED's Agenda 21 states: "[the] integration of environment and develop-ment concerns and greater attention to them will lead to the fulfillment of basic needs, improved living standards for all, better protected and managed ecosystems and a safer, more prosperous future. No nation can achieve this on its own; but together we can—in a global partnership for sustainable development." Quoted in Michael Grubb, et al, *The Earth Summit Agreements: A Guide and Assessment* (London: Earthscan, 1993), p. 101.

12. On Aldo Leopold's land ethic and ecocentric ethics more generally see Aldo Leopold, *A Sand County Almanac* (New York: Oxford University Press, 1949); J. Baird Callicott, *In Defense of the Land Ethic: Essays in Environmental Philosophy* (Albany: State University of New York Press, 1989); Holmes Rolston III, *Philosophy Gone Wild: Essays in Environmental Ethics* (Buffalo, N.Y.: Prometheus Books, 1986).

13. Harold Gilliam, "The Real Price of Free Trade," and Gilliam, "The Bottom Line for Indigenous Cultures," *This World, San Francisco Examiner,* January 2, 1994, pp. 13–14.

14. On the land ethic as a case of "environmental fascism," see Tom Regan, *The Case for Animal Rights* (Berkeley, CA.: University of California Press, 1983), p. 262. For a response see J. Baird Callicott, *In Defense of the Land Ethic* pp. 92–4 and Callicott, "Moral Monism in Environmental

Ethics Defended," *Journal of Philosophical Research*, 19 (1994). 51 60, see p. 53. On anthropism
as the ground for an emancipatory green politics, see Eckersley, *Environmentalism and Political
Theory: Toward an Ecocentric Approach* (Albany: SUNY Press, 1992).

15. The idea of a partnership between women and men as the basis for a new society, but without
   explicit attention to environmental ethics, has been developed by Riane Eisler in *The Chalice and
   the Blade* (San Francisco: Harper and Row, 1988). The concept of relation as a foundation for
   ecofeminism and the relational self has been developed by Val Plumwood in *Feminism and the
   Mastery of Nature* (London: Routledge, 1993). On the connections between ethics and narrative,
   see Jim Cheney, "Postmodern Environmental Ethics: Ethics as Bioregional Narrative,"
   Environmental Ethics, 11 (1989): 117–34. On the importance of seeing the local community as
   connected to a global capitalist system see, James O'Connor, "Socialism and Ecology,"
   Capitalism, Nature, Socialism, 2, no. 3 (1991): 1–12.

16. George Perkins Marsh, *Man and Nature* (New York: Charles Scribner's, 1864), pp. 35, 36.

17. Herbert Marcuse, "Nature and Revolution," in *Counterrevolution and Revolt* (Boston: Beacon
   Press, 1972), pp. 59, 65, 69.

18. "Preamble to *Agenda 21* and "The Rio Declaration on Environment and Development," in
   Grubb, et al, *The Earth Summit Agreements*, pp. 101, 87.

19. On chaos theory see, James Gleick, *Chaos: The Making of a New Science* (New York: Viking,
   1987) Edward Lorenz, *The Essence of Chaos* (Seattle, WA.: University of Washington Press,
   1993); N. Katherine Hayles, *Chaos Bound: Orderly Disorder in Contemporary Literature and Science*
   (Ithaca, N.Y.: Cornell University Press, 1990); N. Katherine Hayles, ed. *Chaos and Order:
   Complex Dynamics in Literature and Science* (Chicago: University of Chicago Press, 1991); Ralph
   Abraham, *Chaos, Gaia and Eros*, (San Francisco: Harper and Row, 1994). On the difference
   between chaos theory and complexity theory, see Mitchell Waldrop, *Complexity: The Emerging
   Science at the Edge of Order and Chaos* (New York: Simon and Schuster, 1992).

20. On the god-trick of seeing everything from nowhere, see Donna Haraway, "Situated
   Knowledges," in Haraway, *Simians, Cyborgs, and Women: The Reinvention of Nature* (New York:
   Routledge, 1991), pp. 183–201, esp. pp. 189, 191, 193, 195.

21. For the diversity-stability hypothesis, see Eugene P. Odum, *Fundamentals of Ecology* (1953) and
   Odum, "The Strategy of Ecosystem Development," *Science*, 164 (1969): 262–70. On shortcom-
   ings of equilibrium theories in ecology, see Seth R. Reice, "Nonequilibrium Determinants of
   Biological Community Structure," *American Scientist*, 82 (September-October 1994): 424–35. On
   the history and disruption of the balance of nature theory, see Daniel Botkin, *Discordant
   Harmonies* (New York: Oxford University Press, 1990); S.T.A. Pickett and P.S. White, eds. *The
   Ecology of Natural Disturbance and Patch Dynamics* (Orlando, FL.: Academic Press, 1985). On
   the problem of a stable world behind socially constructed representations, see Elizabeth Ann R.
   Bird, "The Social Construction of Nature: Theoretical Approaches to the History of
   Environmental Problems," *Environmental Review*, 11, no. 4 (Winter 1987): 255–64. On the histo-
   ry of chaos theory in ecology see Donald Worster, "Ecology of Order and Chaos,"
   Environmental History Review, 14, no. 1–2 (Spring/Summer 1990): 4–16.

22. Braidotti, et al, *Women, the Environment, and Sustainable Development*, pp. 132–34, 90. World
   Commission on Environment and Development, *Our Common Future* (Brundtland Report) (New
   York: Oxford University Press, 1987), pp. 43–44.

23. Braidotti, et al, *Women, the Environment and Sustainable Development*, pp. 116–22, 134, 166–67. Environmental groups from the South include DAWN (Development Alternatives with Women for a New Era), headed by Peggy Antrobus of Barbados, Vandana Shiva's Research Foundation for Science, Technology, and Resource Development in Dehra Dun India, and the Regional Assemblies of women of Africa; the West Asia/Arab World; Asia/Pacific; and Latin America/Caribbean, comprising the Global Assembly of Women and the Environment— Partners in Life.

24. See Charlene Spretnak, *Lost Goddesses of Early Greece: A Collection of Pre-Hellenic Mythology* (Ann Arbor, MI: Moon Books, 1978), pp. 30–1, quoted above, Chapter 1, p. 33.

INDEX

Women are referred as "Mrs." in historical references when they are known only by their husband's name and the title is necessary to identify them. (Example: "Burdette, Robert, Mrs."— but "Harrison, Jane Ellen")

Centre for Environmental Studies (Austraia),
198
Chaos, 3, 34, 44, 82
Chaos theory, xvii, 53-55, 220-21, 266n.19
Charmarette, Christabel, 201
Chaucer, Geoffrey, *The Merchant's Tale*, 65
Chee Yoke Ling, 24
Chemical pollutants, 147, 155, 157-59; DDT,
140, 194; herbicides, 159; PCB spill, 158,
254n.38; pesticides, xviii, 7, 11, 22, 160, 167-
68, 190, 220. *See also* Antitoxics movement
Chesapeake region, 37-38
Childbearing and rearing. *See* Reproduction
Children, 129-30, 180; child labor, 130; psycho-
logical development of, 143-44
Chile, 22, 23
Chipko movement, 18-19, 180
Chippewa Forest Reserve, 114
Chodorow, Nancy, 142
Christ, Carol, "Why Women Need the
Goddess," 172
Christianity, 29, 31, 33, 34, 35, 41, 97
Cities, 23, 79; City in the Garden, 34, 47-51
Citizens for a Better Environment, 10
Civilization, 34, 35; as female, 43-44, 47, 48f,
50; from "savagery" or wilderness to, 38, 39,
40, 43, 44
Cixous, Héléne, 61
Class, social, 80, 157
Clearinghouse for Hazardous Wastes, 165
Cloning, 144
Club of Rome, *Limits to Growth*, 53
"Code of Environmental Ethics and
Accountability, 212, 219, 224
Cole, Thomas: *A Wild Scene*, 38; *The Oxbow*,
38
Colman, Henry, 42
Colonial development, 15, 21, 223
Colonial ecological revolution, 91, 95, 96
Colonial women, xvii, 100-102
Commercialism, 77, 136
Commodities, xxt, 102, 145, 149, 165, 174, 187,
213, 232n.18
Communism, 231n.8
Community service, 197

Compassion, 185, 190
Comte, Auguste, 86
Consciousness, xix, xxt, xxi, 188, 202. *See also*
Mechanism; Narratives; Organicism;
Spirituality
Conservation movement (early), 89, 106, 120,
122-23; battle over Hetch Hetchy Valley, 132-
35; ideology of women in, 105, 128-31, 136;
wilderness preservation in , xviii, 43, 44, 53;

Progressive Era of, 109-10, 214. *See also*
Audubon movement; Forestry movement;
General Federation of Women's Clubs; *and
by individual campaign*
Constructivism, social, xvi; representation and,
64; science and, 71
Consumer goods. *See* Commodities
Consumption, 7, 197, 223, 224
Contraception, 219
Copernican view of the earth, 62
Corn: origin of, 93, 229n.1, 232n.13; planting
of, 94, 95
Corn mothers: deities, xvii, 93, 229n.1;
Indian women farmers, 13, 91, 92, 93-95, 96
Cosmos: celestial cycles of, 94, 97, 99; organic,
76-77, 85, 86, 92, 97, 98
Crévecoeur, J. Hector St. John, 43
Crime, 187, 200
"Critical ecological feminism", 202-6, 207-8
Critical theory, 59-60, 61, 70, 72
Crocker, Emmons, Mrs., 117-18, 127, 135
Cronon, William, *Nature's Metropolis*, 232n.18,
236n.56
Cultural diversity, 217
Cultural ecofeminism. *See under* Ecofeminism
Culture, xvi, xxii; and nature, xv, 10, 50, 61;
nature/culture duality, 49-50, 202-3, 204
Cyclical processes, 88, 94, 97, 99, 107

Dahlgren, Malin, 177
Dalai Lama, 21f
Daléus, Erika, 179
Daly, Mary, *Gyn/Ecology*, 141, 252n.4
Daughters of the American Revolution, 109,
120, 122-23, 129
Davis, Elizabeth Gould, 226n.3
DDT, 140, 194
Dead and Down Timber Act, 114
"Death" of nature, xvii, 35, 85, 86, 89
d'Eaubonne, Françoise, "Feminism or Death",
5, 227n.9
de Beauvoir, Simone, *The Second Sex*, 9,
227n.15
Debt burden, Third World, 222, 223
Decentralization, 14, 90
Deep ecology, 53, 203, 205-6, 207, 215, 223
Defoliation, 159, 170
Deforestation, 190. *See also* Lumber industry
de Lille, Alain, *Nature's Complaint*, 65
Demeter, 57, 69
Democracy, 25, 40, 131
Demonstrations. *See* Activism, ecofeminist
Dept-for-nature swaps, 216
Descartes, René, 60; *Discourse on Method*, 84,
243n.15